DEVELOPMENT PROBLEMS IN LATIN AMERICA

AN ANALYSIS BY
THE UNITED NATIONS ECONOMIC COMMISSION
FOR LATIN AMERICA

Special Publication of the
Institute of Latin American Studies
The University of Texas at Austin

Development Problems in Latin America

An Analysis by the United Nations Economic Commission for Latin America

WITH A FOREWORD BY

CARLOS QUINTANA, EXECUTIVE SECRETARY, ECLA

PUBLISHED FOR THE INSTITUTE OF LATIN AMERICAN STUDIES
BY THE UNIVERSITY OF TEXAS PRESS • AUSTIN & LONDON

International Standard Book Number 0–292–70042–3
Library of Congress Catalog Card Number 71–111930

Manufactured in the United States of America

FOREWORD

There is an obvious need for Latin America to find its own way to development and social change. This will require that Latin America possess a clear understanding of its present situation, develop original lines of thought for interpretation of it, and provide effective guidelines for future progress.

These are the principles that have inspired ECLA's critical studies and its work throughout the more than twenty years of its existence; they continue to be so, as it tackles new tasks and problems today.

More and more, ECLA is sharing its responsibilities with other institutions, with national government agencies, with university research centers, and with an everincreasing number of Latin American professionals and technicians, many of whom have been influenced during their training by the ideas ECLA itself has put forward. As a result, the contributions made to a wider and deeper understanding of the problems of Latin American development have become richer and more productive.

The situations that concern us are not static; on the contrary, new problems are continually emerging, even as the relative importance of existing problems changes—hence the constant need for critical interpretation and review. In tackling these problems, moreover, it is wise to bear in mind what has been achieved so far and to assess how far it is relevant to the new circumstances of today.

All this has created an urgent demand from students and research workers for an analysis of the main proposals put forward by ECLA and an outline of its thinking on a variety of topics, since there are practical difficulties in assembling all the information needed from the large number of publications and reports issued. This book is meant to satisfy the demand to some extent by reproducing a number of the studies, and parts of others, dealing with the main questions with which ECLA has been concerned.

The studies included here reflect what had been done up to ECLA's twentieth anniversary. Subsequently, and especially in connection with the Commission's thirteenth session, held at Lima, Peru, in April 1969, there have been further studies. Although these are still concerned with such fundamental areas as international trade policy, industrial development, basic resources, or the transport systems—usually in the context of Latin American integration—more emphasis is laid on social topics, experience in planning, alternative development strategies, employment targets, income distribution, the problems of foreign investment, and the improvement of administrative institutions and machinery. In this work and in its approach to the whole complex of problems, ECLA's fundamental aim will be—as it has been from the beginning—to seek a genuine understanding of Latin America's problems.

CARLOS QUINTANA
Executive Secretary

Santiago, Chile

CONTENTS

INTRODUCTION

In the publications it has issued in the twenty years of its existence ECLA has been gradually building up a fund of interpretations, criteria, and suggestions which cover many of the most important aspects of the theoretical and practical problems of Latin American development. The present document is intended to be a compendium of the ideas expressed on some of the questions which have been sources of concern to ECLA. Perhaps this will be useful to those who find it difficult to seek out and associate the observations scattered through the many studies that have been issued in the course of the last two decades.

In preparing this book it has been necessary, first, to focus attention on some basic subjects, and to disregard many others which, however important, were not of such permanent concern or which lie mainly within the competence of other international agencies (FAO, IMF, UNESCO, the ILO, and others). This applies to questions in such fields as agriculture, education, and employment. On the other hand, the guiding principle has been to give a faithful reproduction of the texts selected, with only minor cuts, excluding the statistical data they originally contained, as they would have made the compendium too bulky and they can be consulted in the studies cited.*

In the selection and classification of material, several central topics have been chosen, which are the subjects of the different chapters of this document. In broad outline, these topics are as follows:

1. A criticism of traditional theories on foreign trade and, more specifically, on the nature of the economic relationships between the "centers" and the "periphery";

*The English translations of these texts have been revised.

2. A justification of industrial development and an analysis of some of its main aspects in Latin America;
3. Planning as a *sine qua non* for development: its general content and technical direction, and regional planning experience;
4. The *raison d'être* of external financing and investment; ways of meeting economic growth requirements;
5. Regional integration as a primary means of getting away from the "closed' type economy in post-Depression industrial development;
6. The nature of inflation in Latin America: an analysis of its underlying causes and of traditional stabilization policies;
7. The social dimension of economic development: social determinants and effects of the development process, and changes in the structure of employment and of the social sectors;
8. The position of Latin America vis-à-vis world trade policy and trade between developed and developing countries;
9. An over-all and integrated view of development problems in Latin America and the structural changes needed to ensure more dynamic development and an equitable distribution of its benefits.

Although these central topics are dealt with separately, they are clearly interrelated and interdependent. Moreover, a certain sequence may be noted, for the knowledge gained in the first studies and its implications are naturally incorporated in the later ones, and give them greater depth. This does not mean that ECLA started out with or ever had the intention of formulating a cut-and-dried general theory or scheme that would systematically cover all the economic, social, and institutional aspects of Latin America's development. The main factors that have gradually broadened the outlook or sharpened subsequent thinking have been the actual facts, Latin America's experience of the problems and situations as they arose, and the development of the ideas themselves.

The Historical Context

To obtain a clear view from the historical standpoint it may be as well to establish the relationship between these central topics and certain aspects of Latin America's economic and political evolution.

Going back to the time when the Economic Commission for Latin America (ECLA) was beginning to operate, that is, the second half of the nineteen-forties, it is easy to discern a contradiction—or at least a lack of harmony—between the behavior and aims of what are now the economically more advanced countries of the region and the prevailing body of ideas, theories, and doctrines. While these countries, under pressure of the circumstances created by the Depression and the Second World War, had abandoned the outward-directed growth model and set energetically about transforming the structure of their economies, there had been no such process of adjustment on the intellectual plane, where the concepts and theories associated with the old system continued to dominate the scene.[1] In some cases the prevailing thinking had been enriched with some of the new Keynesian ideas, but here too the assimilation of these ideas had been indiscriminate and superficial, and at times they did little more than provide a veneer of respectable theory for inflationary measures. In short, these economies were guided in their new course only by an empirical and pragmatic approach, and this hampered their progress and exposed them to abrupt changes of direction through the action of those who continued to adhere to outmoded formulas.

This is a particularly significant feature when considered in the light of the circumstances following the war. The reactivation of Latin America's external sector, with a few ups-and-downs and disparities between countries, was clearly observable for a fairly long period which extended from the close of hostilities to the middle fifties, that is, almost a decade. This naturally revived the thinking based on the traditional model. Both inside and outside the region, a basis in fact was found for maintaining that the past fifteen years or so had been merely an unfortunate interregnum produced by exceptional factors, and that the "normal" condition—that is to say, the advantageous division-of-labor model of the past—would resume its place.

A convincing illustration of this is that, in nearly all the Latin American countries which had broken with the old system during this phase,

1 "In the midst of the world Depression we did not know the true nature of Latin America's development difficulties: the dominant idea was simply to restore normal conditions, to return to the past" (see Chapter IX).

the political backing for the diversification of the production system weakened, whereas advantage should have been taken of the external sector boom in order to intensify and introduce some method into the previous effort. With a few outstanding exceptions, the change in pace and emphasis was evident in most countries in the early postwar years.

The deep significance of ECLA's early contribution may be assessed at its true value against this backdrop alone. This contribution consisted, in the first place, of presenting a conceptual interpretation of what most countries of the region—more through force of circumstances than in response to a deliberate policy—had been doing since the depression. It showed that they had proceeded, with greater or lesser success or energy, as circumstances dictated. A second and no less decisive contribution was to show that what were considered by some to be emergency measures—for example, industrial development—were really policies that had come to stay and become more sophisticated, since there was no turning back despite the appearance of a relative external boom.

From this standpoint, it is easy to discern the twofold significance of ECLA's postulates in the early stages: on the one hand, it criticized the prevailing theory of the international division of labor—or of foreign trade—as viewed by the countries at the center; on the other hand, it provided a sound basis for a new approach to industrial development and, in general, to the diversification of the production system through the spread of technical progress.

It is worth recalling the reason for the special emphasis placed on all issues relating to foreign trade. It should be borne in mind here that, apart from the essential role played by trade in the development process, perhaps the main *general* feature in the whole diverse complex called Latin America is precisely its structural position in the world market. In other words, one of the key characteristics of the Latin American economies is and has always been their distinctive role as a region specializing in and dependent on the exportation of primary products. Naturally, apart from being a burning economic issue, this factor took on more importance as it became necessary to find a common denominator in the diagnosis of regional problems.

Critique of the Traditional Theory

Under the conventional system of the international division of labor, "the specific task that fell to Latin America, as part of the periphery of the world economic system, was that of producing food and raw materials for the great industrial centers."[2]

In this trade model, two key assumptions could easily be discerned. According to the first, more of the benefits deriving from increases in productivity in the two areas would go to the periphery, because technical progress was more vigorous and widespread in the production of industrial products. The second assumption was that in the centers demand for primary products would grow at least as fast as income, and perhaps faster if consideration was given to the possibility of a depletion in the supply of those goods and increases in their costs and prices.

These two premises are the object of ECLA's main criticism in its first basic studies. No doubt the principal argument was that the agents of production—entrepreneurs and workers—in the industrialized countries tended to absorb the benefits of technical progress and translate them into a sustained rise in income, instead of transferring them to the periphery through a corresponding drop in prices.

Briefly, the weakness of that argument lay in the fact that it was a generalization from particular circumstances. While it is true that the benefits of technical progress are gradually distributed among all social groups and classes in the great industrial countries, the immense gains deriving from increased productivity have not reached the periphery of the world economy in a comparable measure. "Hence the outstanding differences between the levels of living of the masses of the former and the latter, and the manifest discrepancies between their respective abilities to accumulate capital, since the margin of saving depends primarily on increased productivity."[3]

What is the machinery facilitating the retention of these benefits by the centers, which is therefore responsible for the inequitable distri-

[2] See below, Chapter I.
[3] *Ibid.*

bution of the gains deriving from technical progress? The answer to this question embraces one of the most vital and, in its time, most widely discussed of ECLA's ideas: the terms of trade.

If the conventional premise had materialized, independently of any discussion regarding the actual periods and dimensions of the problem, the relationship between industrial and primary prices would have changed distinctly in favor of the latter, for the overriding reason that technical progress and, consequently, the biggest advances in productivity had spread mainly in the centers and in manufacturing and other subsidiary production.

No one denies now that this did not happen and is still not happening, although, as indicated above, some related questions might be raised, such as the processing of industrial products, or the dimensions, consequences, and scope of the problem. The fact remains that far from following that trend, the terms of trade have swung against primary products. Accordingly, not only has the primary expert sector been denied its fair share of the technological progress achieved by the centers, but part of its own increased productivity seems to have been transferred to the centers.[4]

CONCENTRATION OF TECHNICAL PROGRESS AND THE TERMS OF TRADE

This critique must necessarily include an inquiry into the causes of the situation described above and into the processes which brought it about. There are several main hypotheses. The first relates to the second basic premise of the orthodox theory, the optimistic assumption regarding the trend of demand for primary products on the central markets. Flatly contradicting this assumption, ECLA's analysis made it clear that such demand, besides fluctuating periodically and thus causing serious distortions in the peripheral economies, was increasing only slowly and evidently lagging behind the growth of income in the industrial centers. The Commission ascribed this mainly to the following factors:

1. The proportion accounted for by primary commodities in aggregate expenditure or demand decreases as incomes rise;

[4] *Ibid.*

2. Primary commodities are being replaced increasingly by new products;
3. With technical progress, the share of primary inputs in the value of end products is diminishing;
4. Protectionist policies and instruments in the industrialized countries impede access to their markets for the primary products produced essentially by the periphery.

The weak position of primary products on the world markets owing to these factors is aggravated by other circumstances which are dealt with also in the ECLA studies. The sluggish demand for raw materials and foods in the centers goes hand in hand with the periphery's marked propensity to import manufactures. Thus, while demand for the former is increasing at a manifestly slower pace than income, demand for industrial imports in the periphery is rising more rapidly than income.[5] This disparity, apart from other effects which will be examined later, cannot but impair the position of primary products on the world market and strengthen that of manufactures. Consequently, it affects both the terms of trade and the corresponding possibilities of retaining productivity gains in the center and in the periphery.

Another factor heavily emphasized in ECLA's analysis is the effect of redundant manpower on the costs and prices paid and received by primary producers. The proportion of productivity gains which can be retained in a country of the periphery, through wage increases, depends partly on the existence and degree of such redundancy, to say nothing of other factors mentioned above, which also influence the distribution of these gains. In any event, whatever significance may be ascribed to the existing or potential manpower surplus in the primary-export economies, for a proper understanding of the over-all problem it must be remembered that the solution in the major industrial centers is very different, if not the exact opposite. A relative or absolute shortage of

[5] Approximate estimates show that for every 1 per cent increase in Latin America's income its demand for imports tends to grow by 1.8 per cent, whereas for every 1 per cent by which income increases in the United States the demand for imports grows by only 0.66 per cent. See the statement by the Executive Secretary of ECLA to the fifth session of the Commission in the annual report for 1952–1953 (document E/2405–E/CN.12/324), p. 44.

manpower—generally evidenced by technological improvements designed to economize labor—is accompanied by a solid and extensive trade union organization, which plays the role of watchdog and is in a position to claim constant wage adjustments in step with productivity increases.

As some of the extracts reproduced here recall, there was no room for this problem in the orthodox theory, since another of its premises was the mobility of the factors of production. The fact is, however, that neither the labor force nor capital has been transferred, as assumed by that theory. To the almost complete immobility of reserves of active population in the periphery was added an equally marked immobility of the stock of capital and techniques in the industrial centers.

To sum up, the chief factors causing the benefits of technical progress to be retained in the centers under the influence of the terms of trade have been the sluggish demand for primary products in the centers, the disparity between the growth of expenditure on imports in the two areas, and the different positions of the two areas with respect to manpower and social organization.

IMPLICATIONS

From its analyses ECLA deduced some of the main consequences of this particular system of economic relationships between the industrial and the primary-export economies.

One clearly significant result is the disparity involved in specialization, whether in the production of primary materials or of industrial goods. Since demand for the latter increases more rapidly, it is inevitable—as has been proved—that the economies specializing in the production of industrial goods will develop faster than those which continue to be dependent upon primary products. Therefore, in absolute terms, the gap between the central and the peripheral countries will widen in time unless the original structure is modified. This question will be examined at greater length in the section on industrial development.

The second conclusion relates to what may be termed the "built-in disequilibrium" implicit in a system of relationships based on the traditional international division of labor. The foreign exchange earnings of a peripheral economy depend above all on export of primary products, which, as is well known, tends to increase slowly. On the other hand, its demand for imported goods—or, in other words, need of foreign exchange—tends to rise faster than domestic income and export earnings. As a result, depending on the relations between these variables, the balance of payments is subjected to constant pressure, which will be heavier as the gap widens between the amount of foreign exchange available and the increment in domestic income, on the one hand, and the resulting demand for imports, on the other. This is still true today and it is a guideline for the United Nations in taking practical action in the spheres of trade, industrialization, and development.[6]

It is understood that this built-in disequilibrium is due to structural causes: specialization by the central and the peripheral countries each in certain types of commodities for the world markets, and the disparity in the income-elasticity of demand for the two types of commodities.

The problem is also found in another and perhaps more acute form as diversification of the production system gains impetus in a primary-export economy. This point will be mentioned again in connection with the outline of ideas on industrial development.

"Inward-directed" Development

In addition to analyzing the characteristics and implications of the "center-periphery" system, the ECLA studies also stress another fundamental dichotomy: "outward-directed" and "inward-directed" growth. As was noted above, criticism of outward-directed growth is the point of departure for elucidating the nature, problems, and requirements of a new type of economic expansion in the development of much of Latin America.

What are the fundamental implications of moving from one model to another? An approximate first definition might be that it involves substituting one focal center of dynamic development for another. *External* demand for basic commodities no longer has pride of place and is replaced by *internal* demand. From a practical standpoint, the standpoint of the allocation of resources, this change supposes that a

[6] See Chapter VIII, *passim.*

substantially larger proportion of resources is directed toward the production of goods and services for home consumption.

Although unequivocally directed toward reducing the economy's dependence on the external sector—which is the outstanding characteristic of "outward-directed" growth—and therefore toward making the process of expanding and changing the structure of production more autonomous, the new model does not imply, as was sometimes maintained by observers with an oversimplified approach, a move in the direction of autarchy and an underestimation of the importance of foreign trade. As will be seen later, the external sector continues to play a primary role in the new development model, although it is less important than before. Though foreign trade tends no longer to be the only, or, in other cases, the main motive force underlying demand, it continues to play a key role, either as a supplier of supplementary goods and services, or as an actual or potential market for new production generated by structural diversification as well as for traditional products.

NATURE AND MOTIVATION OF INDUSTRIAL DEVELOPMENT

It seems clear that industrial development is the nerve center of "inward-directed" growth, with the result that the two terms tend to be regarded as synonymous, as they are here. However, the far-reaching nature of the process implied by the new approach should not be lost sight of. Although it is true that the expansion of manufacturing is the linchpin of this process, equally important is the fact that corresponding changes take place and are required on all fronts and at all levels, both in economic and in related fields. This consideration is kept in view in the ECLA studies, as is shown by the subject-matter of the final chapters of the present document and, undoubtedly, in other studies not quoted here. This point, although elementary, needs to be made, since the attachment of importance to manufacturing growth alone has led both to unfounded criticisms and to a defective understanding of the nature and implications of such growth.

There are several main reasons why so much importance has been attached to industrial diversification. One, which is of a general nature, is that industrialization is viewed as a transformation of economic structures inherent in the process of development. Another more specific reason is that industrial development is viewed as the indispensable answer to upheavals in the external sector. From this point of view, a distinction can be drawn between two types of situation, both of which are loosely linked with specific historical periods. In the first, which covers the post-Depression and war years, there were fairly considerable difficulties in securing the usual goods and services abroad, either because of the drop in foreign exchange earnings or because of restrictions imposed in the supplier countries. In the second, which covers the postwar period in general, the problem had its origin in a bottleneck in the external sector, in the sense that the foreign exchange available was not sufficient to satisfy the demand for imports generated by the growth of domestic income.

In either case, it is domestic production which must help to supply the industrial goods that cannot be imported with the foreign exchange available.

The necessity of industrial development—as has already been stated—has another basis which is one of the central points in ECLA's reasoning: the spread of technological innovations in primary production and the need to make economic use of the extra labor thus freed and of additions to the labor force resulting from population growth. Industrial development will, of course, take place, even if primary production is expanded, to the extent that technical progress reduces the absolute or relative levels of manpower absorption; and its growth will be even more rapid if, in addition to the spread of capital-intensive techniques, there is a slackening of the growth of demand for primary commodities.

This line of reasoning pointed to the fact that industrialization was the cornerstone of development, even if there were no restrictions or deficits in foreign trade, and this has been more than borne out by the experience of the countries at the center.

SOME ASPECTS OF INDUSTRIAL DEVELOPMENT IN LATIN AMERICA

In the experience of Latin America, restrictions and fluctuations in the external sector have a much greater effect on industrial development than they had in the developed countries. This is the reason for the fundamental fact that in Latin America the diversification of manufacturing takes the form of "import substitution," it is a means of replacing or ensuring the supply of goods that cannot be bought with the foreign exchange available. This circumstance is a determining factor of some of the characteristics and limitations of industrial development in Latin America. For the moment we shall consider only those which are most closely linked with the questions raised in the preceding paragraphs, leaving others to be discussed later.

Of course, since the process of industrial development was not primarily stimulated by the introduction and spread of new techniques in the primary sectors, except in the case of those producing for export, the urgent nature of the expansion of industry accentuated the so-called "dualism" of the productive system and heightened its complexity. As it was inevitable that modern techniques and organization should be used in starting up or expanding manufacturing activities, this widened the gap between these activities and the backward areas of the traditional economy, particularly the agricultural and rural sectors. The social repercussions of this imbalance, which is geographical as well as sectoral in view of the concentration of these new activities in certain areas, are increasingly a matter of concern. Moreover, this imbalance in itself has weakened the base of support for industrialization, whether because it limits the domestic market or because of the shortage it entails in the supply of foodstuffs and various inputs.

This situation has on occasion served to reopen the old debate on the relationship between industrial development and agriculture, and there are those who have attributed the backwardness of agriculture to the support given to industrial development. The question has been discussed in several ECLA studies.[7] Without denying, and even on the contrary emphasizing, the fact that insufficient attention has been paid to the development of agriculture in Latin American economic policy, these studies have pointed to a number of circumstances which have an important bearing on the problem. One such circumstance is the complementary nature of expansion in these basic sectors. From the standpoint of agriculture, any expansion that was not based on an increase

[7] See below, Chapters I and II.

in urban demand would be inconceivable, and such an increase is largely dependent on the growth of manufacturing and related activities.[8] Another is that greater attention to agriculture would inevitably speed up the introduction of new techniques into agricultural production, and this in turn—although in agriculture there is a wider range of possible techniques that are labor-intensive—would have an important effect on freeing labor or reducing the absorption of new contingents. If in these circumstances there are no opportunities outside the sector, the position of agriculture would be worsened by the existence of redundant labor, and by the effect on relative prices. Agricultural prices, for example, would decline, in a kind of domestic parallel to the trend in international terms of trade between the centers and the periphery.

INDUSTRIAL DEVELOPMENT AND IMPORT SUBSTITUTION

It is worth calling attention to some characteristics of industrial development in Latin America which are related to the import control policy often applied because of balance-of-payments difficulties.[9]

To go straight to the heart of the matter, in broad outline one of the most notable effects on "outward-directed" growth in the major Latin American countries was the lack of association between the structure of demand and the structure of production. While the former was considerably diversified as a result of the growth and concentration of income, the latter was overwhelmingly dominated by primary production. This balance between the two was restored by means of imports financed by the primary exports.

When this pattern of relationships led to a depression or showed itself to be inadequate, internal material and human resources were reallocated to meet domestic demand which was unsatisfied because of import restrictions and had been reactivated by the various measures designed to defend the level of national income. There is, moreover, no

[8] There is, of course, the foreign market, but this is conditioned by factors already discussed.

[9] For a more extensive treatment of this and other aspects of industrial development in Latin America, see *The Process of Industrial Development in Latin America* (United Nations publication, Sales No.: 66.II.G.4).

reason to suppose that there was any modification of income distribution.

In these circumstances—defense of the level of income, no change in income distribution, and the reduction or elimination of certain imports—it is obvious that the productive factors tended to be directed toward domestic production of those goods for which there was already an effective demand and which presented fewer problems from the point of view of technology, scales of productions and financing requirements. In other words, the structure of production strove to adjust itself to the previous pattern of demand, particularly as regards manufactures.

Measures for controlling and virtually or directly rationing imports favored this type of evolution and played a fundamental part in it. The reasons for applying such measures seemed eminently justified and even inescapable. If it was desired to "save on foreign exchange" and, on the other hand, to ensure the supply of essential goods, the only feasible solution seemed to be to restrict or eliminate all imports deemed to be of secondary importance or superfluous. However, to the extent that such measures were applied, the elements referred to above came into full and unrestricted operation and directed import substitution and industrial development efforts toward the very activities or ends which trade policy considered inessential or of low priority.

As is well known, this was not the only striking contradiction revealed by experience. The internal inconsistency of the policy had a direct and even drastic effect on the external equilibrium it was designed to attenuate. Domestic production of inessential goods formerly imported doubled the pressure on foreign exchange holdings by stimulating demand for inputs and equipment to expand that production. In short, far from being a saving on foreign exchange, the effect could well be greater demand for foreign exchange, backed by the employment and income being generated in the country.

Despite these inherent contradictions in the process of industrial development in Latin America, it is not easy to devise other economic policy options that would have been feasible in the original conditions under which the problem was posed. They would undoubtedly have required considerable changes in the pattern of income distribution and, in general, in the whole social and institutional framework.

It must also be remembered that, with all its limitations, this *sui generis* approach—with regard to the industrialization of both the capitalist and the socialist countries of the center—succeeded in rescuing their economies from the aftermath of the depression, raising their rates of growth and placing them in a position to resume world trade.

Moreover, during the Second World War in some countries and after it in others, economic policy began to be aware of and to deal fairly effectively with the problems raised by those first attempts at the development of import substitution industries. This is clearly demonstrated by the steps taken to widen the bases of support, which took the form of investment in infrastructure and in such key industries as steelmaking. It was at that time, when interest in planning was beginning to dawn or become more widespread, that some of the main aspects of industrial development strategy began to be formulated. The documents produced by ECLA played no small part in this process of elucidation, and it is worthwhile referring to some of the ideas expressed, which are to be found in greater detail in Chapter II.

INDUSTRIAL DEVELOPMENT OPTIONS

Unquestionably, the driving force behind this effort was the need to steer a largely fortuitous process, determined in the main by external factors, into well-defined channels which would lead to the best possible results. From this standpoint, the primary objective was to lay down certain guiding principles that would make for fuller and more efficient utilization of human and material resources.

The first problem that arose, in manifest connection with the discussion of "inward-directed" development, consisted in "determining to what extent the available factors in a growing economy should be employed in increasing exports, with a view to expanding imports, and to what extent agricultural and industrial production for the domestic market should be expanded."[10]

[10] See below, Chapter II.

In principle, and closely in line with the orthodox argument, any immediate comparison of relative productivity would have shown a balance in favor of using new resources for the export sector. This inference was based on the major assumption—not always explicit or well founded—that there would be sufficient demand for the additional exports and that their impact on prices would not cancel out the apparent advantages of such an allocation of resources. In so far as such forecasts proved unrealistic, the idea of producing for the home market gained adherents. It must be noted that in analyzing this question all or most of the primary producers should be taken into consideration. While it is true that for a single exporter country—especially if its share in the market is small—the assumptions referred to may be valid, the picture is altogether different if all producers are taken into account. In this case, moreover, the temporary gain of one exporter, which would probably be nullified as the others pursued their own path, would end by entailing a loss for all concerned.

This gives rise to a second question. Even if the advantages are really on the side of the allocation of resources to the domestic market, a difficulty comes to the fore: productivity and costs may not compare favorably with those of similar imported goods. This is another of the arguments traditionally adduced in support of the orthodox position.

Without underestimating the importance of the disparities in internal and external production costs, ECLA's analysis focused attention on other factors that seem to carry more decisive weight. First, the imports-domestic production dichotomy was largely fallacious, in view of the limitations of the capacity to import. In many cases, therefore, the real choice was between producing the goods at home, or doing without them. Secondly, even if the productivity of an industrial enterprise was lower than that of its foreign counterpart, the resources assigned to it would represent a more or less significant contribution to the domestic product, which they could not make if they stood idle or were used in "traditional" activities where their productivity might leave even more to be desired.

INTERNAL OPTIONS

This line of reasoning shifted the center of interest to the study of criteria for selecting, among the various ends served by the domestic market, the one that would imply the most productive use of resources. Here the pointers given are categorical, and are based on the principle of marginal social productivity, according to which investment or "the increment of capital should be utilized so as to obtain the maximum product, which is only possible when the marginal productivity of the different investments is equalized."[11]

This is, of course, a very general guide, especially as the starting-point necessarily has to be a given relative price situation which may be affected by a number of factors, such as the influence of economic policies and income distribution. It does, however, establish a clear point of divergence from any consideration based on the profitability of private investment or of a single enterprise, although this does not imply that such indicators are meaningless.

The foregoing rule was not laid down as a rigid dogma, since it was expressly recognized that decisions as to the allocation of resources may be swayed by other considerations—sometimes of overriding importance—such as the expediency of reducing the vulnerability of an economy, increasing its independence and capacity for self-development, and lessening sectoral or regional disparities.

DISCUSSION OF PROTECTIONISM

These remarks on industrial development may be concluded with a brief review of the ideas expounded with respect to protectionism. This subject was a fount of never-ending controversy in the past, and has not yet altogether lost its topical interest. Moreover, it is closely linked to other questions that have been analyzed in the preceding sections.

Even at the risk of harping on points already discussed, stress should be laid on the relation between the various kinds of protectionist devices and the balance-of-payments situation in Latin America. From this standpoint it can be seen that as a rule such expedients were adopted not so much to promote rational industrialization aims as in order to bring expenditure on imports into line with the amount of foreign exchange available; in other words, they merely represented a side

[11] *Ibid.*

effect of the region's chronic external deficit. Naturally, in so far as such measures were applied and substitution activities grew up under their shelter, the interests vested in these industries came to depend upon the existence of a protectionist policy and, with varying degrees of justification, sought to perpetuate it in order to profit by the restriction or total elimination of competition from abroad.

This point is worth making in order, *inter alia*, to underline a first aspect of the contrast with the operation of protectionist machinery in the countries at the center of the world economy. There, such measures are seldom applied because of structural weaknesses in the balance-of-payments, but rather out of regard to the situation of domestic producers who are unable to withstand external competition. Thus, their original motivation is entirely different from the considerations usually underlying protectionist policy in Latin America.

Here the line of reasoning pursued by ECLA goes beyond the "incipient industry" proposition, important though this is. As is pointed out in one of the documents reproduced, instead of considering separate undertakings, "the new approach includes industry as a whole and establishes the need for protection so long as productivity continues to be lower than that of more advanced countries."[12] In other words, it is the general fact of their backwardness in terms of the intensity and extensiveness of technical progress that forces the developing countries to resort to appropriate protectionist measures, with the primary object of facilitating the diversification of the economy and the improvement of levels of productivity.

The ill-effects of overprotectionism are undeniable; but they do not seem to have prevented Latin American industry from making significant technical progress. A glance at its over-all growth will show, for example, that its rate of expansion has easily outstripped its rate of absorption of manpower. This is a suggestive indication of the headway it has made with respect to productivity, with the corresponding reduction of its capacity to provide additional employment opportunities. In this context, needless to say, the far-reaching problem represented by technological dependence is not overlooked. It is considered in detail in the excerpts to be found in Chapter II below.

[12] *Ibid.*

Another vital question which calls for discussion, and which also has implications for the world trade problems that will be noted later, is the analysis of the differences between the effects of protectionist measures when they are applied in the industrial centers and in the peripheral countries. In brief, without reverting to what has already been said, whereas in the first case over-all trade levels will probably be affected, in the second, such a thing is hardly likely to happen. The explanation is simple. "The restriction of certain types of imports in underdeveloped countries is offset—within the bounds set by the capacity for external payments—by increased imports of other commodities. . . . In contrast, restrictions on the import of a given primary commodity into a large industrial center are not necessarily neutralized by greater imports of other primary products, since all imports required to satisfy demand in existing conditions were being brought in before."[13]

Development Programming: Achievements and Difficulties

As has already been pointed out, the transition to a form of development based on industrialization geared to the domestic market will inevitably be subject to the conflicts and stresses that are, to a greater or lesser extent, in its origin and in the economic and social structure of the countries concerned. It is in the light of these facts that concern has been felt about how best to organize and channel the efforts that are being made and thus safeguard the continuity of the process. Hence, the need for general development programming, a concept which was foreshadowed by the formulation and implementation of sectoral plans, particularly for energy, transport, and certain basic industries.

It would not be fitting to lay stress here on the leading role played by ECLA's studies and activities in the advance toward what has been termed a "higher stage" of economic policy. Nevertheless, some of the main stages of this process, which is still going on, may safely be recapitulated.

Theoretical analysis of the broad problems of external economic relations and "inward-directed" diversification was superseded by a more searching diagnosis of the over-all situation in individual coun-

[13] *Ibid.*

tries, and an examination of their prospects and needs in terms of the scale and composition of the investment (and external financing) required to fulfill the projections.[14] Moreover, as early as 1955, a general compendium of the basic concepts and principles of planning had already been compiled. This document has been included in Chapter III; it still preserves much of its original importance and topicality.

The development and study of the technical features of planning need not be mentioned here, since a very full and specialized bibliography is available on the subject. Other questions that are more relevant to the purpose of this introduction will therefore be considered instead.

The first aspect that should be stressed is the relatively rapid and sweeping change that has taken place in the attitude to planning. It may not be out of place to recall that only a short while ago—not more than a decade—the idea that the development of the region should be deliberately regulated rather than left to the mercy of "market forces" was regarded in many circles as smacking of heresy. Although it was clear from the experience of many European countries, such as France, the Netherlands, and the Scandinavian countries, that planning was not the property of economies which had undergone a social and political revolution, there was a tendency to identify planned development with the regimentation of the economy.[15]

These prejudices were completely overcome in a very brief space of time and the formulation of over-all development plans came to be regarded as a prime requisite for obtaining cooperation from abroad. Once the initial reservations had been dispelled and the new situation accepted, Latin America made great headway in planning, as is shown in another document included in Chapter III.[16] The collaboration of ECLA, either in developing theory or in providing assistance, has been an almost constant factor in the region's progress. However, it is clear from the last-mentioned document that the region still lacks experience in planning and the advances it has made do not mean that the magni-

[14] See the country monographs in the series entitled *Analyses and Projections of Economic Development*, which are listed in the Annex to this volume.

[15] See below, Chapter III.

[16] *Ibid.*

tude of the obstacles which still remain or of the efforts which must be made to surmount them can be discounted.

Some important conclusions can be drawn from the gist of the critical review in Chapter III. The first is that planning has been accepted to a considerable and very significant degree among the authorities and in influential circles, progress has been made chiefly with its technical, institutional, and administrative aspects, but planning has not yet completely permeated economic policy and the daily routine of decision-making. In other words, although nearly all the countries have made headway with the technique of development plan formulation and the establishment of institutional and administrative machinery for drawing up and evaluating plans, they still have much to learn about how to put plans into effect and how to obtain the indispensable cooperation of key public areas and the private sector. Cooperation should, in fact, be secured not only from entrepreneurs, but also from all the "social agents," parties, trade unions, and so on that have a part to play in the planning process.

Another salient conclusion to be drawn from the analysis is that although there have been undoubted organizational and operational advances in external cooperation, they have not been sufficient to achieve the requisite standards for effective programming. This point will be raised again later.

However that may be, it would not be going too far to say that ECLA's theoretical and practical cooperation in the work of promoting planned development have established a new landmark in the history of planning in Latin America.

External Cooperation in Latin America's Development

Although the importance of external financing and investment for the development of the region has been emphasized by ECLA ever since its earliest studies, it was not until the mid–nineteen-fifties that the subject began to claim special attention. The excerpt reproduced in Chapter IV, which is taken from an extensive report on international cooperation in Latin American development policy, dates from that time (1954).

It may be helpful to explain why the subject came to the fore then, and why it continues to be one of the most important.

If Latin America's economic development is viewed in retrospect, it is plain that external investment and loans played a leading role during the phase of "outward-directed" growth. Not only did a large proportion of investment in the export sector come from outside the region, much of the process of public capital formation was financed by foreign credits also. Except for distortions produced by the circumstances at the time, exports expanded sufficiently for the countries to meet their debt servicing and repayment commitments without much difficulty. The picture was quite different during the depression and even up to the early years of the postwar period. With a few outstanding exceptions, such as the Eximbank credits, the process of capital formation came to depend first and foremost on domestic savings. Owing to the restrictions on foreign trade and the consequent changes in the structure of imports, the countries were able to earmark a large part of their foreign exchange supply for purchases of equipment and basic inputs. Moreover, many of them had accumulated foreign exchange during the war or added to their holdings in the postwar period. Again, apart from the impetus automatically given to private investment by the development of import-substitution industries, governments began to take a much more active part in saving and capital formation, and often resorted to inflationary devices for this purpose.

By the end of the nineteen-forties, the situation was already in a state of flux and it took an entirely different turn as a result of the changes that accompanied the end of the Korean War. What were the basic reasons for the change, and why did they increase the importance of foreign capital?

The main reasons for the change were undoubtedly the sharp fluctuations during that period as a result of the hostilities in Korea and the first postwar economic recession in the United States. Acting in combination, these put an end to the recovery of the export sector which had begun in the early days of the Second World War. Another major factor was the steady deterioration in the terms of trade, which was particularly severe from the mid-fifties onward.

Furthermore, the change in the over-all balance-of-payments situation is linked to certain features of previous development which have already been analyzed in these pages. In conjunction with the external incentives that had been provided during the war years and immediately afterward, the development of substitution industries had raised income considerably above the levels attained in the nineteen-thirties, and this, for the reasons aforesaid, led to a disproportionate expansion of demand for imports. This process could be kept up as long as countries were in a position to draw on their accumulated reserves or to modify the composition of their external purchases. The situation altered radically once reserves were exhausted or substantially depleted, and the reducible margin of imports grew so narrow as to limit the second of the two fields for maneuver.

The combination of this metamorphosis with the change described above—the weakening of the export sector and therefore of the position with respect to foreign exchange supplies—gives the answer to the first part of the question.

The second part is probably related, in some countries, to the growing difficulty of forming domestic savings by means of inflationary expedients. Such procedures had proved more or less effective as long as they were backed by the recovery of the external sector and the vigorous impetus behind the initial development of substitution industries, and favored by the heedless unconcern of those affected by the inflationary process, but as circumstances changed they lost their efficacy. Moreover, even where recourse to compulsory saving methods continued to enjoy a measure of success, the other stumbling block remained: to turn these savings into investment, a considerable proportion of the funds built up had to be converted into foreign currency, because of the high import component in capital formation.

POSSIBLE FUNCTIONS OF FOREIGN COOPERATION

As part of the response to these new or growing problems, the question of credits and foreign investment comes to the fore.

In the first place, generally speaking, such contributions are viewed as a means of obtaining the additional foreign exchange resources required to maintain a high rate of development and at the same time close the gap between the demand for imports thus generated and the region's own regular export earnings. In other words, the role of the inflow of foreign funds is to relieve the "built-in disequilibrium" described at the beginning of the present analysis.

Still in close connection with the questions previously raised, external cooperation is visualized as fulfilling a second function, interrelated with the first: that of supplementing the most vitally important part of domestic savings—the resources earmarked for imports of capital goods—and reducing or eliminating the need to resort to inflationary expedients or to restrict consumption unduly.

To these two basic functions others might be added. One is linked to the operation of anti-inflationary policies, and is based on the assumption that a timely and adequate inflow of funds from abroad would cushion the depressive impact of an energetic effort to control external and internal disequilibrium.[17] Another outstanding role is that attributed especially to private investment, which can serve as a direct agent for the transfer of new techniques and new organizational patterns.

THE TEMPORARY NATURE OF THE EXPEDIENT

From the relevant ECLA studies it is clear that the functions assigned to external financing are related to the needs of a specific stage in Latin America's development. It may even be said that they are regarded as a device which will help to surmount the difficulties inherent in that stage and to facilitate the transition to another phase, in which their strategic importance would diminish, and development would come to depend mainly upon the mobilization and allocation of domestic resources. This vision of the future is based on the assumption that external cooperation—on an appropriate scale and on satisfactory terms—would simultaneously promote both internal diversification and export opportunities, thus widening the margin of domestic savings and increasing foreign exchange earnings. It would also open up additional possibilities of continuing to remodel the structure of imports in favor of capital goods and such inputs as can be replaced least easily or least economically by domestic production.

[17] See below, Chapter VI.

COOPERATION REQUIREMENTS

Consideration may now be given to ECLA's ideas on the conditions that would have to be fulfilled if external financing was to discharge these possible functions. The subject is discussed in detail in the document reproduced in Chapter IV of the present compendium and there seems to be no need to enlarge upon it further. Reference may usefully be made, however, to one or two major questions.

It should be borne in mind, of course, that the emphasis placed on the requirements which should be met by external cooperation stemmed from a keen awareness of the anomalies and risks involved in any form of borrowing. It was not overlooked that such cooperation might bypass the purposes and functions for which it was intended and become yet another factor making for disequilibrium and yet another obstacle to self-sustained development, in so far as the requirements stipulated were not complied with in full.

What were the conditions laid down in the ECLA documents as essential for the effectiveness of external aid?

The initial stress was laid on the most elementary requisites. The funds contributed should be sufficient in quantity to have appreciable effects on the development process. This carried the additional implication that loan costs and maturities and returns on investment should be kept down to proportions which would maintain the net contribution at the same level throughout the period to be covered. Importance was also attached to the continuity of the inflow of capital, which would enable internal programs or investment to be designed and carried out with the indispensable measure of security and stability.

Together with these basic requisites, attention was drawn to the necessity of setting up new financing institutions, revising the policy of those already in existence, and organizing institutional machinery for assembling, assessing and allocating foreign capital resources. Nor was it forgotten that evaluation agencies would be needed, which would be qualified to issue an authoritative technical verdict on the merits and implementation of programs for which financial assistance might be obtainable.

The fact that some of these proposals have materialized largely accounts for the progress made in organizing the institutional framework for the mobilization of external resources on Latin America's behalf. A number of others still represent distant goals, and it is to this circumstance that many of the existing problems—for instance, the "indebtedness spiral," as it is called,[18] and the inadequacy and unreliability of external financing—must be imputed.

The Time for Regional Integration

It would be impossible to evaluate the significance of ECLA's conceptual contribution and veritable campaign in favor of regional economic integration without considering two prime aspects of development in the last few decades, which had not been deliberately brought into focus before, although they had been receiving attention since the issue of the earliest ECLA documents.

In a way, the first aspect may be considered, without exaggeration, to be a complete contradiction of the inward-directed growth model, in that the structural changes entailed by the development of import substitution industry did not aim at or extend to a key segment of the over-all structure: the export sector. While the economies were being "modernized," in the sense that they were undergoing the changes to be expected with the spread of technical progress and the diversification of the production system, virtually no change took place in the primary-export system, specializing as it did in the production of a small number of primary products almost exclusively for export.

Needless to say, this particular dissociation has not occurred in the evolution of the countries at the center, nor apparently in that of the socialist countries. In both cases, diversification of the structure of production embraces not only the activities producing for the domestic market but export industries as well. The change is widespread: as the structure of production for the domestic market alters, so also does that of the external sector activities: the composition of exports changes. Moreover, although goods may be produced with a definite market in

[18] See, for example, *Economic Survey of Latin America*, 1965 (United Nations publication, Sales No.: 67.II.G.1), Chapter V.

view, in practice there is no out-and-out specialization, and goods are not produced exclusively for export or for the domestic market.

This characteristic is associated with another related feature which, in some degree, represents the other side of the coin: the fact that, at the national level, the changes in the process of inward-directed growth and industrial development take place almost entirely in the "watertight compartments" referred to in ECLA's early studies.

Needless to say, in this respect also Latin America's experience contrasts sharply with that of the centers, which adopted and still maintain a relatively "open" industrial development model.

This is not the place to analyze the causes of such striking contrasts. It may be noted in passing, however, that dissociation or dispersion in Latin America is due not only to geographical factors but also to the fact that the different countries had forged their own separate links with the centers during the phase of outward-directed growth. On the other hand, the absence of an outward-looking approach to industrial development in the Latin American countries may be ascribed both to their lack of experience and to their late arrival on the manufacturing scene, when other countries had already reached considerably higher levels of productivity. Latin America's industry is developing in unfavorable circumstances for its foreign trade, and it is based on small markets precisely at a time when economies of scale are beginning to be a prerequisite for the application of up-to-date techniques.

IMPLICATIONS OF THE CHARACTERISTICS AND OPTIONS

From an appraisal of the characteristics described above, it is not difficult to see that they were bound to give rise to further contradictions.

In the first place, the more vigorous growth deriving from the development of import substitution industries, in giving rise to an increasing demand for imports, was hampered by the slow growth of the traditional export sector. Secondly, inward-directed growth itself, besides being curbed by the limitations of the capacity to import, was to become more difficult as the "easy" stages of import substitution were passed and other problems of greater magnitude and complexity had to be faced, such as the size of the market required by this process, the volume of resources needed to finance it, and the technological requirements.

As noted in the previous section, a diagnosis based on these and other related facts led to more emphasis being placed on the external contribution. It was not, however, enough—or feasible or satisfactory in the long run—to leave the matter to decisions taken beyond the radius of national policy. Hence the need to seek sounder and more lasting formulas.

If more consideration is given to the contradictions indicated above, it can be seen that the main lines of a solution were fairly obvious. On the one hand, it was necessary to extend the structural changes to the export sector and diversify its essential base. In that way it would be possible to increase foreign exchange earnings and to make the Latin American economy less vulnerable than it is with the present high degree of concentration. On the other hand, the national markets would have to be broadened in order to satisfy the basic requirements for progressing to more advanced stages of industrial development.

Some ideas on how to do these two things began to take shape. One possibility was to give more impetus to foreign trade by expanding the traditional exports and placing new products, mainly manufactures, on the competitive and difficult world market. Another was to make a determined effort to incorporate in the market those populations or areas which had been left behind or bypassed by earlier development, an important matter in countries where this problem affects large groups or areas.

These activities were and continue to be necessary, a fact which is borne out by the attention they are given in various ECLA studies,[19] but apparently they were not enough. To achieve both objectives, regional integration emerged as the indispensable and virtually irreplaceable instrument, or the only measure capable of bringing about a qualitative change in the real situation and in the problems under consideration.

Apart from the thorough examination contained in Chapter V of this compendium, ECLA defined the essence of the problem as fol-

19 On the question of foreign trade, for example, see Chapter VIII.

lows, in one of its other documents: "An expansion of inter-Latin American trade based on an accelerated substitution process in respect of imports from other parts of the world, but carried out at regional level and by means of more intensive trade in traditional commodities . . . would have the advantage of enabling the substitution process to be carried farther, without detriment to specialization possibilities, than would be possible within the sphere of each country's individual market."[20]

By following this course, the basic framework of inward-directed growth for the countries of the region is expanded and modified. This concept is no longer confined to an individual country but extends to the whole common area. Substitution, therefore, would imply carrying out the process in and for each economy and also for the whole region. As countries proceed with import substitution for the region, they will be developing exports which will make it possible, and indeed necessary, for the other Latin American countries to finance and increase their imports from the region itself. Thus they would not have to extend the import substitution process along the whole front, which would have been essential—supposing it were possible—if each country was compelled to act on its own.

It is unnecessary to go deeply into many aspects of regional integration, since they are examined in greater detail in Chapter V. The main purpose here is merely to bring into focus the close relationship that exists between this question and the previous over-all analyses of Latin American development procedures and problems, which actually led to integration.

It is common knowledge, moreover, that the analysis and justification of this objective were accompanied by energetic and continuing action to create appropriate institutional machinery. In this respect, the establishment of both the Latin American Free Trade Association (ALALC) and the Permanent Secretariat of the General Treaty on Central American Economic Integration (SIECA) was primarily the result of ECLA's efforts.

20 *The Latin American Common Market,* (United Nations publication, Sales No.: 59,II.G.4), p. 67.

International Trade Policy

ECLA has recently been devoting special attention to questions directly connected with those just discussed in the preceding section. They concern the need to take advantage of new opportunities to reactivate the external sector by strengthening the position of primary products, promoting industrial exports to the world centers and devising more satisfactory formulas to ensure the effectiveness of external cooperation in the development of the peripheral countries.

The address delivered by the Executive Secretary of ECLA at the second session of the United Nations Conference on Trade and Development is quoted extensively in Chapter VIII of this book. It represents both the product and the gist of a whole series of studies which have acted as catalysts of Latin American thinking.[21] Particular mention should be made of the documents presented at the two sessions of UNCTAD, and of other special studies concerned with transport and external financing problems. The major postulates of these studies could hardly be more clear-cut; they are summarized below.

The first may be defined as follows: if the outdated pattern of the international division of labor is still, in essence, preserved intact, it is right and proper that at the very least the industrial centers should do their utmost to facilitate the access of primary products to their markets, especially as the result will be a more than proportional increase in demand for the manufactured goods they themselves produce. Clearly, any step in this direction, rather than representing a graceful concession, will mean that the industrialized countries are putting the interests of their economies as a whole before the individual interests and the existence of secondary economic areas or activities. In this connection, one of the documents reproduced draws attention to the vitally important and paradoxical fact that "while the industrialized countries have agreed upon decisions of enormous importance for the liberalization of their trade, which will certainly promote a new surge of rapid technical progress and economic growth in the developed areas of the world, no such agreement has been reached for adopting the measures

[21] See below, Chapter VIII.

or establishing the institutions which would make for equal progress in the developing countries."[22]

The second postulate relates to another patent fact, obviously linked to the preceding one: the countries at the center of the world economy should throw their markets open to industrial exports from the periphery, without demanding reciprocal concessions, not only because the impact of such a move on their over-all economies would be very slight, but also because its indirect effects would include an expansion of demand for the more complex goods in which their production systems specialize.

The third premise is no less relevant: in so far as the terms of external financing are not modified on the lines mapped out in an earlier section, inflows of foreign capital—which are inadequate, costly, unreliable and not always consonant with development priorities—may become yet another factor making for disequilibrium and possibly for strained relations with the suppliers of the capital in question.

A Panoramic View of Development Problems

Together with the effort to pursue the central line of analysis of Latin American development farther and in greater depth, ECLA has shown a tendency to broaden the scope of its studies so as to take in other relevant factors and questions, not only of an economic but also of a social and political nature. This progressive broadening of its approach is largely attributable to a reconsideration of the scale of the obstacles to growth and of the conditions under which they can be surmounted.

To elucidate this point, a contrast may usefully be drawn between the attitudes to the region's development prospects current in two significant periods. Up to 1950, a relatively optimistic view was taken of the future of industrialization and of the new development pattern. While the difficulties and limitations were recognized, the predominant feeling was one of confidence that the dynamism of the process itself, and the changes already brought about in the structure of production, would make it possible to forge ahead and to remove or reduce the

[22] *Ibid.*

most formidable barriers to progress. By 1960, a different mood seemed to prevail. Prospects were evaluated with a good deal more caution, and the magnitude and the varied nature of the obstacles to development, and of the requisites for the continuance of the process, aroused far more concern.

What was the reason for this change of front? To borrow the approach adopted in one of the studies included in the present compendium, it may be ascribed to a critical revaluation of the "effects" and the "conditions" of development.[23]

From the standpoint of the effects of the process, it can be seen that many significant and disquieting phenomena gradually took shape. There were, of course, the general circumstances that with certain exceptions—few in number and related, moreover, to very special situations—the economies of the region found great difficulty in attaining, and still more in maintaining, satisfactory growth rates. The prospects of establishing the process on a sound footing thus receded into a more distant future. Furthermore, in a number of countries—mainly those that had done most to diversify their structures of production—development trends became less firm as the gravity of the threats represented by inflation and external disequilibrium increased. Whenever the economic policy-makers sought to control such distortions, they found themselves forced to choose between two alternatives which in practice, although not in theory, were incompatible—stability and development; and in many cases the solution adopted furthered neither of these possible ends, but was detrimental to both, in the sense that the unfavorable effects on development strengthened one of the basic factors of instability.[24]

It was felt, moreover, that the difficulty of keeping up a steady and satisfactory rate of development without undermining stability was linked to the persistence and indeed the aggravation of certain external problems. In particular, the terms of trade, which had been deteriorating since the mid nineteen-fifties, had once again become a major handicap. Internal obstacles also seemed to loom larger. In several countries,

[23] See below, Chapter VII.
[24] See below, Chapter VI.

with the completion of what has been called the "easy" stage of import substitution, the margin for further diversification of the structures of production was growing narrower, while at the same time the whole development process was affected by the internal stumbling blocks deriving from lack of flexibility in the agricultural sector, a small market, and inadequate capacity for saving and capital formation.

While these were—and to a large extent still are—the general features of the process, others were also discernible which related to its economic and social content. One of these, for example, partially invalidated the theory that the expansion of a "modern sector," mainly built up around industry, would exert a vigorous promotional influence on the whole body of economic activities, and would thus tend to unify the system at a higher level of productivity. In practice, the tendency in many countries seems rather to have been toward what has been described as the concentration of technical progress and its benefits. This again is in striking contrast to one of the characteristics of development in the central economies. The disparities that used to and still do exist in these countries are not on the same scale or of the same kind as those observable in Latin America. In short, sectoral and regional disequilibria, instead of righting itself, has become worse, a development which accounts for the increasing attention devoted by economic policy-makers in the various countries to means of remedying this trend.

Furthermore, in close relation to the foregoing difficulties, a twofold problem arose: the inhabitants of rural and backward areas were strongly attracted by the more populous urban centers, while in these latter the "modern sector," and in particular the more capital-intensive and dynamic branches of manufacturing, showed a very limited capacity to increase employment opportunities.[25] The most visible and serious form assumed by the combined effect of these factors was the proliferation of the marginal settlements ("shantytowns") which are a more or less salient feature of large towns in Latin America.

There is another important question which may be regarded as the outcome of some of the foregoing situations and as a factor that has

25 With reference to the linkage between this situation and the problems relating to the assimilation of imported technology, see below, Chapter I.

helped to create and aggravate them: namely, the marked concentration of income distribution which has been prone to occur at all the relevant levels (personal, functional, sectoral, and regional).[26] This is another basic respect in which the hopes of those who expected the history of the industrial centers to repeat itself were doomed to disappointment. While economic development in Latin America has undeniably raised income levels in a segment of the middle-income groups and in the upper stratum of manual workers—especially those employed in the "modern sector"—it is equally true that the proportion of total income falling to the privileged minority is much larger than in the industrialized countries, and, above all, that about 50 per cent of the population still receives only a tiny share, which in absolute per capita terms is estimated at an average of not more than $140 a year.

The social significance of this situation needs no comment; nor do its implications with respect to political tensions and the difficulties of achieving a minimum degree of collective unanimity, solidarity, and participation in the arduous task of national development and self-realization. Its economic repercussions are no less obvious and important. Suffice it to recall the population sectors that virtually play no part in the development process, and all that they represent for the domestic market, at once as ballast and as a potential reserve; or to consider how they affect public expenditure and welfare services—which do not always strike at the root of the problem—by diverting resources from more advantageous investment possibilities.

In the present cursory review, allusion must be made to a problem which is relatively new in the stage of industrial development based on import substitution, but is plainly significant at several levels. This is the question of foreign enclaves in the most dynamic key sectors of the new manufacturing structure and the complementary financial and business activities. The existence of such enclaves produces innumerable repercussions relating to the balance of payments, technological dependence, dependence on decisions, and criteria that are not necessarily in the best interests of the national economy concerned. Furthermore, it has another consequence to which due weight is not always

[26] See below, Chapter IX, and "*Estudios sobre la distribución del ingreso en América Latina*" (E/CN.12/770 and Add. 1).

attached. It hampers the development of national entrepreneurial skills.[27]

In this context, a factor must be noted which has lessened internal independence in a different way, and which has its origin in the shortcomings of the external cooperation system. This is the "indebtedness spiral," as it is called, which has already been mentioned in these pages, and is particularly serious in some countries.[28]

If the new circumstances are considered from the standpoint of the general and particular "conditions" required for a development process, it is easy to see that almost all the key variables or factors mentioned in the foregoing analysis, which was preeminently economic—such as rates of saving and capital formation, the channeling of investment, the responsiveness and flexibility of the sectors of production, the efficacy of programs and machinery for the allocation of resources—were conditioned, if not determined, by a complex of social, political, and even psychological factors whose implications could not be ignored or shirked if development policy was to bear fruit.

The new approach to the problem of Latin American development, which began to take shape in the early nineteen-sixties, was crystallized by Mr. Raúl Prebisch, then Executive Secretary of ECLA, in the document he presented to the Commission at its tenth session (Mar del Plata, Argentina, March 1963), the introductory chapter of which summarizes this approach and is reproduced as Chapter IX of the present document.

Mr. Prebisch's study is a coherent presentation of the central line of thinking and analysis already described, with the addition of new circumstances, problems, and tasks which subsequently appeared. Its point of departure is that the lack of dynamism in Latin American development and its various distortions "are not determined by circumstantial or transient factors. They are an expression of the critical state of affairs in our time and of the incapacity of the economic system—owing to structural defects that it has been beyond our ability or our

27 For a discussion of various aspects of this problem, see Raúl Prebisch, *Towards a Dynamic Development Policy for Latin America* (United Nations publication, Sales No.: 64.II.G.4), pp. 53 *et seq.*

28 See *Economic Survey of Latin America, 1965*, pp. 91 *et seq.*

power to remedy—to achieve and maintain a rate of development consonant with the growth of the population and with its demands for a speedy improvement in its levels of living."[29]

What are the main aspects or factors determining this "critical state of affiairs"? On the one hand, it is a product of the numerous anomalies and deficiencies in trade, financing, and foreign investment, and of the obstacles to accelerating and extending Latin American integration. On the other, it stems from certain features of the social structure, which still predominate in Latin America but which vary in intensity according to the conditions in each particular country. The question of social structure includes a number of topics which received too little attention in the past, and it is, therefore, worthwhile to comment on it.

One of the features referred to is the excessive rigidity of the social structure, which prevents the emergence of new dynamic elements and deprives the bulk of the population of the social mobility which would ensure the expansion of the ruling groups and infuse them with new life, and would also establish another level of effective participation in development decisions and tasks. In fact, those who can participate and carry some weight in public affairs represent a relatively small proportion of the various social groups and interests. This means that the great majority of wage-earners, agricultural workers, technicians, professionals, and even entrepreneurs, are still not directly linked with the growth process and do not participate in that process as active and united agents. This situation may have been compatible with development in times gone by but does not seem to be so today, given the size of the undertaking and the absolute necessity of the bulk of the people being consciously associated with development objectives and efforts.

The most striking and significant socioeconomic expression of this "closed" society is what the authur calls "a situation of privilege in the distribution of wealth." These distributional privileges are both a consequence of the structure described and a cause of the greater or lesser isolation of the masses from development goals and tasks.

The analysis touches upon the diagnosis and implications of the prevailing pattern of income distribution in Latin America, but it also goes

[29] See below, Chapter IX.

on to discuss the design and content of a new kind of distribution policy to meet the demands of development and social justice.

With regard to the diagnosis, the study stresses two outstanding elements of the present distribution structure: the striking concentration of income in the upper income groups, which represent only 5 per cent of the population, and the meager participation and absolute level of income of the "base of the pyramid," or lower-income groups, which represent 50 per cent of the population.

The study also stresses the somewhat paradoxical fact that the marked inequality of distribution, far from strengthening savings and capital formation, led to the creation of consumption levels and patterns similar to those of the upper-income groups in the industrialized countries, and often even more exaggerated. Thus, the social sacrifices and the restrictions on the expansion of the domestic market which are a consequence of this great inequality of distribution are not even hypothetically offset by a high rate of capital formation.

To reduce or eliminate these distributional privileges seems, therefore, to be an essential task of economic policy. The strategy does not, however, consist in "taking income away from the upper minority and simply distributing it among the broad masses of the population, for with per capita personal income in Latin America as a whole barely amounting to $370 a year, the benefits of such a redistribution would not stretch very far. But if, on the other hand, restrictions on the consumption of the privileged groups were reflected in a steady increase in net capital formation, the standard of living of the bulk of the population would rise progressively faster."[30]

To avoid any misunderstanding, it should be made clear that this transfer of surplus consumption to capital formation does not imply any lack of consideration for the social aspects. On the contrary, it opens the way, in the first place, to solving the crucial problem of unemployment. In other words, despite the uses of investment and its "technology-intensive" nature, only a substantial increase in capital formation and in productive capacity can help to raise the uncertain rate of absorption of the labor force in productive and steady employ-

30 *Ibid.*

ment. Second, it does not ignore the significance and place of social investment. It is explicitly stated that "the first concrete expression of an income redistribution policy should be in this field, through social investment in the development and training of human resources and in the provision of effective means of access to education at all levels. This would bring about a new order of things in which the dynamic elements that reach the upper strata would be proportionate to the numerical size of the social strata from which they come."[31]

The new "state of affairs in our time" which is in sight will finally emerge only as a result of far-reaching changes in the region's economic and social structure. This is the message of the document that concludes this compendium.

The changes that are advocated include the transformation of the system of land tenure, which has been the keystone of all attempts to put an end to underdevelopment. It is imperative for three main reasons: to make use of the saving potential and encourage social mobility, to satisfy demand in a rapidly growing population and to raise the levels of living of the rural masses, which still constitute almost half the population of the region and so far have been more or less excluded from any share in the development process.

This is not the only reform that brooks no delay. If the potential sources of capital formation represented by the concentration of income are to be tapped, tax, financial, and other machinery must be established to divert these funds from nonessential consumer expenditure to investment that is economically and socially productive. This shift will, in its turn, involve not only technical and organizational problems but also what is perhaps the main issue, namely, the social and political changes that are required to make the new pattern of spending a practical possibility.

[31] See Prebisch, *Towards a Dynamic Development Policy for Latin America*, p. 46.

DEVELOPMENT PROBLEMS IN LATIN AMERICA

AN ANALYSIS BY
THE UNITED NATIONS ECONOMIC COMMISSION
FOR LATIN AMERICA

CHAPTER I

FOREIGN TRADE AND THE DEVELOPMENT OF LATIN AMERICA

The Periphery and the Spread of Technical Progress

A New Stage in the Spread of Technical Progress[1]

The spread of technical progress from the countries where it had its source to the rest of the world has, from the point of view of each generation, been relatively slow and irregular. During the long period which elapsed between the Industrial Revolution and the First World War, the new methods of production in which technique has constantly found its expression reached only a small proportion of the world's population.

The movement began in the United Kingdom, continued in varying degrees of intensity in Europe, received an extraordinary impulse in the United States, and finally reached Japan, which strove rapidly to assimilate Western methods of production. Thus the great industrial centers of the world grew up, while the vast and heterogeneous peripheral areas of the new system shared to only a slight extent in the improvement of productivity.

In these peripheral areas, technical progress affected only small sec-

[1] *Economic Survey of Latin America,* 1949 (United Nations publication, Sales No.: 51.II.G.1), pp. 3–5.

tors of the vast population, as it usually penetrated only where it was needed to produce foodstuffs and raw materials at low cost for delivery to the great industrial centers.

If this economic pattern which the world had developed before the First World War could have been considered the ideal system of the division of labor, any departure from its principles would, of course, have had to be considered as a deviation from the economy's normal way of functioning. However, there could be no sound, scientific reason for believing that this was a final pattern. All that happened in that period was that the world economy passed through a singularly important stage in its growth, but in spite of the significance of its effects, it could hardly be called a final stage since, to a certain extent, it had left untouched the vast peripheral area, with its enormous potential capacity for assimilating technical progress, so as to raise the very inadequate level of living of the great masses of its population.

Carefully considered, the economic development of the peripheral countries is one more stage in the worldwide spread of the new form of productive technique, or, if preferred, in the organic development of world economy. A few early signs of this new stage had already appeared in the primary producer countries before the First World War. But it was the war, with the consequent difficulties of maintaining imports, which revealed the industrial possibilities of those countries, while the great economic Depression of the 1930's strengthened the conviction that those possibilities had to be used, in order to offset, by means of internal development, the manifest failure of the external incentive which until then had stimulated Latin American economy; this conviction was confirmed during the Second World War, when Latin American industry, with all its improvisations and difficulties, nevertheless became a source of employment and of consumption for a large and increasing part of the population.

Latin America has, therefore, entered a new stage in the worldwide spread of technique, though technical methods are still far from having been assimilated completely in primary production, for, as explained above, new production methods tend to be adopted in activities connected in one way or another with the exportation of foodstuffs and raw materials rather than in other activities. In the performance of this function as a primary producer which is actually the function of Latin America, there was from the beginning a strict selection of aptitudes. Vast regions were coupled to the world economic system, while others, no less large and generally more densely populated, have up to the present time remained outside the system. Hence, development was very uneven. New and fertile lands, which became accessible during the second half of the last century through the development of transport, acquired human resources, technique, and capital with which to undertake agricultural and mineral production to satisfy the evergrowing European demand, whereas the impressive process of the extension of capitalist technique and economy bypassed other lands, which had been cultivated and had supported their populations for centuries, but which suffered from a low level of productivity or difficulties of access. Thus in Latin America there remain extensive regions, with relatively large populations, in which the methods of working the land, and consequently the standard of living of the people, are essentially precapitalist. Accordingly, economic development in these countries requires first and foremost technical progress in agriculture and other related activities, including means of communication.

Experience has repeatedly shown, however, that as modern technique increases productivity, a surplus of labor, no longer needed by agriculture, is created. It then becames the task of industry and other activities to absorb this labor productively. Hence, agricultural improvement and industrial development are two aspects of the problem of economic development. One need only consider the large number of people engaged in agriculture in Latin America, with the exception of a few countries, to realize the magnitude of this problem and the vast effort which will be necessary to solve it.

Through the force of circumstances, with the spread of technical progress, an increasing proportion of the economically active population of Latin America, as part of the peripheral area, will be diverted from agriculture toward industry and other urban occupations. Yet that would not constitute a full solution, unless certain precapitalist or semicapitalist methods of production (still used by a large part of the population) were to evolve toward methods characterized by a high level of capitalization per person, and high productivity. Though this is indeed very important, the problem of the economic development of Latin America cannot be limited to these terms, for to do so would be to ignore other fundamental aspects. This is not surprising, for though there are certain common denominators in the appearance of the problem in the different countries, there are also specific differences which must be considered lest unwarranted generalizations are arrived at.

Past Trends and New Developments[2]

In Latin America, reality is undermining the outdated pattern of the international division of labor, which achieved great importance in the nineteenth century and, as a theoretical concept, continued to exert considerable influence until very recently.

Under that schema, the specific task that fell to Latin America, as part of the periphery of the world economic system, was that of producing food and raw materials for the great industrial centers.

There was no place within that schema for the industrialization of the new countries. It is nevertheless being forced upon them by events. Two world wars in a single generation and a great economic crisis between them have shown the Latin American countries their opportunities, clearly pointing the way to industrial activity.

The academic discussion, however, is far from ended. In economics, ideologies usually tend either to lag behind events or to outlive them. It is true that the reasoning on the economic advantages of the international division of labor is theoretically sound, but it is usually forgotten that it is based upon an assumption which has been conclusively proved false by facts. According to this assumption, the benefits of technical progress tend to be distributed alike over the whole community, either by the lowering of prices or by the corresponding raising of incomes. The countries producing raw materials obtain their share of these benefits through international exchange, and therefore have no need to industrialize. If they were to do so, their lesser efficiency would result in their losing the conventional advantages of such exchange.

[2] Raúl Prebisch, "The Economic Development of Latin America and its Principal Problems" (United Nations publication, Sales No.: 1950.II.G.2), *Economic Bulletin for Latin America*, VII, No. 1, (1962), 1.

The flaw in this assumption is that of generalizing from the particular. If by "the community" only the great industrial countries are meant, it is indeed true that the benefits of technical progress are gradually distributed among all social groups and classes. If, however, the concept of the community is extended to include the periphery of the world economy, a serious error is implicit in the generalization. The enormous benefits that derive from increased productivity have not reached the periphery in a measure comparable to that obtained by the peoples of the great industrial countries. Hence the outstanding difference between the level of living of the masses of the former and of the latter, and the manifest discrepancies between thier respective abilities to accumulate capital, since the margin of saving depends primarily on increased productivity.

Thus there exists an obvious disequilibrium, a fact which, whatever its explanation or justification, destroys the basic premise underlying the schema of the international division of labor.

Hence the fundamental significance of the industrialization of the new countries. Industrialization is not an end in itself, but the principal means at the disposal of those countries of obtaining a share of the benefits of technical progress and of progressively raising the level of living of the masses.

Analysis and Appraisal of Estimates Based on Traditional Economic Theory[3]

The Premise of the Mobility of the Factors of Production

A good many of the peripheral countries, including those of Latin America, appear to have decided to make their own economies the basis of the development of industry, but it is not without interest to discuss briefly the conditions which would have to be fufilled in order to carry out the opposite policy: namely, that the existing industrial centers should continue increasing their industries, while the periphery continued to devote itself to primary production.

[3] *Economic Survey of Latin America*, 1949, pp. 13–14 and 46–61.

It has already been seen that when technical progress is extended to primary production, it produces a surplus of gainfully employed population in that sector, which can be absorbed by industry and other activities. If these other activities were not developed in the periphery, they would automatically have to develop in the centers, which would consequently have to absorb the surplus manpower, in addition to that part of the natural increase in population which could not be absorbed in their own primary production.

This presupposes complete mobility of population; in other words it would mean not only that the unemployable surplus of the population must be willing to emigrate from the periphery, overcoming a rooted unwillingness, but also that the countries of the center must be prepared to admit large masses of immigrants who, accustomed to low wages, would compete to advantage with the workers of the center.

This demonstrates that the idea that the peripheral countries should continue to act as primary producers as they did during a particular stage in the process of the extension of technique, according to the precepts of the international division of labor, is based upon certain assumptions which do not appear compatible with the economic and social reality of the world as this has emerged since the process started.

The logical consequences of the premise of the mobility of the factors of production, which is the postulate on which the theoretical concept of the international division of labor is built, are very far-reaching and must be borne in mind in any attempt to interpret the significance of this reality by theory.

If this premise of mobility had been an actual fact, the economic and social effects of technical progress, and the way it spread, would certainly have been very different from what actually took place.

The Spread of Technical Progress and the Terms of Trade

We have already stated that it is not possible to understand the problems connected with Latin America's economic development without first investigating this process and its consequences. One of these consequences, without a doubt, is the constant tendency of the terms of trade to deteriorate. The phenomenon is purely dynamic and we hope to prove that ultimately it can be explained by the relative slowness of the world's industrial development to absorb the real or potential surplus of population gainfully employed in primary occupations. Technical progress, as we have seen, tends to decrease the amount of labor engaged in primary production. However, this decrease has been extremely slight over the years. In the meantime, new productive techniques are evolved which make further readjustments necessary in the distribution of employed population.

Thus there is a relative abundance of potential labor in primary occupations, tending constantly to exert pressure upon wages and the prices of primary products and preventing the periphery from sharing with the industrial centers the advantages of the technical progress attained by the latter. Furthermore, the periphery is unable to retain a part of the benefits of its own technical progress.

Significance of the Price Relationship between Primary and Industrial Goods

From the outset one must be careful not to attribute to this statement implications which can only be understood later. Therefore, a short explanation will be useful before going more deeply into the subject. If prices reflected only decreasing costs resulting from technical progress, then prices of manufactured goods should fall more than those of primary goods, since, as is generally recognized, the increment of productivity is greater in the former than in the latter. The price relation would thus seem to swing in favor of primary production, and its index or that of its equivalent, that is, the index of the terms of trade, would consequently rise. A rise of, say, 100 to 150 would indicate that the same amount of primary products as before could purchase 50 per cent more manufactured goods. Primary producers would then be able to share equally with the manufacturers the profits derived from technical progress, as they would be able to purchase larger amounts of goods of higher quality. If, despite the greater decline in the cost of manufactured goods, the index of the price relationship were to remain at 100, it would mean that producers of manufactured goods would have retained for themselves the advantages of greater quantity and higher quality of manufactured goods. Should the index fall below 100, then not only would primary producers not have received any share from increased industrial productivity but they would have been unable to retain for themselves the full profits of their own technical progress, since they would have surrendered a part of it to the manufacturers. This does not mean that primary producers are worse off than they were before. Everything depends on the degree of increased productivity reached and the extent to which it is transferred to industrial manufacturers. If the index falls to 80, for instance, primary producers will be able to obtain 20 per cent less manufactured goods than they did before, for the same amount of primary goods. However, if to obtain that same amount they need work only half as long as before, one hour's labor would now allow them to produce 60 per cent more manufactured goods, instead of 100 per cent more, as would have been the case had they received the full benefits of their own technical progress; or an even greater quantity had they been able to share in the benefits of technical progress achieved in the industrial sector, should such progress be greater than that achieved in the field of primary production.[4]

The indices available seem to indicate that in the past seventy-five years something of this sort has occurred; that is to say, if, as is likely, technical progress in primary production at the periphery has been less than that of industry at the center, then the periphery will have transferred to the center part of the benefits of its own technical progress. Unfortunately, owing to the lack of data concerning the increment of productivity in primary production, it is not possible to ascertain the extent of such benefits and what part of them has remained in the primary producer countries. We will return to this aspect of the question later. Meanwhile, we shall try to explain the causes of this phenomenon, which is so vital to the economic development of Latin America.

The Real or Potential Surplus of Gainfully Employed Population and the Terms of Trade

We have already stated that a surplus of labor generally exists in primary production and that this excess exerts an unfavorable pressure

[4] For a fuller analysis of this phenomenon, see Prebisch, "The Economic Development of Latin America," p. 2.

on primary wages and costs. This tendency derives on the one hand from the relatively large increase of population in the regions of primary production and on the other from technical progress, which reduces the number of persons required to obtain the same quantity of products. The absorption of such a surplus in fact becomes the task of industry and the occupations directly or indirectly depending on the development of industry.

The surplus may be either real or potential, that is to say, it may already have become a reality through the application of new techniques in primary production or occur when new methods are introduced either spontaneously or as a consequence of industry's labor requirements which, by drawing labor from primary production, cause wages to rise, and force an improvement in methods of production. This latter case seems to have occurred frequently in the United States, where industrial areas attract population from the peripheral zones of primary production in the country. A real surplus of gainfully employed population could also occur if technical progress in primary production was not accompanied by either prior or simultaneous development of industry and its related occupations, in which case neither would then be capable of absorbing the excess labor as it arises.

In either case, if the gainfully employed population were perfectly mobile and did not show reluctance or deliberate opposition to migration, and if the rapid development of industry and its related occupations could immediately absorb the aforesaid real or potential excess of gainfully employed, then there would be a marked tendency toward a leveling of primary and industrial wages, even making allowance for differences in skill. Both would benefit from the general increment to productivity if, instead of wages rising with the increase of productivity, prices fell together with costs.

However, an examination of the situation in the world as a whole shows that both industry and its related occupations have developed relatively slowly, so that absorption of the real or potential surplus of gainfully employed population in primary production has been considerable in the great industrial countries; but the process is only just beginning in Latin America and the rest of the periphery.

The large countries, given the present structure of the world's economy, limit the process to their own population. Within their frontiers, industry and its associated activities do not develop in such a manner as to absorb the population of the periphery, so that the peripheral countries have no means of absorbing the surplus of their gainfully employed population except by developing their own industrial activity. It is not possible for them to employ this surplus in expanding primary production since the distribution of the active population is not arbitrary but depends on productive technique, as has been pointed out above.

Consequently, the relatively slow spread of technical progress has carried more weight than the factors which tend to distribute its benefits over the world, and the periphery not only has been generally unable to share with the industrial centers in the advantages derived from the technical progress in these centers, but has even been compelled to cede to them a part of the benefits deriving from its own progress, owing to the insistent pressure of the real or potential surplus of gainfully employed population.

Degree to Which Benefits of Technical Progress Are Transferred

The magnitude of this cession by the periphery to the center of a part of the benefits derived from technical progress in primary production is not uniform. On the contrary, the intensity of the movement varies in proportion to the strength of two opposing forces. On the one hand, we have the growth of primary production and, on the other, the demand for primary goods in the industrial centers. Should the latter increase more than the former, the amount ceded decreases; and the centers might even transfer to the periphery a part of the benefits of their technical progress, a phenomenon which would become manifest in the improvement, for the periphery, of the terms of reciprocal trade. However, if demand in the industrial centers increases relatively less than primary production, or is slow to recuperate after an acute depression, the price relationship will deteriorate for the periphery, and the degree of the transfer to the center will increase in inverse ratio to the proportional or absolute weakening of the dynamic industrial factor.

There is, in fact, a dynamic element in industry which is not found to a comparable extent in primary production. The latter, as its name would imply, covers the initial phases of the productive process, while industry accounts for subsequent stages. Because of this relative position of the two activities, the increase in industrial activity stimulates primary production, but the latter has not the power to generate industrial production. When industrial entrepreneurs, stimulated by the normal economic forces, or by extraordinary factors as in times of war, undertake to increase production, demand for primary products increases; as profits are consequently greater, entrepreneurs in the periphery seek to increase primary production. The spontaneous increase of the latter, on the other hand, does not cause a similar rise in industrial demand which would be capable of absorbing that increase, as can easily be seen from the following example. Let us assume, exaggerating the proportions to simplify matters, that in a total selling price of 1,000 units for a finished product, 500 correspond to the periphery and the rest represent values added during the various stages of the productive process, corresponding to industrial sectors. Let it further be assumed that the periphery on its own initiative intends to increase its production by 10 per cent, giving its productive factors an added income of 50. To simplify even further, let it be assumed that this increase of income is entirely absorbed by the consumption of finished goods from the center. It is clear that the demand for such goods will only increase by 5 per cent at most, whereas primary production will have increased by 10 per cent. There would, therefore, be no increase of industrial demand sufficient to absorb the increased primary production and the latter's terms of trade would deteriorate. In actual fact, the share of primary production in the value of finished goods is less than that given in our example, and the increase in income is not absorbed entirely and immediately by the consumption of finished goods. In reality, the periphery's influence on the center would be weaker and the consequent disequilibrium would be correspondingly greater.

The foregoing affords us a better understanding of the effects of increased production in the periphery deriving from either increased population or from improved technical progress, and shows that if such an increase of production is not accompanied by an equivalent increase in the demand for primary goods in the industrial centers, the position of the periphery is weakened and it cannot resist the pressure of factors which tend to take from it the benefits of its own productivity.

Dynamic Importance of Industrial Growth

From our remarks concerning the dynamic significance of industrial development, it may be seen that this development makes itself felt in two ways: first, by what we have called demand from the center—this covers both raw materials for industry and foodstuffs required by the center—and secondly, by the absorption of surplus manpower from primary production. Let us look at this second point.

It has been shown that the centers absorb their own surpluses but not that of the periphery. However, they may have an indirect influence on the number of the gainfully employed in the periphery, through the demand for primary products. If industry and other activities at the center develop to such an extent that they not only absorb the surplus manpower of their own primary production but also the population which that production requires in order to meet the increased industrial demand, then the centers would have to import from the periphery a greater proportion of primary goods to meet the increase of their own requirements. In this way the periphery would obtain relief from the pressure of its surplus population and at the same time the deterioration of the terms of trade would be halted.

Phenomena of this nature must have occurred in the development of those countries which have now become great industrial centers; but there are other, better known, and perhaps more important ways in which industrial development has functioned as a dynamic factor, absorbing surplus population from primary production. It is a well-known fact that when the Industrial Revolution was in full swing in the nineteenth century, the European population increased considerably. An increasingly large part of this population increase was absorbed by industry and other related occupations developing at the time, and the rest was engaged in primary production not only at the center but also in the new overseas countries which technical progress in transport had thrown open to international economy, especially in the latter half of the century. Large numbers began to emigrate from the older regions of primary production in Europe (which were gradually becoming more and more industrialized) to the newer areas which had become either complements or substitutes in the production of primary goods. If we look at the phenomenon as a whole, however, we perceive that the proportion of persons gainfully employed in primary production tended to decrease, whereas that in industry and related economic activities tended to increase. Nevertheless, the decrease was not sufficient to avoid a relative drop in primary prices.

Productivity in the new lands was higher per capita than in the older regions, and progress in transport enabled goods from the former to reach the European markets easily and cheaply. It is possible that this increase in production, probably greater than that of demand at the center, greatly influenced the deterioration of the terms of trade which occurred after the eighteen-seventies and continued until the First World War.

Then, as now, the growth of industry probably did not have sufficient impetus to prevent the terms of trade from changing, to the disadvantage of the periphery. If industry and related occupations at the centers had absorbed more of the population employed in primary production, emigration toward new countries would have been less, and consequently they would have had fewer people available to increase primary production; thus primary production would have been in a more favorable position vis-à-vis demand from the center.

A good deal of this will remain conjectural until further research has been undertaken. Nor should we forget that, in the case of some primary goods at least, the increase of productivity indirectly attained when the new countries were opened to world trade by technical progress in transport, may possibly have been greater than that attained by certain industrial sectors. This would not, of course, invalidate this analysis since, if a part of the benefits of technical progress in primary production in the periphery is transferred to the industrial centers, both when the increase of productivity in primary occupations is greater than in industry and when the increase is less, the reason is probably that the real or potential surplus of gainfully employed population engaged in primary production exerts a persistent pressure on wages and prices.

Not all the countries then opened up to the international economy were predominantly exploited by immigrant labor from the older regions of Europe. In the Latin American countries with old settled populations that had come to live there before or after the Spanish conquest, there is more than ample potential labor to work the land, whether in agriculture or mining. For this and other reasons, these countries do not attract immigrants from Europe, or at least not to the same extent as do other countries. This fact cannot be overlooked in a study of the changes in the terms of trade of the various primary products, according to the type of product, the pattern of production, and the degree of technical progress attained. Yet we must disregard it in this summary explanation, which for the moment has no other purpose than to clarify certain fundamental ideas for a better understanding of the problem of the terms of trade.

The period during which the new lands were opened up on a large scale in Latin America may be taken as ending somewhere between the First World War and the Great Depression. There are remarkable contrasts between this period and the subsequent period. During the latter the deterioration of the terms of trade was much more pronounced than before, since the marked deterioration during the First World War was followed by that caused by the Depression. There is not only a transfer to the center of the benefits accruing from technical progress in transport and other activities which made possible the better utilization of the increased productivity of the new lands, but also a transfer of part of the increase in productivity directly obtained from improved technical methods of exploitation, or perhaps the whole of the increase and even more, as may have occurred in some cases.

Exports, which in the previous period had generally increased more than the population, continued increasing, but at a slower rate than the population; the serious consequences of this fact in conjunction with the adverse trend in the terms of trade have already been pointed out. In addition, income from land, expressed in terms of constant prices, decreased instead of increasing. All these circumstances combine to place an entirely different complexion on the economic development of Latin America compared with the earlier development of other countries.

Wages and Income from Land in the Development of the Periphery

In this first analysis of the terms of trade, it can be stated that in Latin America the export industries to which these terms relate have, as a general rule, kept wages at a fairly low level compared with wages at the centers, even in cases where there has been an appreciable increase in productivity. We should not forget, however, that there have always been marked differences from country to country and that, in recent times, increases have been achieved where the organization of labor and other favorable factors made them possible. A number of factors account for such differences between the wage levels, among these the extent to which the industrial development of each country has progressively absorbed the surplus population and tended to raise wages relatively when competitive conditions in the international sphere allowed.

The fact that wages have remained at comparatively low levels during the primary development of the Latin American periphery does not mean that technical progress has not been able to increase other sources of income considerably. In those areas which are opened up to agricultural or mining exploitation, a sharp increase has occurred in income from land whereby the value of the land itself, previously worth little or practically nothing, was greatly enhanced. The income from the economically new lands is, in the last analysis, the expression of their greater productivity as compared with the older lands. Technical progress in transport is largely responsible for this increase of land income. A part of the benefits derived from this progress remains in the hands of the landowners, while another part flows into the industrial centers, by means of a relative lowering of prices.

The economic and social repercussions of this fact are indeed vast, as increasing returns from the soil give a very special character to the penetration of the capitalist technique in the export industries of the peripheral countries.

The relatively low level of wages in primary production was therefore compatible with the high increase in income from land, to the advantage of certain social classes.

Thus we find considerable sources of income springing up during the primary development of certain countries in which more advanced forms of economic development may later thrive, whereas in other countries, even though income from land also greatly increases, an appreciable part of the increase flows into the industrial centers, especially in the development of certain mining enterprises.

Terms of Trade in this New Stage of Extension of Technical Progress

It has been shown that technical progress had been predominant in Latin America's primary export activities, though with varying intensity. There is still much room for technical improvement in these occupations; but if present world economic conditions continue, it is possible that these improvements will not guarantee the permanent raising of wage levels. On the contrary, wages may even be lowered and a large part of the profits derived from technical progress lost, if the surplus population created by these very improvements cannot simultaneously be absorbed into industry and its associated occupations.

Still, the periphery is immense, and the population which will have to be absorbed by its industry and associated occupations as modern technique expands is also large. If a country proposed to raise its wage levels by increasing the productivity of its export occupations and absorbing into industry the surplus of gainfully employed population accruing therefrom, it might be seriously hindered by other countries, also engaged in improving their techniques, but making no effort to raise the very low level of their wages.

This might be the case for areas which are at present engaged in a process of primary development similar to that which began about the middle of the nineteenth century in the Latin American periphery. In these areas there is no industrial development to absorb the surplus population, and this lack may contribute to the maintenance of low wage levels. This is one of Latin America's most serious problems, especially owing to its influence on the phenomenon described above in connection with the terms of trade of certain important products.

The same thing does not occur in the case of primary production for domestic consumption in these same countries where, in general, little technical progress has been introduced, as compared with export industries. It is obvious that if the surplus of gainfully employed cannot be absorbed there, prices will drop as productivity rises, to the advantage of other social groups; but in this case the phenomenon can be counteracted by the development of industry and its related occupations, ensuring that primary producers obtain all the benefits deriving from technical progress without interference from competitor countries.

Nevertheless, even in the case where the benefits of technical progress in export industries flow abroad, a net increase of income would be possible by employing in industry and its associated occupations the surplus of labor created by technical progress in primary production. In other words, despite the possible deterioration of the terms of trade, the peripheral countries can obtain for themselves the full benefits accruing from technical progress in primary production for the domestic market, as well as from technical progress in industry, as applied to the surplus gainfully employed population; but it is obvious that the net increase in income will be proportionately greater in accordance with the country's ability to counteract the tendency of the terms of trade to worsen.

Another Form of Transfer of Benefits of Technical Progress

At the outset, we cautioned against any tendency to attribute to the terms of trade, without further study, any implication other than a mere statement of fact. The preceding analysis now permits us to study the possible implications, beginning with those which seem unacceptable.

First let us take the ethical implications. The fact that the centers tend to retain the benefits derived from their own technical progress does not mean that they are taking something that does not rightfully belong to them. From the ethical standpoint, there might be more than one justification for this procedure. However, this point is irrelevant to the present report. Our purpose is rather to point out that this method of appropriating those benefits was not assumed in theories which have had great influence on certain currents of economic thought. According to these theories, the benefits accruing from technical progress should flow equally to the whole community in the form of lower prices or increased incomes. This is what has, in point of fact, generally taken place, but only in the industrial centers which have retained the benefits of their technical progress. The same theories furthermore assumed the absolute mobility of factors and products, and the abstract world based on this assumption is substantially different from the one in which we live. It would, therefore, be necessary to revise the theory *ab initio* before applying it to the study of problems of economic development in the periphery. If the world division of labor had been effected according to this theory, the distribution of economic activities throughout the world would perhaps have been very different from what it is today, and the problems presented by the differences in the rate of increase of productivity and income, which so profoundly affect the world economy, would not have assumed their present proportions. The difficulties would have been of another kind, perhaps far more serious than those with which we are now faced.

This difference between the abstract world of absolute mobility and of leveling tendencies, on the one hand, and the complex reality of the present economic organization, on the other, makes it difficult to compare the results which, in given circumstances, would correspond to that theory, with those which are, in fact, observed.

It might be argued that, if the centers did not retain the benefits of their own technical progress, every peripheral country would be able to attain far better terms of trade than at present and its income level would approach that of the centers; but it might similarly be contended that the peripheral countries derive a lower income than that of the centers from their export industries because their productivity is lower. According to the above-mentioned theory, no country, region, or industry could maintain its position in a state of absolute mobility of the factors of production if its technique was inferior to that of other countries, regions, or industries, since it would no longer be able to export and its factors of production would be transferred to other countries, or to other regions or industries in that same country.

Furthermore, according to the same theory, if the benefits derived from technical progress flow from one party to another, similarly, benefits derived from a greater productivity of the latter must flow toward the former. There is reciprocity in this movement and in no case could the transfer be a premium on inefficiency in production.

Since the theory must not be applied only in part, we will do no more than keep it in mind as an aid to understanding the differences between the facts and the assumption in order to acquire a more accurate knowledge of actual conditions.

Conclusions Drawn from the Preceding Analysis

The foregoing leads to a first conclusion. The theory as outlined above assumes reciprocity of transfer whereas, in fact, such reciprocity does not appear to exist. Given the dynamic changes which are constantly taking place in the world economy, the slight mobility of the factors of production, and the slow development of such occupations as can absorb the surplus of gainfully employed persons, the periphery tends to transfer a part of the benefits accruing from its technical progress to the centers, while the latter retain their own benefits for themselves. The more the periphery seeks to increase its productivity, thus increasing the surplus of its gainfully employed persons, the more intensive will be the transfer, other things being equal. Therefore, in order to raise the income level in primary production in Latin America it is not sufficient merely to increase productivity; it is also necessary to absorb the surplus of gainfully employed persons in expanding industry and allied occupations.

There is also a second conclusion to be drawn in relation to the economicity of developing industry. The argument demonstrates, with unimpeachable logic, the economic advantages to be derived from a natural division of international labor, given perfect mobility of the factors of production. It is evident that, if a country obtains all the advantages of technical progress achieved by other countries and in return affords them the advantages of its own productivity, it will not obtain any additional advantage if, by means of protective measures, it engages in the production of goods already produced by others. On the contrary, it can be proved conclusively that economic losses will follow. However, if there is not absolute mobility of the factors of production from country to country, the development of industry may help to bring incomes in the primary producer countries up to the level of industrial countries. In so far as this occurs there will be a net profit for the primary producer. Nevertheless, for this leveling to take place, it would be necessary for other competitor countries in primary production not to force competition in their own favor by lowering wages. That is precisely the difficulty facing the periphery, as has been indicated earlier. But there is another source of net profit which is less problematical, since industry and its allied occupations add a net increase to incomes previously earned when employing the surplus population formerly gainfully employed in primary production and dislodged therefrom by technical progress. This increase will be proportionately greater as the productivity of the new industries reaches that of those industries in the countries which are more advanced technically, and it represents a net profit even though productivity may be inferior. Consequently, owing to the lack of international mobility of the factors of production, we have to apply a criterion of economics to the development of the periphery, instead of the criteria suggested by the above theory.

The third conclusion relates to the way of extending technical progress. In the theoretical argument we have been examining, the fact that a group of occupations increases its productivity presupposes that the resulting lowering of prices will immediately benefit all other activities, creating an additional margin of income available to increase demand or savings; but in fact, if prices do not fall in the large centers as productivity increases and income rises, then greater demand and savings capacity will be developed only in the centers. This would mean that the peripheral countries have, on the one hand, remained unaffected by such advantages while, on the other, they are faced with the problem of assimilating an advanced industrial technique which requires extensive development of both demand and savings.

To sum up, the discrepancy between the theoretical argument based upon absolute mobility of the factors of production and the realities of economic experience is so significant for the theory of economic development in Latin America in particular, and in the periphery in general, that we shall have to give our theories a thorough overhaul. A revision of this nature, being based upon premises closer to reality, will help us to state, on sound premises, the essential lines of a policy of economic development.

The Economic Cycle and Fluctuations in the Terms of Trade

In reviewing the theory from the standpoint of the development of the periphery, the study of the economic cycle must be given special consideration. Even though the low mobility of the factors of production, as technical progress spreads, suffices to explain the great differences between incomes at the center and those of the periphery, these differences are actually created during the cyclical movement. In other words, the cycle has, in fact, been the mode of growth of the capitalist economy. These phenomena are of great interest to the Latin American countries, and hence we shall consider some of them here.

It is a well-known fact that, during the cycle, price relationships move in favor of primary products on the upswing but, on the downswing, generally tend to fall more than they had previously risen. Thus, as the relative price level falls during each depression more than it had risen during the preceding period of prosperity, we find that over a number of cycles there is a continuous tendency for the terms of trade to worsen, as has been shown above.

This periodic deterioration in the price relationships is the result of the way in which, in cyclical downswings, the benefits of technical progress are transferred from entrepreneurs to other social groups. During the upswing, despite increased productivity, prices rise and the profits of the entrepreneurs rise concurrently. If increased productivity brought immediate improvement to wages and salaries, these would have to rise more than prices. This does not usually occur during the upswing, when prices frequently rise more than wages, so that the benefits accruing from technical progress remain in the hands of the entrepreneurs. It is during the cyclical downswing that these benefits are transferred to wages, which decrease less than prices, and a more favorable wage relationship is thus established; more and more advantage is taken of this as a new phase of prosperity absorbs the unemployment which marks the cyclical downswing.

In other words, during a depression, wages lose only a part of the benefits obtained during a period of prosperity and thus can reap the benefits of technical progress. Naturally, not all the benefits go into wages. The State has been taking an increasing proportion of the benefits derived from technical progress and so has been able to widen the scope of its activities. Other social groups also take their share, to a greater or lesser extent, and, furthermore, as competition between entrepreneurs is limited, these are left with a greater share than they would otherwise have had. However, we are not concerned with the distribution of benefits in the centers but rather with the sum of the respective increments of productivity which remains there, as compared with that remaining in the periphery.

Let us assume that after a period of depression, the net increase in income at the centers is equivalent to the increase in production obtained by greater productivity. It is evident that, if the full benefits remain in the centers, the periphery will obtain no share at all. Now let us assume that the net increase in income at the center is greater than the increase of production there; this would mean that the periphery must have transferred part of its increased productivity to the center and even part of the real income which it formerly enjoyed.

The question now arises: what are the forces which allow the industrial centers to exert such pressure on the periphery, retaining the profits of their own technical progress or even appropriating part of the benefits accruing to the periphery?

To answer this question, let us recall some observation made in a previous document regarding certain manifestations of cyclical phenomena at the centers and in the periphery.[5] During the cyclical upswing, demand for finished goods in the centers is greater than supply. There exists, therefore, an excess demand which increases the profits of the entrepreneurs and gives rise to other phenomena; these phenomena, in which the periphery plays an important part, eventually transform this excess demand into insufficient demand, and so lead to the cyclical downswing, wherein demand becomes less than the aggregate supply of finished goods at the price offered. As the value of the aggregate supply, swollen by the higher profits of earlier stages in the production process, cannot be easily reduced by lowering prices, stocks

[5] *Ibid.*, pp. 18–22.

of finished goods, temporarily unsaleable at those various stages, are accumulated.

There follows a series of reactions which tend to lower the aggregate supply price until demand once again begins to absorb current production and the surplus stocks are gradually reduced.

This way of decreasing the aggregate supply price of finished goods is of great importance to the periphery. In actual fact, this price, as mentioned before, was augmented at the centers by the addition of profits; but some of these were converted into increases in wages and other forms of income. For the sake of brevity, and to avoid entering upon any unnecessary complexities, we will refer merely to the increase of wages, this being the more significant phenomenon. If the aforesaid decrease in the supply price was in proportion to the increases of profits and wages which had previously raised that price, the situation would once more be what it had been at the point of departure, and both the centers and the periphery would share equally in the benefits of technical progress, whatever their amount in either place.

However, this is not the case, owing to the mechanism of the cyclical downswing and the nature of the forces affecting it. The accumulation of surplus stocks causes the sellers of finished goods to scale down their demand for goods from their immediate suppliers; these in turn scale down their requirements of goods from their own suppliers, and so on, to the stage of the entrepreneurs engaged in primary production in the periphery. In each of these stages through which the cyclical downswing is transmitted, there is a fall in employment and profits.

It is a recognized fact, however, that at the centers there is great resistance to any lowering of wages, despite unemployment, and, in some sectors, to the reduction of profits. This constitutes an obstacle to the lowering of that part of the aggregate supply price which is accounted for by the centers, and when it cannot be brought down far enough to bring the supply price more closely into line with aggregate demand, surplus stocks will continue to accumulate. It follows that the greater the volume of these surplus stocks, the more production, and therefore the demand for primary products, will be curtailed, and the greater will be the fall in the prices of these primary products.

In the periphery, lower prices for primary goods naturally mean lower profits and adverse pressure on wages in communities in which labor organizations, where they exist, are far less powerful than in the cyclical centers.

The greater part of production costs corresponding to the stages completed in the industrial centers is accounted for by the wages paid at those stages. Therefore, the fact that wages suffer a relatively small decrease means inevitably that it is for the periphery to reduce the aggregate supply price, so that the greater the wage increase during the cyclical upswing, and the more rigid the wage levels during the downswing, the greater will be the pressure exerted by the centers on the periphery, through the reduction of their demand for primary goods and the consequent decline in the price of these goods.

All this occurs while the other factors which influence the intensity and duration of the cyclical downswing remain equal. For instance, if, during the upswing, only a relatively small part of the profits has flowed into wages, the fact that during the downswing profits may become inelastic would have even more serious consequences than the rigidity of wage levels as, during the depression, profits are generally not spent, and there is a falling off in demand.

Having made this qualification, let us continue the analysis. If, on the one hand, at the centers we have this relationship between the net increase in wages and their resistance to any decline, and, on the other hand, we have the intense pressure exerted by the centers on the periphery, it is not difficult to understand that if the net increase in wages is greater than the increase in productivity, in accordance with a previous assumption, the pressure on the periphery will be so great that the lowering of prices will take from the periphery an everincreasing share of the benefits of its own technical progress, or even more, as has been shown above.

How far does experience show that the periphery can resist this pressure? There have been cases in which large stocks of primary products have been accumulated in the periphery in preference to selling at prices considered too low. But when the periphery resists the constriction of its own supply price, the total supply price of finished goods at the center does not fall sufficiently to eliminate the difference between it and demand. Hence stocks of finished goods and also of goods in course of manufacture continue to accumulate and there is a steeper decline in the demand for primary products.

Though this explanation is rather general and each individual case would have to be examined separately, the Great Depression of the 1930's showed clearly that the pressure on the primary producer countries can be so great as to compel them to devalue their currency in order to be able to adapt themselves to the fall in prices imposed by the decrease in demand at the cyclical centers. In this way, the whole population is affected by the consequences of a readjustment which would otherwise be catastrophic for those who derive their income from primary production.

It would not be admissible to generalize this inference and argue that the chronic tendency toward monetary depreciation, recorded in the annals of some of the Latin American countries, can be attributed to the particular manner in which this reduction in selling prices occurs during the cyclical depressions. But neither would it be reasonable to suggest that financial distortions and resulting inflation are exclusively to blame for that phenomenon, without admitting the influence of the pressure which is automatically brought to bear on the periphery during the cyclical downswing. The whole problem offers a most interesting field for study.

It is evident that if there had been notable increases of productivity in the periphery, this area would have been better prepared to withstand the effects of such pressure by surrendering to the centers the benefits recently acquired through increased productivity. But if there are no such advantages, the periphery will be compelled to surrender a part of the benefits acquired in the previous phase of development. This is one of the reasons why the world economic crisis affected Latin America and other peripheral countries so seriously. Depressions prior to the First World War had been shorter and far less intense. One must go back to the eighteen-seventies to find a depression that was as long—though less intense. However, the downswing of the seventies coincided with a period during which Latin America was rapidly increasing its indirect productivity, by incorporating new areas into international productive activity. There was, therefore, a wider margin of benefits derived from technical progress in the periphery to be shared with the centers.

Here we have another case where the course of events subsequent to the world economic crisis, when contrasted with those leading up to it, offers us a better vantage point from which to analyze the problem of economic development in Latin America. Yet this is not the only important comparison, as has been shown above.

Technical Progress, Industrialization and Disequilibrium[6]

It has been said that technical progress is compelling the Latin American countries to resort to industrialization as a means of development, and that in this form of economic development there are certain inherent and persistent tendencies to external disequilibrium.

The origin of these tendencies to disequilibrium lies in the changes brought about by technical progress itself: on the one hand, in the methods of production and in demand and, on the other, in the distribution of the gainfully employed population to meet this demand within each country and the sphere of the world economy.

External disequilibrium must be eliminated; a regular and orderly form of economic development is to be achieved. Thus far, the Latin American countries have sought to correct the disequilibrium only after it has occurred, and at considerable cost, as may be deduced from the experience of the past twenty-five years. However, this experience provides valuable lessons in how to avoid this phenomenon, or at least how to attenuate it.

Before considering these practical aims, it is necessary to analyze the nature of this disequilibrium, which may be found in certain aspects of the technique of production that are of great importance to primary producing countries. In a broad sense, technical progress has been reducing the share which the value of primary products represents in the

[6] See ECLA, "Theoretical and Practical Problems of Economic Growth" (E/CN.12/221), May 18, 1951, pp. 28–32.

value of finished goods. In other words, the share of primary products in the real income of the population has been declining, especially in the great industrial centers. There are various reasons for this tendency, among which the following should be cited:

(*a*) The technical changes involved in the constant creation of new products result in a progressively more complex or sophisticated elaboration of the raw materials required in the productive process, whose contribution to the value of the finished article is therefore diminished. In relation to the total value, the proportion of raw materials used in the manufacture of an airplane is therefore lower than in that of a locomotive, and lower in the case of a locomotive than in that of a horse-drawn vehicle.

(*b*) Technical progress makes for better utilization of raw materials, subproducts and byproducts, so that the same amount of raw material is now equivalent to a proportionately greater value of finished goods than heretofore. Though there is no reason to assume that cotton piece goods contain a smaller quantity of cotton than one hundred years ago, in our time the same amount of raw material provides industrial byproducts or subproducts which make the total value of the finished products considerably greater than previously; and

(*c*) Synthetic materials such as synthetic nitrates, artificial fibers, and plastics, are replacing a number of natural products in increasingly important spheres of industrial activity.

Thus new forms of production and certain changes which technical progress has brought about in the structure of consumption are responsible for reducing the scale on which primary products are being utilized. Technical innovations are undoubtedly the dynamic factor which has caused the greatest changes in demand. Moreover, the increase in productivity and per capita income which these innovations bring in their train has made it possible to satisfy demand in new ways. Thus it is a well-known fact that, when the level of income rises (a) demand becomes more diversified, and while beyond a certain point there may be only a relatively small increase in demand for ordinary foodstuffs, demand for the wide range of articles produced as a result of constant technical innovations rises sharply. Furthermore, these innovations imply an increasing industrial processing of foodstuffs for the sake of hygiene, preservation, or convenience, thus widening the gap between the rates of growth of the primary product and of real income; and (b) the growth of demand for personal services also tends to become more diversified, and therefore the proportion of primary products in the supply of the population's aggregate demand diminishes.

The combination of all these factors, arising from advances in the technique of production, has consequences of vital importance to the periphery, since imports of primary products in the industrial centers tend to expand at a lower rate than real income. In other words, the income-inelasticity of demand for primary imports in the centers tends to be lower than unity.

Other facts must also be mentioned which are partly the result of technical progress. Productivity increases are observable in the primary production of the industrial centers themselves, and this often enables them to compete successfully with the periphery on foreign markets, despite the low salaries prevailing in the peripheral areas. In other cases, where this does not occur, the industrial centers resort to the application of import tariffs in order to maintain or stimulate their primary production, thus protecting the domestic market against competition from the periphery. This is another of the consequences of the unequal distribution of the increase of productivity in various domestic activities and in various countries, and of the slight international mobility of human resources.

As a result of the protection of primary production in the great industrial centers, the proportion of the population gainfully employed in these activities has not decreased to the extent it might have otherwise, and consequently the increase of the population gainfully employed in industry, services, and other activities has not been so great as might have been expected. Had no such measures been adopted, there would not now be such a pressing need in the periphery for labor to obtain employment in secondary and tertiary occupations when no employment opportunities are available in primary activities. It should be borne in mind, however, that the protective tendencies of the industrial centers merely accentuate the compulsory migration of the peripheral population from primary to secondary production and services, since ultimately this movement is occasioned by the spread of technical progress.

As has been said, imports of primary goods in the centers tend to increase more slowly than real income. Thus, if the Latin American countries expanded only as a result of primary exports, as usually occurred before the world economic crisis, their rate of economic development would be considerably lower than that of the industrial centers.

However, these countries, as a whole, seem to be in a position to expand at the same rate, if not more rapidly, than the centers, owing to the stage of development which most of them have reached. The rate of growth of the population is much higher, and as its productivity is relatively low, there is more room for growth.

In practice, experience during the twenty years following the world economic crisis shows unquestionably that the export activities of the Latin American countries, even allowing for their exceptional development in Venezuela, have been insufficient to provide employment for the natural increase in the gainfully employed population and for the surplus manpower resulting from the spread of technical progress in primary production.

Hence the vital need for industrialization, in order that economic development may take place at a faster rate than the expansion of primary exports. Industrialization absorbs a part of the available population, enabling another part to be absorbed by associated activities such as transport and trade, which expand with it. The increase in average productivity resulting from industrialization, together with the increase of productivity caused by technical improvements in primary production, raise per capita income and lead to a growing demand for services, thus creating new sources of employment. Thus industrialization is linked with various phenomena inherent in economic development, and if reference is made only to this aspect, it is for reasons of brevity and not because the importance of other phenomena has been overlooked.

CHAPTER II

INDUSTRIALIZATION AND DEVELOPMENT

Some Major Questions[1]

Industrial Development Options

Besides absorbing population growth and surplus labor from other activities, industrialization also provides a developing country with the manufactured articles that it cannot obtain abroad, owing to its limited capacity to import.

The ultimate objective is the attainment of the maximum real income, that is, the goods and services which the population requires, according to its pattern of demand.

Two problems arise in the obtaining of this maximum. They both involve the best method of utilizing productive factors. The first consists in determining to what extent the available factors in a growing economy should be employed in increasing exports, with a view to expanding imports, and to what extent agricultural and industrial production for the domestic market should be expanded. Once this first problem has been solved, the second problem lies in ascertaining which goods can most advantageously be imported and which should be

[1] From ECLA, "Theoretical and Practical Problems of Economic Growth" (E/CN.12/221, May 18, 1951), pp. 35–67.

produced internally (given optimum quantities of imports and domestic production), in order to maximize real income.

With regard to the first problem, primary producing countries as a group are faced with the very limited option of either employing the increment of their productive factors in increasing exports so as to acquire supplementary imports, or alternatively, of increasing production for domestic consumption.

A brief explanation would help to elucidate the problem. Let it be assumed that countries producing a specific article obtain $100 annually per worker employed in production for export, and that they use this amount to obtain an equivalent volume of imports. Assume that one million workers are employed, in other words, that the total product is $100 million, and that there are, in addition, 100,000 workers and available capital that can be employed either in increasing exports and obtaining additional imports, or in the production of these goods domestically.

Let it be further assumed that the productivity of these 100,000 laborers in domestic production is merely $70 per capita,[2] which is lower than the value accruing from export activities. It is evident that if exports could be increased 10 per cent by making use of these 100,000 workers, without allowing per capita yield to be lowered by a fall in prices, then it would be more profitable to employ the labor force in export activities than in domestic production. On the whole, however, this is hardly likely to occur, if the increase in production exceeds the increase in consumption in the importing countries, in terms of the expansion of income and other factors which determine the volume of demand. It would be sufficient for prices to fall 9.1 per cent, thus reducing the yield per man to $90.9 for the total value in dollars to be decreased to the 100 million prevailing earlier, despite the increase in the volume of goods.

It is evident that instead of increasing production for export it would be more convenient for primary producing countries to employ these 100,000 laborers in production for domestic consumption, despite the

[2] Computed on the basis of the value of imports of identical goods of foreign origin.

fact that the yield per worker (\$90 in export activities) is greater than that accruing from domestic production (\$70).

This simple conclusion is of interest, since the opposite might be argued from the current theory, that the optimum solution lies in a distribution of productive effort whereby the marginal yield per worker in export activities is equal to the marginal yield per worker in activities supplying the domestic market, taking into account the differences in skill required by these activities.

If the industrial centers and the periphery are viewed as a whole, this latter theory would be correct, as it would thus be possible to obtain the maximum volume of goods or of real income. However, because of the price-inelasticity of demand in the industrial centers, the latter would have been favored in the distribution of these goods, to the detriment of primary producing countries.

Undoubtedly, in the case of absolute mobility of the factors of production, income or remuneration would tend to be uniform in a given country and as between several countries. Thus, provided that skill is uniform throughout, the same wage level would obtain. Consequently, if in the foregoing example the yield of export activities declines, together with the wage level, there would be a displacement of the factors of production from these to other activities. Since these factors could not be employed in additional production for domestic consumption, where, because of the lower yield, wages would similarly be lower, excess labor would migrate to other countries, until wages were equalized.

It is therefore evident that an example such as the above could not occur, if the assumption of absolute mobility of the factors of production obtains. But this assumption is unrealistic, whereas the example reflects conditions which are very similar to those found in developing countries.

Let us consider the example again for a moment. For the increase in exports to be advantageous to the periphery, export prices should not fall below a per capita yield of \$97.3. Thus the increase in the value of exports and, therefore, of imports, would amount to \$7 million, which is the same increase in value to be derived from production of these goods for domestic consumption. Beyond this neutral point, it would be advantageous to utilize the productive effort in domestic activities. If at the neutral point a worker engaged in export activities could obtain \$97.3 worth of imported products through trade, in domestic activities he would obtain only \$70 worth of the same products, that is to say, the cost of the latter would be 28 per cent higher. Consequently, domestic production could not be fostered unless it was protected against foreign competition.[3]

Economics of Industries Where the Level of Productivity is Lower than in the Centers

It has been shown that, in view of the factors which determine the demand for primary products in the industrial centers and the very small margin of international mobility of the factors of production, it might be expedient for a peripheral country to employ its extra manpower in domestic production, even where the cost of such production is higher than that of the imported articles. A cursory examination often leads to a condemnation of industries in which production costs are higher than the prices of similar imported goods as uneconomic. Despite its seeming validity, this conclusion does not take account of the fact that the productive factors employed in these industries could not be put to better use. It is therefore to the advantage of the economy to produce at relatively high cost rather than to leave productive factors lying idle or use them in ways that would adversely affect the terms of trade and, consequently, the capacity to import.

If complete mobility existed, this proposition would be inadmissible.

[3] It is necessary to realize that the free interplay of economic forces might give rise to another solution which would render protection unnecessary. It would be sufficient for the excess population to exert pressure freely on the wage level, until it was lowered to such an extent that the cost of domestic production would equal that of foreign production. However, this would involve a serious deterioration of the terms of trade and it would be greatly detrimental to total production, further involving other considerations which are alien to the main thesis of this work. There is considerable theoretical interest in this particular example of the free interplay of factors in the peripheral countries, associated with their low mobility as between these countries and the industrial centers.

Given the tendency for wages to equalize, the economic impossibility of increasing exports beyond a certain limit would cause the gainfully employed population to seek higher incomes in other countries. It logically follows that the total volume of production and of real income for the whole world would be optimum, if certain other conditions obtained. However, actual conditions differ from this theoretical model, and they are influenced by other factors, often more important than the purely economic. If industrial costs are higher than import prices, this does not mean that it is necessarily uneconomic for a country, as is sometimes assumed. On the basis of that criterion, industrialization would be practically impossible in Latin America at the present stage of economic development. The economic development of the periphery is therefore not compatible with this theory. The problem, as has been shown, must be considered from another standpoint. It is not so much a question of comparing industrial costs with import prices as of comparing the additional income obtained from the expansion of industry with the export earnings that would have resulted from applying the same productive resources to export activities.

Costs in a great number of Latin American industries and in large sectors of agricultural production are, in fact, higher than those of imports under the present terms of trade. The prevailing low incomes cannot offset the relatively low productivity in these activitities. This does not imply that such activities are necessarily uneconomic. It simply means that goods which cannot be obtained from abroad, because of the limited capacity to import, must be produced by domestic industry at a higher cost than if exports could be easily increased in order to provide the means of obtaining the necessary imports.

The concept of economics should be based on the total supply of available goods. It has been shown that a greater volume of goods is obtained despite higher costs. But it is evident that this volume could be increased proportionately with the raising of Latin American productivity to a level closer to that obtaining in the great industrial centers.

This general proposition is not incompatible with individual solutions. In a given country and in given circumstances, it might be possible to achieve a steady marked expansion of exports, out of proportion with the rate of increase of income in the industrial centers.

Optimum Distribution of the Factors in Different Sectors of Domestic Production

Attention should now be given to the second problem presented. In view of the optimum volume of imports on which a country may rely under given circumstances, and the increased capital it could muster, it is necessary to ascertain in what sectors of production investments should be made so as to maximize real income.

The principle of marginal social productivity would appear to meet this requirement fully. The increment of capital should be utilized so as to obtain the maximum product, which is only possible when the marginal productivity of the different investments is equalized.

This criterion offers a basis on which to determine the best means of utilizing the limited capacity to import, that is, which products that were formerly imported should be replaced by domestic production, and which it is more advisable to continue importing. The advantage of developing an iron and steel industry instead of a heavy chemical industry, or of developing domestic production of all the footwear required by the population, or of the cultivation of all the wheat at present imported will depend on the comparative increase in the social product which would be obtained from the different activities, according to the various alternatives open to the investment of the available capital and other conditions influencing productive efficiency. If the amount of capital required by the iron and steel industry would give rise to higher productivity in that industry than in other import substitution activities, its development would be economic, despite the fact that the cost of the domestically produced article might be higher than that of the imported product. It may be higher, but not so high as in other cases, given the average level of productivity in the country.

These considerations are also applicable to agricultural production, which, in some Latin American countries, may be relatively easy to increase. In other countries, however, the increase in agricultural output involves extensive irrigation works or other improvements. If it is expedient to replace an import by agricultural production, or by the development of industrial production, how the two may best be combined can only be determined by comparing the levels of productivity.

However, the maximization of productivity in the form described previously does not always imply that the most satisfactory solution has been found. Certain productive activities, in which the level of productivity is lower than in others, may nevertheless be eminently advantageous, owing to the fact that they diminish a country's vulnerability to foreign fluctuations and contingencies. The experience of the Latin American countries is very instructive on this point, and it is easily understandable that such a consideration may prevail in certain specific cases.

Optimum Capital Intensity per Gainfully Employed Person in Latin America

The validity of the principle of the social yield or marginal social productivity of capital has already been acknowledged in connection with the planning of an investment policy for the Latin American countries. This principle demonstrates that if savings are distributed in such a way that the social productivity of the marginal increment of capital per gainfully employed person is the same in all branches of economic activity the maximum product will be obtained. The optimum degree of capital intensity per gainfully employed person in each branch will thus have been attained, that is, the exact amount required in order to obtain the highest possible product for the economy as a whole.

However, the mere statement of this principle does not suffice for an analysis of the concrete investment problems encountered in the economic development of the Latin American countries. Outstanding among such problems is the determination of the most suitable intensity of capital per gainfully employed person, in relation to the amount of capital available.

As a result of technical progress, the optimum intensity of capital has tended to rise continuously in the great industrial centers. Thus, a constant increase in productivity has been achieved which, by raising per capita income and expanding the margin of savings, has facilitated the introduction of new techniques, thus increasing further the intensity of capital, the process being repeated again and again.

This process takes a different form in the underdeveloped countries. In those countries technical improvements do not appear gradually, as they did in the development of the great centers, and thus the under-developed countries do not have to go through the successive stages of evolution which the centers went through in developing their capital goods. In carrying out their investment programs, these countries find that they must import the same equipment as that which was developed by the industrialized countries over a long period. Thus, equipment which is highly capital-intensive and which is compatible with the high level of per capita income in the industrial centers, is equally available to the underdeveloped countries, in which per capita income, and therefore the capacity to save, are evidently lower.

In other words, it is theoretically possible for the Latin American countries, in view of their relative scarcity of capital and abundance of manpower, to have a lower capital intensity than the more advanced countries. However, given the nature of technical progress and its irreversible character, there is little likelihood of underdeveloped countries actually attaining their optimum capital intensity. It is true that in some cases they are in a position to use less complex equipment and other outdated techniques involving low capital investment. However, if they seek to modernize the equipment because of the very low productive efficiency of the methods in use, they are often faced with the necessity of acquiring highly capital-intensive machinery, since, given the nature of the productive techniques utilized, each unit of equipment is generally indivisible, and therefore its intensity cannot be reduced to the level compatible with a relatively small volume of available capital.

Were sufficient capital available for investment in capital-intensive machinery in all branches of the economy, no such problem would arise. It would only be necessary to assimilate the technical methods of the more advanced countries in order to obtain approximate, if not equivalent, levels of productivity. This, however, is not the case. The problem of capital intensity arises precisely because there is shortage of capital, but this problem varies considerably from one Latin American country to another. In some of these countries, 60 per cent of the gainfully employed are working in activities where productivity is low and capital is scarce, whereas in others, capital formation and productivity are approaching the levels of the more advanced countries. This means that the following generalizations must be qualified in the light of the actual situation in the different countries.

The diffusion of modern production techniques gives rise to a paradoxical situation. Countries rich or potentially rich in labor and short of capital are faced with production techniques which, especially in the United States, are primarily concerned with saving as much labor as possible, by means of increasing the capital outlay per worker. Undoubtedly technical progress also seeks to increase the volume of production per unit of capital, while reducing the amount of labor required. However, though these two aims call for increasing capital investment per gainfully employed person, and though in the abstract they may be considered separately, technical development has linked them in such a way that, as a rule, it would be impossible to break down investment into the part which is aimed at increasing production per unit of capital and that which is directed toward saving labor. Undoubtedly sufficient capital has been available in the great industrial centers to realize both of these aims progressively. In other words, these objectives have been combined in a manner and to a degree compatible with capital formation. Thus, with the exception of brief intervals, investment to reduce labor consumption tended to be made in accordance with the availability of the capital necessary for this purpose and, at the same time, for the absorption of the labor thus displaced.

In view of the fact that these aims have been pursued simultaneously and in view of the indivisibility of technically advanced equipment, the combinations adopted in the economy of a highly industrialized country, with a high per capita capital intensity, cannot be undone arbitrarily and transformed into other combinations which are better suited to prevailing conditions in a less developed country, where per capita capital intensity is much lower. It is logical that if the combinations prevalent in the former were to be transplanted to the latter, there would not be sufficient capital to absorb the amount of labor saved. In order to avoid this self-defeating consequence, it would be necessary to invest in equipment that would increase production rather than reduce labor consumption per unit of capital.

This, then, is the problem which faces countries in which there is a relative scarcity of capital, since, as a rule, the characteristic indivisibility of equipment prevents the adoption of any combinations other than those produced by the evolution of the great industrial centers.

Technical Unemployment and the Role of Capital Industry

Turning again to the saving of labor, which is generally entailed by capital-intensive equipment, it should be noted that this problem is typical of the underdeveloped countries. This does not imply that, in the large centers, the introduction of such equipment has not occasionally given rise to a surplus of labor. However, the problem is not the same. The form of technical unemployment which generally occurs in these centers, especially during the cyclical downswing, is not superimposed on a structural problem of a large force with little capital and low productivity, as occurs in the underdeveloped countries. It is a transient phenomenon, which will persist until new investment creates job opportunities for the unemployed. If surplus labor is not reabsorbed rapidly, it is not owing to a deficient capacity to save, but to flaws in the operation of the system. On the other hand, in the underdeveloped countries, where capital is inadequate for the intensive absorption of low-productivity labor, an excessive reduction of labor, through new capital investment or the replacement of equipment, accentuates the structural problem.

In the development of the industrial centers, it was possible to incorporate capital-intensive equipment into productive activity because savings were sufficient to introduce it into all the branches of the economy in which the entrepreneur found it advantageous. This equipment, therefore, corresponds to a high income and a high capacity to save. On the other hand, such equipment is out of line with the relatively low income and low capacity to save characteristic of underdeveloped countries. The fact that certain entrepreneurs may be in a position to acquire such equipment does not by any means imply that there is sufficient capital available to generalize its use. It is necessary to distinguish between the interests of the entrepreneur and the general interests of the economy. The entrepreneur is only concerned with minimizing his production costs and increasing his profits. As a rule, the question of how to combine an increase in production with a reduction in labor consumption per unit of capital, in order to achieve his objective is, for him, usually a secondary or unimportant consideration. If his action causes technological unemployment and the unemployed cannot be absorbed because of the scarcity of capital, the entrepreneur will nevertheless have increased his profits, even when the capital invested in saving labor instead of increasing production involves a misuse of capital from the standpoint of the country's economy, apart from the social repercussions of the phenomenon.

This phenomenon is not so evident when the reduction of labor consumption, entailed by the introduction of this equipment, instead of causing technological unemployment, prevents the absorption of labor displaced from occupations with a lower productivity. This absorption might have taken place if the capital invested in reducing labor consumption had been used to increase production.

However, in cases in which there are no better alternatives from an economic viewpoint in the underdeveloped countries, the latter, as was pointed out, are compelled to employ this equipment or fall back on techniques which waste capital by reason of their very low yield. In other words, even though capital-intensive equipment does not offer the best solution to the problems of development in countries where labor is plentiful, it may constitute the least harmful of the feasible means of increasing productivity open to the entrepreneur.

There are still other differences between the underdeveloped and the more advanced countries. In the latter, technological unemployment tends to disappear as a result of new investment. The development of capital-goods industries must provide the strongest element of absorption, since employment in these industries has expanded more intensely than in consumer-goods industries. Moreover, the increased profits accruing to entrepreneurs with the reduction in costs, resulting from the introduction of new techniques, are to a large extent reinvested, thus stimulating demand in the capital-goods industries. The underdeveloped countries, lacking capital-goods industries, except perhaps for the initial stages of such industries, find themselves in a very unfavorable position from the point of view of their internal development, because the profits accruing from the cost reductions mentioned above, when employed in acquiring capital equipment, are transferred to the great industrial centers producing the equipment, thus stimulating employment there and not at home. Consequently, in countries where no capital industries exist, the reinvestment of profits does not tend to reduce unemployment as it does in the great centers, except to the extent that it is directed toward building, and manufacturing the small amount of equipment produced and used domestically.

It might be argued that these countries have vast possibilities for absorbing technological unemployment in existing consumer-goods industries or in those which might be established with a view to replacing imports. This is true; but it brings us back to the starting point, lack of capital. If the investment of profits in imported capital equipment offered a means of absorbing the technological unemployment resulting from the utilization of the same profits, the problem would be relatively simple; but this is not the case. There is a considerable difference between the profits accruing from the displacement of a single worker and the capital required in order to reemploy that worker. Profits accumulated during the course of several years would be required for that purpose. In this as in other aspects of economics, the time factor is of the greatest importance. Substantial capital investment is necessary if time is not to be wasted. Undoubtedly the existence of profits for the amortization of investments over a period of time is a favorable factor in stimulating investment. However, in order to absorb unemployed workers, an immediate increment of capital, several times greater than the wages saved, would be necessary.

The foregoing considerations show that the problem of investment in the present stage of Latin American development has several distinctive features which make it impossible to draw general conclusions from the experience of the great industrial centers. We do not propose to examine all these features, but merely to draw attention to the most important: first, capital intensity, which was analyzed above, and secondly, the obsolescence of equipment, which will be considered below.

Obsolete Equipment and the Shortage of Capital

The persistent utilization of certain types of obsolete equipment as well as other highly efficient equipment is often encountered in Latin America. This is generally put down to the habits of entrepreneurs, and this explanation might be acceptable were it not for the fact that the same entrepreneur often uses obsolete and modern equipment in the same factory, or more significantly that he seeks to invest in other fields of productive activity and acquire the most advanced equipment obtainable instead of investing his profits in replacing his old machinery. There is undoubtedly an explanation in each specific case. At the root of the whole problem, however, the common denominator is the shortage of capital—not a shortage of capital in the case of individual entrepreneurs, but a general shortage in the country.

From the economic standpoint of an underdeveloped country, if capital equipment, despite its obsolescence, is in sufficiently good condition to continue operating, the solution of the problem lies in an analysis of the alternatives. Evidently, the replacement of obsolete equipment would considerably increase the total product, disregarding for the moment its labor-saving effects. However, it could well be the case that the same amount of capital invested in other sectors of economic activity in which capital resources are limited and productivity low would lead to an even greater increase in the product. It is ultimately a question of ascertaining how the greatest increase in the product of the economy as a whole may be produced by investing a given amount of available capital; whether by replacing equipment which, though old, is still productive, or by investing this capital to absorb part of the real or potential surplus labor force. In many cases, it might be preferable to keep the outdated equipment in operation, since its elimination would involve the destruction of existing capital, when capital for new investment is scarce. This possibility is nevertheless limited, since the productivity of obsolete equipment might be reduced to such an extent, in the course of time, that, by substituting new equipment for it, the net increase in output would be greater, and would exceed that which might be obtained in other branches of the economy.

In other words, in countries where scarcity of capital gives rise to the employment of a sizable part of the labor force in primary production, where capital is scarce and productivity low, and to disguised unemployment in other occupations, there is no reason to destroy existing capital equipment, despite its obsolescence, if the labor employed is more productive there than in other activities, and if the increase in productivity which new investment would bring about in the latter activities is greater than that which would result from the replacement of obsolete equipment. If, in addition to the increase in the product, the labor-saving effect is also taken into account, the problem becomes more complex. Even though there may be more suitable fields for investment from the general economic standpoint, the entrepreneur may find it advantageous to discard the obsolete equipment and replace it by modern equipment, simply because he will thus be able to obtain a substantial saving in labor costs.

Problems of this nature will continue to arise in the underdeveloped countries while there are still substantial internal differences in the degree of capital intensity and in the productivity of different sectors of the economy. Therefore, a clear distinction should be made in investment policy between the interests of the entrepreneurs and the general interests of the economy.

In the more advanced countries, where technology and productivity have developed gradually and have been extended to all branches of economic activity, the problem does not arise in the same way. There are no vast sectors in which the scarcity of capital offers a wide field for investment, the rate of growth of the population is lower than in the underdeveloped countries, and the high level of income determines an appreciable margin for savings. Consequently, there is sufficient capital to replace equipment normally, and even to shorten its normal span in order to introduce technical innovations that increase productivity, and at the same time to absorb the labor thus saved. This does not imply that the problem under discussion never occurs in the more advanced countries, since, in the great centers, there are well-known cases in which obsolete equipment has been retained in certain sectors which, for specific reasons, such as the decline of exports, have lagged behind in technical improvements.

The Special Case of Export Activities

Since it is not our purpose to make a complete analysis of the problem of productivity and the consequences of a shortage of capital, but rather to stimulate discussion of these topics, there are important aspects and specific situations which cannot be included in this brief outline. However, the special case of export activities warrants separate consideration, since the introduction of labor-saving equipment in these activities may be essential in order to enable them to compete favorably on the international market and in order to expand exports themselves, whose fundamental importance in economic development is generally accepted. The reduction of labor consumption in primary export activities intensifies the problem of the real or potential labor surplus which should be absorbed by industry and other activities, therefore increasing the amount of capital required for economic development. On the other hand, exports may procure a wider range of savings and facilitate the use of such savings for importing capital goods. The measure in which this may be done depends on the extent to which the effects of the reduction in labor consumption and of the increase in production per unit of capital can be retained within the country, in the form of increased income, rather than transferred abroad, to the detriment of the terms of trade.

The Problem of Investment in Agriculture

The duality of the aims of technical progress, mentioned earlier, is clearly perceptible in the case of agricultural investment but, in practice, it is possible to distinguish the purpose for which such investment is made. Some investments are designed to increase the volume of production per unit of land, while others are aimed at reducing labor consumption per unit of land and per unit of production, by different degrees of mechanization, ranging from the use of better implements to the use of the most advanced technical equipment. Despite this division, there are ways in which the two objectives are related which, for reasons of brevity, will not be taken into account in the following general observations.

Increase in yield is a general necessity in the Latin American countries, where, with a few notable exceptions, production of foodstuffs is relatively low. There is also a general need for mechanization, since, in the course of economic development, it offers a means of obtaining a labor surplus to be productively absorbed by industry and other activities.

From the general economic standpoint both aims have a very different significance, though for the agricultural entrepreneur both the reduction of labor consumption and increased yield per hectare achieve the same results, namely, a reduction in costs and an increase in the profits accruing to him.

The absorption of agricultural workers by industry and other activities will create a powerful incentive to mechanize agriculture and improve primitive farming methods. However, the experience of some countries has shown that this incentive is not enough in itself: without technical action in the rural sector on the part of the State, the incentive might misfire, and even hold up the development of agriculture, since the introduction of new techniques requires careful preparation and perseverance.

From the general economic standpoint, and aside from the individual advantage to the entrepreneur, the degree of agricultural mechanization which it is desirable to attain depends, as was stated before, not only on the capital available to purchase equipment and thus to free labor, but also on the capital available to enable industry and other activities to absorb the surplus labor. If mechanization is extended beyond the capacity to absorb this surplus labor, a problem of technological unemployment is created, similar to that described in the section dealing with equipment. Moreover, in agriculture it is easier to avoid this problem, since the investments are divisible and it is not necessary to resort to self-defeating reductions in labor consumption in order to increase production.

This is a very important aspect of the extension of technical progress in Latin America and one which has not yet been given the consideration it warrants. It is probable that, in view of the scarcity of capital with which to absorb the labor freed by the mechanization of agriculture, the reduction in labor consumption may in some cases have given rise to disguised unemployment in rural areas or in densely populated urban areas.

There are, nevertheless, cases in which the absorption of surplus labor by industry has been very intense while mechanization has lagged behind. In other cases, the opening up of new farmland in sparsely populated regions has led to intensive mechanization, since that has proved to be more economic than the transfer and settlement of large groups of the population which would otherwise have been required. There have also been cases in which mechanization was essential, not in order to reduce labor consumption, but because of the need to cultivate foodstuffs on what was formerly pasture land, or to shorten the period of cultivation and thus reduce weather hazards.

However, given the abundance of human labor on the land and the scarcity of capital, mechanization should be given careful consideration in economic development programs, especially since the scanty capital available might perhaps be more advantageously employed in increasing production, particularly when the limit beyond which surplus labor cannot be absorbed has been reached.

Investment to increase production must also be considered from the general economic viewpoint. The land immediately available for this purpose is fairly scarce throughout most of Latin America, with several notable exceptions; and this factor, together with the scarcity of capital, constitutes one of the most serious obstacles to economic development.

It is therefore necessary to use the scarce capital available to obtain the maximum increase in yield. Investment for this purpose may be divided into two main groups; investment designed to increase the yield per hectare, by technical improvement of the methods of cultivation, including seed selection and the use of pesticides, and investment designed to enlarge the arable area by irrigation, drainage, deforestation, and rehabilitation of areas affected by erosion, or to prevent erosion from reducing the arable area and diminishing the actual volume of production.

Together with the need to increase the amount of capital per worker in order to increase his productivity, it is also indispensable to avoid what might be called the natural depletion of the land, i.e., the loss of its productive capacity. Erosion is the most important agent of this depletion. Erosion takes different forms, and the very abundance of land resources may have helped to increase erosion. For instance, from the point of view of the individual, over the short term the most advantageous procedure may be to take land, exhaust it by harmful farming methods and then move on to other land, since it must be admitted that the labor and capital invested in the new land would produce more than the same amount invested in preventing the land already farmed from deteriorating. However, in the long run and from the point of view of society as a whole, such procedures are not recommendable because they destroy enormous quantities of natural wealth. This is another fundamental problem, which, if not solved in time might prove a very serious obstacle to efforts to increase productivity and raise the level of living of the population.

The relatively slow growth of agricultural production in these countries, together with the generally low levels of nutrition, emphasize the need to stimulate investment in technical improvements of farming methods, especially in cases where this represents the more economic of the two methods, given immediate possibilities of increasing the yield. In all cases where a persistent effort has been made, substantial results have been obtained, compared with the relatively small amount of capital per hectare needed by such investment. Undoubtedly, little has been done in comparison with the magnitude of the task which the experts maintain must be carried out, as may be seen from the small amounts spent by most of the Latin American countries on agricultural research and experiments and on agricultural extension, in relation to their total public expenditure.

Nevertheless, the improvement of methods of cultivation may also involve the opening up of new land, in order to achieve satisfactory results. In many countries, rainfall is sparse and the land exhausted by age-old methods of cultivation, or impoverished by the type of crops grown, or by erosion. Where it is possible to achieve improvements, large amounts of capital will have to be invested to introduce mechanization, for the above-mentioned reasons.

It will be seen then, that here, as elsewhere, generalizations can be dangerous. Each country, and even the different regions within a country, has individual characteristics which must be taken into account in order to understand the concrete problems of economic development.

Not infrequently, there are cases in which an increase in agricultural output depends largely on improved utilization of the available resources rather than on new capital investment. There are regions where the land is used uneconomically, not in relation to the improved methods of cultivation which might be adopted, but in terms of current practices in that region or country. There are cases in which, before undertaking costly irrigation works (which might be justified at a later date), it is necessary to make better use of the water in lands which are inadequately irrigated; in other instances, land is wasted in areas of abundant rainfall, and in still other cases, land appropriate for artificial pasture of higher yield is still used for natural pasture.

Thus, increased investment is not a panacea; the rational utilization of existing resources must also be considered. However, this solution encounters in many Latin American countries a serious obstacle in the system of land tenure. In some areas, there are vast stretches of well-cultivated land, whereas in others a poor or average utilization of a fraction of land allows the large landowner to derive a substantial income from it. This point is so familiar that it needs no further development. There would be no reason for the industrial entrepreneur to allow part of his capital to remain unproductive, except in periods of reduced demand. But, as a rule, the productive value of land does not decline if the land is not worked; in some cases, on the contrary, it may even improve, and its value be enhanced, in the course of time, commensurate with that of cultivated land, especially where inflation helps to accelerate the normal increase in the income derived therefrom. In many Latin American countries, this feature, together with other social factors, causes a considerable portion of arable land to remain in the hands of a relatively few persons. This system of land tenure and the high value of the land in relation to its present yield (because of the present capitalization of future increases in its value) make land almost inaccessible to the landless farmer. He is compelled to invest his limited resources in holdings which are too small to enable him to attain a higher level of living than that of the agricultural wage-earner, which is very low in most of these countries. Hence the extraordinary phenomenon of the subdivision of a small part of the total area into numerous small, uneconomic holdings, while a relatively small number of landowners hold the greater part of the available land.

There is little doubt that this problem may be solved as industrial development continues to absorb agricultural labor, but the process is slow and can only be speeded up by a sharp acceleration in the rate of development of industry and other activities. Ultimately, it is a problem of investment, which, by increasing the demand for labor in activities of considerably higher productivity, will compel the large landholders to mechanize and to increase the yield of the land. The high proportion of the labor force employed in agriculture is only a part of the general problem of economic development. Little progress can be made in raising the standard of living of the agricultural population, especially in areas where the soil is poor and where age-old methods of agriculture prevail, unless the surplus population can be displaced by technical progress, and unless that portion not required for work in the new areas opened up for cultivation can be reabsorbed into activities where productivity is high.

This does not imply that the problem of land tenure in the Latin American countries can be postponed. On the contrary, it should form an integral part of economic development programs, once an objective and impartial consideration has been made of the different aspects of the vital problem of increasing agricultural production. In regions where the land-tenure system itself is not at fault in retarding progress, but rather the lack of investment and of technical action on the part of the government, a different solution will be required from that applicable where the land-tenure system constitutes the major obstacle. It is surprising that so little has been done to explore practical possibilities in this field, although much has been written and planned with regard to the problem of land tenure. In other words, when there is possibility of assimilating modern productive techniques, extensive holdings may offer the most economical means of raising the level of productivity.

Immigration and the Surplus of Human Labor

In this brief outline of some of the aspects of the problem of productivity in Latin America, reference has been made to the real or potential abundance of human labor, in relation to the shortage of capital and of arable land. It would now be of interest to ascertain if, in these circumstances, there is any point in discussing the possibilities of immigration, especially in countries where the disequilibrium of these factors is greatest. It is evident that if the productive capacity of these immigrants is comparable to that of the population which economic progress tends to displace from primary to secondary production within the country, then there would be no call for such immigration, since it would affect the process of migration within the country, and unnecessarily intensify the problem of the relative shortage of capital. However, if their productive skills are greater, then the case is different. In countries which need to assimilate better agricultural or industrial techniques, immigrants with such skills would be very useful, as has been shown by past experience. Experience has also shown that within the mass of immigrants, not only are there efficient laborers who tend to raise the average level of productivity, but many laborers who have since become entrepreneurs, exercising considerable influence on the general direction and pace of economic development. However, immigration is essentially a problem of greater capital, as are all problems of economic development. The addition of each worker to the labor force generally calls for an increment of capital, and if there is not enough capital to achieve a satisfactory rate of absorption of surplus labor from primary production, this same capital could hardly absorb immigrants. Therefore, without the necessary capital, immigration would be unproductive. It should be remembered, however, that the capital required for immigration is lower than that generally needed for internal migration, since in the latter case capital is required not only to free labor from primary occupations, but also to reemploy it in secondary activities. The cost of freeing labor does not arise in the case of foreign immigrants. Moreover, if the productivity of the immigrant is higher than that of the domestic worker and helps to raise the general level of productivity, the resulting increase in real income will help to promote increased capital formation in the future, to the evident advantage of economic development.

Trade Policy and Industrialization[4]

Industrialization and Protectionism

There are two principles, the frank recognition of which would exert a substantial influence on the policy of the Latin American countries as regards their trade relations both with industrialized countries and with each other. First, in differing degrees according to individual countries, industrialization is an inevitable feature of economic development. Second, a reasonable measure of protection is generally indispensable for industrialization.

Once these fundamental principles are recognized, the problem arises of determining how and to what degree industrialization should be accomplished. This is the key to an industrial policy, although only the aspect of tariff protection is considered here.

The major justification for protection lies in the differences of productivity between less developed countries and those which have developed to a greater degree. These differences are explained basically by the great disparity in the capital per person engaged and in the technical skills which they possess.

In the abstract, it is possible to conceive a case in which a decrease in the wage levels of less developed countries could offset these differences in productivity. On this supposition a given country could entirely abolish its protective tariff, always provided that the decline in wages would compensate industrial establishments for the losses which would ensue. But, in addition to being impracticable for social and political reasons, such a policy would have serious economic consequences. If a

[4] From *International Co-operation in a Latin American Development Policy* (United Nations publication, Sales No.: 1954.II.G.2), pp. 60–62 and 67–70.

decline in domestic wages was followed by a fall in prices, real wages might recover their former levels, assuming that adequate adjustments could be made. However, this wage decline could in turn affect export activities, causing a drop in export prices through the workings of the wage-price mechanism. Since this would not be accomplished by a corresponding fall in import prices, a deterioration of the terms of trade would result, with adverse effects on investment and the rate of development of the country.

Therefore, if the spontaneous development of industry is impracticable and uneconomic, protection alone, either through customs tariffs or subsidies, would remain to offset the differences in productivity, since direct import restrictions are usually less advisable as a measure of industrial policy, unless they are only temporary.

Such is the type of protection required by Latin America's industrial development. Within the classical school of economic thought, protective measures are condoned during the initial phase of industrialization until such time as industry can be strengthened and has the ability to meet foreign competition. It is certainly possible that, in a developing country, a given industry may achieve the same capital density and the same productivity as in the large industrial countries. In such a case, in view of lower wages, it would cease to be an infant industry requiring protection, even before reaching the same degree of productivity. But this could hardly be the case for all the industries which a developing country requires, to expand, as a means of absorbing the actively employed population not required by other sectors. For this purpose it would be necessary to obtain a volume of capital per person engaged similar to that of highly developed countries, and also the necessary technical skills. It is not difficult to show that such a situation is theoretically possible, but it is hardly likely to occur in the foreseeable future, since, while productivity grows in underdeveloped countries, it also increases in the industrially advanced countries—and sometimes with greater rapidity.

As a result, the argument employed to demonstrate the inevitability of protection enlarges the scope of the classical argument. Instead of considering one isolated industry, the new approach includes industry as a whole, and establishes the need for protection—so long as productivity continues to be lower than that of more advanced countries—and to the extent that the difference in productivity is not offset by differences in wage levels.

A sound development policy must recognize the need for protective measures, which are in no way detrimental to world trade so long as they are kept within the limits required by development. Within such limits, which will be discussed later, they do not reduce the imports of a developing country but only change their composition in accordance with the structural modifications of the domestic economy. Customs tariffs decrease or eliminate some imports for which domestic substitutes are found, allowing for an increase in other imports with a very elastic demand in relation to the growth of per capita income.

Thus, if protection does not exceed these limits, it does not affect the total volume of imports. This volume is mainly determined by the exports of primary products from developing countries (as well as capital investment and other positive elements in the balance of payments which are omitted here to simplify the reasoning).

Consequences of Protectionism in the Industrial Centers

Protectionism in the industrial centers and its consequences for world trade, especially the trade of the developing countries, should now be considered. It has already been stated that a general characteristic of the centers is for imports to increase at a slower rate than income. This tendency may be either neutralized or accentuated by trade policy. In Great Britain during the nineteenth century, the elimination of customs duties upon imports of primary products encouraged these imports to such an extent that for a number of decades they increased more rapidly than income and their coefficient rose steadily. The influence thus exerted by Great Britain, not only directly, on the periphery, but also indirectly on other industrialized countries, was one of the outstanding features of economic history of that period. This was the period when the Latin American countries received a strong impetus to outward-directed growth in response to a rapidly expanding world demand. Countries such as the United States, whose growth began to be more inward-directed, were favored by this strong stimulus to world trade, which has slackened to a great degree today when it is Latin

America's turn to follow a similar process. Despite such favorable conditions in the international sphere, industrialization in the United States has systematically resorted to protectionist measures, the theoretical rejection of which at that time is clearly evident in the many criticisms of the classical school.

If Great Britain at that period is an example of how trade policy may alter the tendency of primary imports to increase at a slower rate than income, the United States, now the principal economic center as a result of its prodigious growth, is an example of the opposite trend. The protection of primary production has accentuated this import trend in the United States, where the import coefficient is at present almost 3 per cent, in contrast with the 35 per cent recorded in 1880 in the principal economic center during the nineteenth century.

The results of this phenomenon cannot be interpreted in the light of the previous explanation of protectionism in the peripheral countries. Another distinction of decisive importance must be introduced. The effects of protectionism on world trade are not the same in an industrial center as in countries in the course of development. While primary imports to the center tend to increase less than its income, its exports of manufactured goods have a tendency to rise more rapidly than the income of peripheral countries, as has already been pointed out at some length. This disparity in trends creates contrasting problems. Imports to developing countries tend to expand more than their exports, while the opposite tends to occur in the industrial centers, although to a very different extent (with exceptions which will be indicated later), and to the degree in which the changes in the composition of imports from the periphery affect their industrial exports.

Thus, in industrial centers whose exports are particularly in demand in developing countries, the tendency for exports to grow faster than imports of primary products is greater than in other centers.

Under these conditions, there might be other motives for supporting measures to protect domestic primary production, although very different from the underlying motives for protectionism in developing countries. Naturally there is no tendency whatsoever toward a negative disequilibrium in the balance of payments, but rather the exact opposite. Further, the active population which technical progress is gradually eliminating from primary production spontaneously moves toward other domestic occupations and to the industrial export activities favored by foreign demand.

Consequently, while protective measures in underdeveloped countries—within the limits previously established—result in maintaining the close relationship between imports and exports, without retarding the rate of growth in world trade, for an industrial center with these characteristics, they reduce imports below the capacity for external payment and have an unfavorable effect on world trade.

In other words, given the substantial income-elasticity of demand for industrial goods in general, the restriction of certain types of imports in underdeveloped countries is offset—within the bounds set by the capacity for external payments—by increased imports of other commodities which could not previously be acquired in the same volume. In contrast, restrictions on the import of a given primary commodity into a large industrial center are not necessarily neutralized by greater imports of other primary products, since all imports required to satisfy demand in existing conditions were being brought in before; the restrictive measure will not be offset unless it is combined with others designed to encourage imports of manufactures or semimanufactures.

The consequences of such a protectionist policy on the part of a large industrial center are obvious. Developing countries are compelled to strengthen their own protectionist policies because of a new and weakening factor for their export trade. They must clearly exert stronger pressure on imports: to reconcile them with a potentially lower capacity for external payments, and to encourage the additional use in industry of productive factors which would have been absorbed by export activities in more favorable circumstances.

The United States and Trade Reciprocity

It is of interest to examine the breadth of the functional differentiation already noted. A large industrial center, the United States has a decisive influence on world trade. Confining the argument to Latin America, it is a well-known fact that its industrial imports depend closely upon exports of primary products. But, as already stated, the opposite does not hold true. If Latin America independently increases its purchases from the industrial center, this does not imply that the center will acquire more primary exports from Latin America. The volume of these exports is governed by other factors which are so important that fluctuations in Latin American demand are insignificant in comparison. Therefore, the only effect of an independent rise in Latin American imports, not caused by a previous increase in exports, will be a disequilibrium in the balance of payments.

The position of the United States as the principal dynamic center of the world economy lends particular emphasis to the concept of trade reciprocity. Upon examination, reciprocity is found to be implicit in the functional nature of the center, since, if exports are increased at the same time as imports, compensation is spontaneous and there is no need for the tariffs of other countries to be adjusted in order to avoid market disruptions. It was a function of the British center also to provoke the immediate reaction of the periphery when industrial exports from Great Britain were subject to very intense demand.

Thus the tariff concessions granted by the United States to developing countries as a counterpoise and world purchasing power generated by greater United States imports will tend to transform itself directly or indirectly into greater international demand for United States exports. In fact, the position of the United States vis-à-vis the economic development of Latin America could not be more advantageous. While Latin American countries maintain their policy of protection within the given limits, rather than their tariffs it will be their volume of exports to the United States which will determine their *quantum* of imports. It is true that if Europe strengthened the competitive position of its industry, some of the dollars generated by the United States would be diverted to Europe, but those dollars would soon be transformed into European demand for United States exports, as indicated by the foregoing reasoning and also by experience. This is a well-recognized fact.

Clearly, since Latin American tariffs are the instrument for modifying the composition of imports, United States export activities must undergo the process of readaptation already mentioned. In this respect also the United States holds a favorable position as compared with other industrial countries, not only because of the slight incidence of its exports in the national income (approximately 5 per cent), but also because, as has been said, its exports are attractive to Latin American countries, even to an exaggerated extent. This does not imply that in certain cases the United States may not have a particular interest in promoting certain exports in preference to others, and the exports it wishes to promote may be precisely those whose domestic output a Latin American country may desire to stimulate. This is a matter for trade negotiations, which would be far easier if agreement were reached on the fundamental principles of an economic development policy.

If it was a recognized fact that the volume of Latin American imports is not determined by tariffs but by exports, it would not be difficult to find an agreement of interests. Suppose that, as a result of United States tariff concessions, a Latin American country increases its exports and is therefore in a position to import more; but suppose also that this country wishes to reduce rather than raise imports of certain goods which can be replaced by domestic production through a reasonable measure of protection. It is probable that, with this object in view, the protective duties on such goods will be increased. What will happen to the other imports? There will be a tendency toward an over-all increase, without any need for a reduction of customs duties. Nevertheless, it is evident that if the duties on certain goods were to be reduced or eliminated, imports of these commodities would increase at the expense of others. An increase could therefore take place in imports of luxury goods mainly consumed by those in the higher-income brackets —goods not indispensable for popular consumption. The resources could have otherwise been advantageously employed in acquiring capital goods. Once again the importance of considering all the aspects within a development policy is apparent, as it takes account not only of present requirements, but also of the evident need to introduce future changes in the composition of imports.

To return to protection, the maintenance of high duties on goods to avoid overencouragement of imports might cause their domestic substitution and thus prevent productive factors from being used to the country's greater advantage. A good development policy can use domestic fiscal instruments to deal with such cases and thus eliminate one of the difficulties which often arise in trade negotiations.

The ability of the United States to obtain spontaneous reciprocity for its tariff concessions is a result of the fundamental changes that have taken place in the short span of one generation. Interested as the United States is in a vast peripheral development policy, it is logical that its trade policy should also be modified in accordance with its new international situation. But to assume that this merely consists in accommodating a policy to new principles would be an artificial oversimplification of a real and very complex problem. There is every reason why exporters in general—and especially those encountering tariff obstacles elsewhere—should react in a manner which coincides with their immediate interests. This attitude is even more understandable in a country whose foreign trade policy only a few decades ago had necessarily to be focused upon the encouragement of exports.

CHAPTER III

PLANNING CONCEPTS AND EXPERIENCES

Economic Development Programming[1]

Development Programs and the Regimentation of the Economy

There is a certain amount of confusion between the concept of a development program and that of rigid state control of the economy. Such ambiguity must be dispelled. A program of economic development is the expression of a single idea, namely, the desirability of increasing and judiciously regulating capital investment, so that stronger impetus and greater order may be given to the growth of a country. Undoubtedly, the State may thus encompass a very wide sphere of action and to a great extent supplant the role of private enterprise; but this is by no means inherent in a development program. In fact, state intervention may even take place without economic development as a definite objective, and there may be no clear direction of investment. Conversely, a program may be put into effect with the minimum of state intervention. That the sphere of action of private initiative and

[1] From the series *Analyses and Projections of Economic Development*, I. *An Introduction to the Technique of Programming* (United Nations publication, Sales No. 55.II.G.2), pp. 3–9.

free enterprise in a program may actually be very wide does not imply that the State ought necessarily to limit itself to the traditional attitude of laissez-faire. On the contrary, a program calls for the firm application of a development policy; but this is possible without shackling private enterprise, which may, in fact, be stimulated into undertaking certain activities, and be offered access to essential resources. The State possesses effective instruments for this purpose, namely, its fiscal and tariff, monetary and credit policies, and domestic and foreign loans, apart from its direct participation in those basic investments which, for one reason or another, cannot be effected by private enterprise. Well handled, these can become the chief instruments of a program conceived in terms of a development policy.

Here, too, it would be as well to avoid confusion. There are two kinds of state intervention: that which involves the use of such instruments and creates a favorable environment for the evolution of private enterprise, enhancing its ability to fulfill certain goals or objectives; and that of a regulatory character which tends to prescribe what private initiative may or may not do. The system of exchange permits and price controls is characteristic of this latter kind of intervention. A good program, far from strengthening or insisting upon imposing this type of control over the actions of individual entrepreneurs, could, on the contrary, create favorable conditions for its elimination, by means of a more systematic and intensive growth of the economy.

The field of programming techniques is so vast that this chapter will be limited to the preliminary techniques of programming and to a general commentary on the problems involved.

Development Targets and Investment

The first problem in the technique of formulating a program consists in determining the possible targets of development in a given economy. Such a problem cannot be resolved without a prior review of past events and present possibilities, and its solution must be the result of painstaking analysis. First, to undertake what might be termed a diagnosis of the national economy, an examination must be made of the way in which a country has evolved, and of the dynamic factors which have played a part in its growth. Of special importance is the determination of the most recent rate of growth, as well as of the efforts made by the economy to attain it. Secondly, a study must be undertaken of probable future trends, and of the possibilities of change or of persistence in the internal and external factors that have played a role in recent years. An over-all survey of these elements will enable the economy's growth potentialities to be assessed, and the degree of effort required to attain various rates of growth to be defined.

The possible conclusions to be derived from the results of such an analysis are many and varied. It way well be that, on account of favorable circumstances—internal or external in origin—the country has attained what might be considered a satisfactory rate of growth, but that a continuation of this promising trend is unlikely. In that event, the aim of a program might be to maintain development at the rate attained, which would necessarily imply a greater effort on the part of the economy as a whole. Another possibility is to accelerate the rate of growth, because it is thought that the economy could either make a greater effort or achieve a better organization and distribution of its resources. These two instances are perhaps the most typical in Latin America.

At all events, it is likely that the study of recent and future trends in a country's development will suggest various alternative patterns of growth, depending upon the degree of effort employed. One of the decisive factors in the evaluation of these alternatives is the level of investment required to ensure that a given rate may in practice be achieved.

Careful calculation of the total investment required would be a laborious task; but simplified procedures exist which, established upon past experience of a country's economy, make an approximate computation possible. These methods are based on the relationship between the stock of capital and income over a representative period. This relationship will give an approximation of the volume of new investment required to attain a given increase in income. Thus, taking Latin America as a whole, it can be estimated—according to experience later than that of 1935—that to obtain an increase in income of 1 per cent, about 2.3 per cent of income must be devoted to capital investment, apart from the amount which must be invested to offset the loss of depreciation in the stock of capital.

With the coefficient thus derived it is possible to make a preliminary estimate of the volume of income that would be obtained from year to year according to each rate of growth, as well as of the aggregate annual investment required to attain it. In this way projections of income and investment are drawn up, on the basis of past experience, which by their very nature are general and aggregative. The next step is to establish projections for individual sectors of the economy, with more detailed estimates of the capital required by each, so that the general projections of investment can be subsequently amended; but this comes at a more advanced stage of programming, and meanwhile work must proceed with aggregate projections.

To return to the previous question—it is in this matter of the investment required by each growth alternative that economists responsible for programming encounter the first limitation to their range of alternatives. To attain a higher rate of growth, the coefficient of investment must be raised. This implies a corresponding increase in saving, which cannot be achieved without a restriction of present consumption. On paper, it is easy to see how the lowering of average per capita consumption by a given amount could raise the coefficient of investment, so that, within a few years, income would increase and consumption return to its former level, subsequently expanding at a higher rate than before. The numerical demonstration of the acceleration of growth is a very simple concept; but in expressing numerical hypotheses in terms of practical reality considerable stumbling blocks are encountered. In the first place, preference for the current pattern of consumption is very strong and the population will not readily accept any modification of its habits of consumption and saving unless there is an appreciable change in the volume of income or in its distribution among the different social groups. This attitude is all the more understandable in countries such as those of Latin America, where the level of consumption—although it has risen in no small measure—still remains very low, notwithstanding the fact that the pattern of income distribution would suggest that the higher-income groups are capable of much greater saving than at present. In the second place, very strong pressure exerted on consumption may lower it to a level below the installed capacity of consumer-goods industries, so that the stimulus provided by this important sector of production would be lost.

These practical difficulties are among the fundamental reasons for believing that savings must be supplemented with foreign capital to attain a higher rate of growth. Another reason will be examined at a later stage. The additional contribution of foreign capital to a development program is usually considered as a transitory expedient which allows of a higher rate of growth without the curtailment of existing consumption. Its impermanence rests upon a simple principle. The growth of income must be accelerated with the aid of foreign capital until it reaches a point beyond which all the investment required for further growth at a higher rate of development can be covered by domestic saving, without resort to additional foreign capital. From this point of view the aim of the foreign capital inflow is to create conditions favorable to an increase in the savings coefficient. In a program, the time required to raise initial domestic saving to the level necessary to achieve the target rate of growth will be called the period of transition.[2]

In other words, foreign capital must facilitate an increase in the coefficient of domestic savings, without its being necessary to reduce current consumption. Nevertheless, it will be essential to restrict the expansion of consumption as income rises. A larger share than previously of the increment in income obtained from greater investment should be devoted to savings. If this is not accomplished and the savings coefficient remains at the same level, the inflow of foreign capital must continue indefinitely in order to maintain the desired rate of growth. This would be hardly practicable for a series of reasons. Among them figures the increasing burden of remittances abroad, which could be borne only on the assumption that the foreign capital inflow would continue to increase without interruption, not only to meet the deficit in saving, but also to contribute to the payment of these remittances.

2 This treatment of foreign capital as a transitory phenomenon should be understood as a methodological approach and not as a principle of economic policy. It is quite conceivable that, after the period of transition, the inflow

Between the assumption of a continued and indefinite rise in the inflow of foreign capital and the hypothesis that consumption would be restricted in order to accelerate development without resort to foreign investment, there are other, intermediate courses. Everything depends upon the share of the increase in income to be set aside for saving during the period of transition. The higher this proportion and the more rapidly a country's domestic saving reaches the savings target for a higher coefficient of investment, the smaller will be the foreign capital required to attain this objective. Here also the question of feasibility must be borne in mind, which, as in the preceding example, is inevitably affected by political and social, as well as economic, considerations. The programming expert must present the different possibilities as objectively as possible, to facilitate the decisions of the responsible authorities. Consideration must be given not only to this aspect, but also to that of import substitution or of an increase in exports. Domestic savings alone are not enough; the possibility of transforming them into capital-goods imports is indispensable.

The Vital Need to Raise the Domestic Savings Coefficient

It was stated above that domestic saving would have to increase until it could cover the investment needed for an accelerated rate of growth. This is one of the most delicate points in a development policy, in view of the tendency to adhere to a set pattern of saving and consumption. It would not therefore be possible to count too much on a spontaneous rise in saving resulting from the gradual and moderate increase in income achieved by a program. The lower-income groups will be inclined to use their earnings to improve their level of living, and very little in the way of saving can be expected from them. The higher-income brackets have a greater capacity for saving, but they too will tend to increase consumption in the adoption of new and luxurious ways of life. These obstacles to an improvement in domestic saving have sometimes led to the replacement of voluntary saving by inflationary methods of financing which result in lower real incomes for the poorer and

---

of foreign capital should be continued to make possible a higher rate of growth and the introduction of new techniques.

more populous sectors. In the experience of some Latin American countries, the consequences of such a policy were either that saving rose at an extremely high social cost or that dangerous conditions of foreign and domestic instability were created. Both situations retarded development over the long term.

It is thus part of the technique of programming to discuss the means available to a government for modifying saving in terms of the existing data on income distribution. Some examples will serve as a better illustration of these possibilities. It should be recalled that much private financing takes the form of reinvested profits, which firms or enterprises retain in preference to distributing them as dividends. An incentive to this type of saving could be most effective, and doubtless the tax system could play a decisive role by reducing or eliminating taxes on income that is reinvested. This is one of the most important objectives of fiscal policy in a development program. The fiscal instrument might thus be employed to encourage saving by the entrepreneur before income flows toward consumption. But taxes can also be used directly to discourage consumption, above all in the high-income groups, insofar as they have rejected investment. If the coefficient of saving in the high-income sector is relatively low, and the means for discouraging consumption cannot increase it, fiscal policy might be of considerable help in achieving this end, if a substantial proportion of the tax on such income were used for purposes of investment. In this way, the State would divert to investment those resources which would otherwise have been used for consumption. Moreover, the investment could also be made through private channels if the resources thus obtained were placed at the disposal of those entrepreneurs who would know how to invest them, instead of resorting to familiar inflationary expedients in the banking system.

Nevertheless, the fiscal instrument may also exert an unfavorable influence on development. The excessive growth of current government expenditure in relation to a country's income can adversely affect the savings of the population and will thus retard the rate of development. It is extremely difficult to demarcate clearly what is and what is not excessive in this field. There is obviously much need for governmental services in Latin America, but equally vital is the necessity to increase the consumption of goods and of certain private services. Consequently, changes in the proportion of government services to total income should be a matter for careful consideration. A program must be based on certain assumptions of the relationship between the rate of development of governmental services and the expansion of income; should these assumptions cease to be valid, the program must be revised.

The nature of this relationship is usually determined by motives other than economic development; but the projection of its influence on the rate of development, together with the analysis of growth, may contribute persuasively to the argument that the policy of fiscal expenditure should not be considered independently from the problems of a country's growth.

Limitations to Development Arising from the Capacity to Import

Another problem involved in the technique of programming must now be examined. It was explained earlier that one reason for resorting to foreign capital was the practical difficulty of reducing consumption in order to increase saving; but if this difficulty was overcome, others would crop up in its place, since the additional saving obtained in this way would have to be used for the purchase of capital goods abroad at the expense of other imports. This point is of such practical importance that it must be dwelt on at more length here. If the coefficient of imports to aggregate investment was equal to the coefficient of imports to aggregate consumption, there would be no difficulty in using the increase in saving for buying foreign capital goods, since the additional saving would be divided between the imported and the locally produced capital goods in the same proportion as the sacrifice made by the consumer would be divided between national and imported goods; but this does not happen. Even in the Latin American countries where capital-goods industries have been vigorously developed, the coefficient of imports in investment is much higher than the coefficient of imports in consumption. A reduction of consumption in favor of saving does not therefore lower imports as much as the growth of investment increases them. This has two fundamental consequences. First, greater saving, and its transfer abroad, weakens the demand for domestic consumer goods, without being offset by a corresponding increase in the demand for domestic capital goods. Second, imports will rise. These are two aspects of the same phenomenon, in which the deficiency in domestic demand is equivalent to excess in demand for imports.

This excess is the important point. The shift of income from consumption to investment implies additional imports. It is conceivable that nonessential imports might be restricted in order to offset this increase. Nevertheless, apart from the fact that such a process does not occur spontaneously but requires selective state intervention, the margin for control is very narrow in countries where severe restrictions upon the expansion of imports are already in force because the capacity to import is fully absorbed. Such is the case in some Latin American countries. However, this is only one aspect of a more general problem, namely, that of the limitations imposed on economic development by the capacity to import. Even when greater imports of capital goods are offset either by a reduction of imports of other goods or by the use of foreign capital, only a temporary difficulty has been removed. There still remains an obstacle of major importance to economic development: as per capita income expands, demand for imports tends to rise more than the capacity to import. This disparity makes the replacement of imports by domestic production inevitable, so that income may continue to grow at a rate which is adequate in relation to the capacity to import.

A development program calls for an assessment of how much substitution should be effected in order to attain a given rate of income growth. For this purpose two series of hypothetical calculations must be made. First, the probable expansion of the requirements for imported goods must be determined by means of a series of projections, to which further reference will be made. Second, the probable growth of the capacity to import must be estimated in terms of exports and their relative prices, as well as of the volume of foreign capital necessary to carry out the program. In view of the probable increase of these requirements and of the capacity to import, the difference between these two estimates will give the volume of imports to be replaced by domestic production. Alternatives will be available in selecting the most suitable items for replacement and, in some cases, in deciding whether it is preferable to increase import substitution or encourage exports. Apart from other considerations, the essential criterion should be the increase in income obtained from the alternatives. The greater the increment obtained by a given addition of capital, the greater will be the volume of goods and services available for the community. Since further reference will be made to this subject, it is now sufficient to note that the calculation of import substitution, as of other fundamental estimates in a program, rests upon a series of hypotheses. These must be carefully prepared on the basis of past events and future prospects, but it is not worthwhile to discuss whether or not they are true in practice. It is therefore necessary to introduce an element of flexibility into a program, which, while affecting its primary aims as little as possible, will allow it to be adapted to any changes that may occur.

The Projection of Demand in Terms of the Rate of Growth

The problem mentioned above forms part of a much greater whole, from which it has been isolated inasmuch as it has certain different characteristics that give it special significance. This problem appertains to the assessment of the growth of demand for available goods and services, in order to calculate investment requirements in the different sectors of economic activity and in the different branches of each sector.

The aggregate projections give a first approximation of the volume of capital required to obtain a given rate of growth and its corresponding coefficient of investment. A second approximation must then be made by calculating capital requirements by sectors. Once this is done, either the first calculation or the rate of growth must be adjusted. In this way, the aggregate projections of income and over-all capital requirements are transformed into projections by sectors. Only then may more elaborate calculations be made with the assistance of specialists in the different activities. To enable such specialists to work satisfactorily, it is essential to provide them with clear and precise information on what each activity must attain in terms of the probable rise in demand and the capital available to meet this growth.

At this stage the part to be played by the projections may be seen more clearly. It is not possible to project expansion of demand in each sector of economic activity without first having determined the general rate of growth which it is desired to achieve. The target for per-capita-income growth determines the form and intensity with which the sectoral expansion of demand can be forecast. It is thus necessary to pass from the general to the particular, in order to return once more to the aggregate projections and introduce the necessary adjustments there.

If future demand were to expand proportionately to current consumption, its calculation would be very simple, since the rate of growth in the aggregate projection could be applied to individual sectors. Obviously, this is not the case. With a given increment of income, the expansion of demand for different goods and services varies; in some cases demand increases more than income, while in others it rises either proportionately to or less than income. The income-elasticity of demand according to the principal groups of goods and services must therefore be calculated; but this is no easy task, given the unreliability of Latin American statistics. The same is true of the estimates of capital needs in the different sectors.

This method of summarizing the principal problems of the technique of programming was adopted in the interests of clarity and does not imply that in practice these problems should be considered in the same order. In reality, once the rate of growth has been determined, they must be analyzed according to the relationship imposed by their interdependence. Thus, the assessment of capital needs, to which reference has just been made, cannot be separated from an analysis of the availability and productivity of labor. This is another problem to be raised in the present chapter, and a discussion of it follows.

Productivity and Transfer of Labor

Two main stages distinguish between economic development in underdeveloped countries and the growth of more highly developed countries. By the very way in which technical progress penetrates the less developed countries, Latin America's primary activities, except those producing for export, are generally characterized by a relative abundance of labor, a relative shortage of capital, and low productivity. As a result, a high proportion of the labor force is engaged in these primary activities. As technical progress advances, the proportion gradually falls, and the labor force shifts to industry, trade, transport, and services. In the latter sectors the intensity of capital per gainfully employed person is usually higher than in primary activities, with a consequent difference in labor productivity. Therefore, as the working population shifts from activities with a low productivity to others where it is higher, average productivity throughout the whole economy also rises, although it may not have improved in any individual sector. For this effect to be achieved, it is sufficient for the increment in the population that cannot find employment in agriculture to be absorbed by the other more productive activities. But in reality this process is accompanied by an improvement in the productivity of the different sectors; the shift of the active population from primary production becomes greater as the same productivity can be attained with a smaller labor force. The same is true of the other sectors, although to a varying degree and, as these effects are added to those of the normal displacement of the labor force, both elements unite to raise productivity.

Given the degree of progress in productive technology, there is a limit to the reduction of the active population engaged in primary activities, which cannot continue to decrease without adversely affecting the relationship existing between production in the different sectors. The complete assimilation of techniques in primary activities will enable such activities to surrender virtually their entire surplus labor, and thus the initial phase of economic development will be accomplished.

During the second stage, there are no great shifts in the labor force. There is a certain technological homogeneity in all activities, compatible with the degree of technical progress in the different branches. Naturally, a certain amount of displacement will occur, owing to the different intensity with which this technical progress is introduced and the different rates of expansion of demand. Nevertheless, the large and unilateral shifts from primary activities to others will have disappeared. There will be no further outstanding increases in productivity as a result of the mere transfer of manpower, but only through the improvement of skills and of the capital intensity in the individual sectors and branches.

The Latin American countries are now in the first stage, although some are reaching the end of it and are ready for gradual entry into the second stage. In other words, they have the problem of a shift in the labor force from agriculture to industry, trade, transport, and services.

In general terms, therefore, the labor force is not usually a factor restricting development—at least from the point of view of its size. The limiting factor lies in the capital required to free labor from activities with low productivity, and at the same time to raise productivity in the other sectors by increasing the capital intensity.

Herein lies one of the principal motives for drawing up an over-all program which can coordinate partial plans and make them compatible. How, for example, could per capita productivity in agriculture be raised, if a simultaneous attempt were not made to reabsorb in other activities the labor force which agriculture, with its own rate of expansion, could no longer retain? From another standpoint, how could industrial development be accelerated if it was not known how much of the labor force could be withdrawn from agriculture or from broad categories of personal services with a low economic yield?

The essence of the problem is as follows: given the probable increase of demand in the various activities, and the higher productivity to be expected from each of them should their capital intensity be increased, how should manpower be distributed among them, what shifts will be necessary, and how and where can the displaced labor force be absorbed?

Productivity and Investment Alternatives in a Program

To solve this problem, the concept of productivity and the influence of capital formation upon it needs prior explanation. This is a basic concept in programming development. Once the rate of growth to be reached within a given period has been determined, and a preliminary estimate made of the capital requirements, a criterion for directing the distribution of the capital among the different sectors and branches of each sector must be established. An estimate will naturally be available of the expansion of the requirements for goods and services in the different sectors and branches. To meet these requirements, various courses of action are open, and one of the most important considerations in choosing among them, but not the only one, is productivity.

There are two courses of action. The first is the satisfaction of requirements by domestic production and imports, although it is known that the present volume of imports cannot be maintained, since the capacity to import expands more slowly than the demand for imported commodities. Import substitution must therefore take place, and various possibilities offer themselves. Should the domestic production of a particular foodstuff instead of a particular raw material or manufactured product be undertaken or increased? What should be the selective criterion if, given the estimated increment in the available capital and labor force, the aim is to achieve a maximum rise in income? These are the first possible courses of action which must be examined by the economist in charge of a program.

A second choice is closely linked with the first, although it does not encompass the whole economy but is concerned with each of the individual branches. The problem lies in the existence of different solutions for the production of a given commodity or service, each of which involves a different capital intensity per worker. What criterion should be adopted so that the series of investments will be accompanied by a maximum increment in production?

A discussion of this aspect must include the two principal forms of productivity, namely, product per worker and product per unit of capital. To increase productivity in either of these forms it is generally necessary to raise the capital intensity per worker; but an increase of this kind does not always have the same effect on the product per worker and the product per unit of capital. For the economy as a whole, the final objective of technical advance is a progressive increase in the product per worker, that is, a reduction in the amount of labor per unit of production. However, to obtain a given increment in the product per worker may require disproportionate increases in capital. The ideal situation would be for a given increment in the product per worker to be achieved with the minimum increase in capital, which implies a maximum increment in the product–capital ratio. But either because of reasons inherent in the process of introducing improved techniques, or because the latter is aimed mainly at achieving the greatest possible increase in labor productivity, capital increments which do not bring about an increase in the productivity of capital and which even result in a decline in the product–capital ratio are not only conceivable, but are also of great importance in more economically developed countries.

In the United States, the product–capital ratio, notwithstanding continual fluctuations over short periods, tends rather to remain constant, owing to factors of another order. This would appear to indicate that those effects of an improvement in technique which tend to increase the product–capital ratio have been offset by others having the opposite results.[3]

This is one of the most interesting aspects of the dynamics of development. If the guiding principle of the capitalist entrepreneur was the choosing of those investments designed to obtain increases in the unit product proportionately greater than the increment in capital, thus obtaining the maximum increase in the product for the economy as a whole, he would not resort to investments of another type. However, under the impetus of improved techniques and with a large supply of capital at his disposal, he is not obliged to follow this line of action. If technical progress enables him to raise labor productivity by reducing costs and increasing profits, he will do so without regard to the product–capital ratio. This procedure has profound dynamic consequences. If labor productivity is increased in this way, wages will tend to rise, so that labor will be drawn away from activities with a lower product per worker, albeit with a higher product–capital ratio. Thus, these activities, in turn, are compelled in many instances to seek methods whereby labor productivity can be increased and competitive wages paid, although this may imply a decline in the product–capital ratio. At an elementary stage of productive technique, in which the capital per worker is scanty—a situation which is still characteristic of Latin American farming for the home market and of handicrafts—the product–capital ratio is relatively high. As modern technology becomes more widespread, this process will be repeated and, in order to expand labor productivity, it will be necessary to lower the product–capital ratio. This takes place, for instance, in the mechanization of agriculture, but

[3] The following explanation of the same phenomenon would be more in line with traditional theory: since the capital factor has tended to grow with greater rapidity than the labor factor, and in view of the law of diminishing returns, the productivity of capital will tend to decline over the long term. The fact that statistical evidence reveals this productivity as having in practice remained constant can be attributed to technological advances offsetting the drop in the productivity of capital.

this same example is an illustration of the compensatory factors at work, since technical progress in agriculture is continually offering new means of increasing the product per unit of land and of labor with a relatively small amount of capital.

This historical development of technology and its effects on the economic process have taken place gradually in the more highly developed countries, until the present high standards have been reached. But the underdeveloped countries have no reason to follow the same pattern. Advanced technology is available, and there is no need to pass through all the stages of its development. Such countries lack the necessary capital to assimilate it, and even if the requisite resources were available, technology in all its complexity could not be rapidly absorbed. In 1953, Latin America had an average per capita income of $247 at 1950 prices; taking into account changes in purchasing power, it would be necessary to go back as far as 1840 to find a comparable figure in the United States. But during that period per capita investment was barely $505, whereas at the present time it has reached $3,330 (both at 1950 prices). Latin America, in common with other underdeveloped areas with an income level equivalent to that of the United States more than a century ago, is therefore confronted with the results of a technological development which calls for high per capita investment.

This demands a very intensive investment effort. But it would not be possible to attain the capital intensity required and the corresponding level of productivity within the short space of a few years. The amount of capital available would fall short of requirements and therefore any examination of the capital increments necessary to obtain an increase in the product per worker touches upon one of the most vital aspects of programming development.

This leads to the question of alternative investments in a given branch of activity, to which reference was made earlier. Investments of varying intensity may be made in the same branch. In some cases the intensity may be very high, accompanied by a high level of productivity per worker, although the product–capital ratio is lower than in other investments or in the rest of economic activity. It is evident that if there was sufficient capital to attain the highest possible intensity in all activities, the problem would be solved. This is not the case, however; to obtain maximum income in the economy as a whole, in certain sectors it would be necessary to adopt solutions giving a higher product–capital ratio, even at the expense of forgoing increases in the product per worker.

However, it is not always possible to find solutions of this nature, since technological research in those countries where capital is relatively abundant is directed more toward labor-saving processes than toward capital saving.

At this point it may be useful to digress a little so that the point just made can be placed in the context of technical development. A British transport authority recently showed that if underdeveloped countries assimilated the road-building techniques of other countries such as the United States, many of them would be unable to meet the resultant cost. Progress in the field of motor transport, together with the abundance of capital in the United States, has given rise to heavier and faster vehicles, and this has created new problems in the technique of road-building, with a consequent increase in investment per unit of surface. This is a further manifestation of the glaring discrepancy between the modest per capita income of underdeveloped countries and the high investment level required by modern productive techniques.

Thus it may be necessary to adopt solutions involving a product–capital ratio which would be much lower than that of other new investments, owing to the lack of a selection of courses of action in the same branch of the economy. On the other hand, the techniques involving a high capital intensity, combined with a high product per worker, are as attractive to the Latin American entrepreneur as they were to his counterpart during the evolution of capitalism. But in the latter case, technical progress took place gradually and in easy stages, whereas the underdeveloped countries have sought to absorb advanced technology as quickly as possible, in view of the prospect of greater profits. It happens with relative frequency that entrepreneurs, whose own individual resources are adequate, choose the courses of action involving high capital intensity, while the economy as a whole has sufficient capital only to effect investments corresponding to a much lower intensity. Owing to this shortage of capital, the dynamic effect which the entrepreneur obtained in the highly developed countries by raising the wage level in the rest of the economy cannot be achieved—or can be achieved only to a very small extent; moreover, available capital is not distributed in a manner conducive to obtaining the maximum increment in the product.

Obviously, this will not result in the most economical distribution of the small stock of capital. In a development program, all possible attention should therefore be devoted to this problem, particularly in those instances where the government effects direct investments or guides investment policy by means of its tariff, fiscal, or credit measures.

The other types of alternative are of equal importance, although they are not applicable in a single branch of activity, but among different branches, especially in connection with import substitution. Here, too, of course, the product–capital ratio must be considered, but in the following special way.

If, for a country to attain a given rate of growth, a certain amount of substitution must be effected, it would be essential, above all, to select those items involving the highest product–capital ratio. Nevertheless, as these substitutions are carried out, the ratio might decline until it was lower than that obtained by the new investments in the rest of domestic activity. The only alternative would then be to export, always provided that a product–capital ratio could be obtained which would be superior to that in the replacement activities. Should this be impossible, the reduction of the product–capital ratio would be vital to the continuation of growth. As long as this phenomenon is accompanied by an increasing labor productivity, there is no cause for alarm; but it is a different matter if the decline in the product–capital ratio coincides with a fall in the product per worker. This is not an arbitrary assumption, but something that might well take place if substitution is expanded in those countries whose markets are not sufficiently wide to absorb the production deriving from investments of high capital intensity. The smallness of markets is therefore one of the gravest obstacles to the development of the economy beyond certain limits, which in some cases are not very wide.

All the foregoing considerations demonstrate that analysis of productivity is of fundamental importance in a development program.

However, there is very little material available in the Latin American countries upon which such an undertaking could be based, and a more resolute effort must be made to study and analyze the subject if a better understanding of economic development problems is to be achieved.

The Neutrality of the Programming Technique

In the foregoing pages, frequent reference has been made to a choice of solutions which the economist charged with the preparation of a program should submit with all possible objectivity to the authorities responsible for making the final decisions. In some cases, the terms of these alternatives are of a strictly economic character; in others, social and political factors are involved. These decisions are of no concern to the experts as such, although the technique of programming must provide a sound basis for judgment so that a full knowledge may be had of the extent of the factors at play and of the consequences to be expected from any decision.

The first impartial step of the programming technique is to discuss the possible rates of growth and to decide whether recourse must be had to foreign capital and, if so, to what extent, to attain these rates of growth. As has already been seen, from the economic point of view various solutions exist, and their selection will inevitably depend upon social and political considerations. The role of the expert is to submit the selected courses of action with all objectivity, explaining the requirements and probable effects of each one. It must be ascertained, for example, whether current consumption would have to be restricted in order to attain a given rate of growth, if no recourse is to be had to foreign capital; or what amount of foreign capital would be required according to the way in which consumption is to be permitted to expand in relation to savings, as a result of the additional increase in income. Similarly, with respect to this problem of increasing saving, the programming technique must permit an unprejudiced examination of the various possibilities offered by taxation or other expedients, pointing out in each case the probable effects on the distribution of income and consumption in the different social groups.

This attitude of impartiality in the technique of programming is not only necessary in defining functions; it is also commendable inasmuch as it strengthens the moral authority and increases the powers of persuasion of those drawing up the program. Programming is an extremely complicated procedure, requiring the collaboration of strong social forces. In obtaining this cooperation, it is indispensable to give an unbiased presentation of the possible targets and the different methods for attaining them. The final objective of any program is to obtain a substantial increase in future consumption, and this inevitably requires the raising of the level of investment by restricting the growth of consumption. The support of vast sectors of public opinion for a development program necessitates a clear understanding of the need to improve the investment coefficient. Without this support, no development program could be effectively implemented, no matter how rational and well-conceived it might be.

Planning in Latin America[4]

Past History

The need for a development planning policy has only recently been recognized in Latin America, as the result of a combination of internal and external factors.

During the forties, the need to enlarge the economic infrastructure, particularly the transport network and power supply, and to adapt it to new development conditions, as well as to encourage relatively large-scale projects in key industries led to the preparation and implementation of some partial programs dependent mainly on public investment.

It later became increasingly apparent, particularly toward the end of the fifties, that the Latin American economies lacked the necessary dynamism to maintain moderately satisfactory rates of growth, to remedy critical imbalances in their foreign trade and external financing, to contain inflationary pressures, to provide sufficient productive employment for a rapidly increasing labor force, and to improve living

[4] "Planning in Latin America" (E/CN.12/772), *Economic Bulletin for Latin America*, XII, no. 2. (1967).

conditions, and at the same time fulfill rising expectations created by a knowledge of the tremendous possibilities opened up by technical advances. Economic policy thus came to hinge on development in its most comprehensive sense as an economic and social concept, and to take into account both internal and external limitations. ECLA, whose objectives are to obtain a fuller knowledge of Latin America's development problems, determine technical criteria for a development strategy, and suggest methods of projecting future needs, helped to instill that more comprehensive outlook. Although its work was focused on analysis rather than planning, the increasing use of projections as a method of anticipating certain problems and analyzing policy alternatives helped prepare the ground and provide a methodological tool for the formation of plans.

Bolivia, Chile, and Colombia were the first Latin American countries in the fifties to formulate national development plans and to establish the necessary planning machinery, largely with the help of international technical assistance. However, it was not until the Punta del Este Conference, 1961, that the Latin American governments acknowledged that planning should be the fundamental instrument for mobilizing national resources, making structural changes, enhancing efficiency and productivity, and securing more international financial cooperation.

Since then, virtually all of the Latin American countries have prepared plans of different kinds and scope. These plans have also been analyzed and evaluated by regional organs, which have helped to sustain planning efforts by bringing them into line with the volume and orientation of foreign financial assistance.

A valuable fund of experience has thus been built up, but its true significance may be hard to appreciate, because planning is a relatively recent phenomenon and began in very special circumstances. Until fairly recently, no experience had been obtained in this field, apart from some preliminary experiments and certain sectoral programs, and the very idea of planning was resisted. There were no background data on which to draw for planning purposes, and no methodology had as yet proved its worth in the particular circumstances of Latin America. Nor was there a flexible administrative structure which could be adapted to functions and methods other than those enshrined by custom and tradition. Nonetheless, this period was marked by the preparation of the technical bases for planning and the training of cadres on an ever-increasing scale. All the countries now have the necessary machinery for the preparation and orientation of plans (offices and general plans); the criteria used in the allocation of resources are becoming more rational, especially in the public sector, and, last but not least, planning has become a widely accepted idea.

Obstacles to the Implementation of Plans

Although planning in Latin America has made a number of important advances in certain aspects, it still has serious weaknesses, and the improvement of planning and the implementation of plans are still being hampered. Of late, the planning process has been experiencing a period of stagnation, and in some cases can be seen to have lost ground. The impetus to prepare the over-all plans has spent itself, and the same fervor has not been applied to the tasks of translating over-all planning policy into specific economic policy programs and short-term operational plans, and to establishing efficient instruments for the periodic review and updating of plans and the evaluation of their implementation.

It is in such tasks that the different limitations and obstacles are most apparent. Some of them stem from internal factors, ranging from those of a general nature that include the degree of political security and support that planning efforts actually enjoy to those with a more direct bearing on the operation of planning machinery. In assessing the latter, it is important to remember that little time has elapsed since planning first began, whereas, in other countries, efficient planning is the fruit of many years' sustained effort. Moreover, the attainment of planning targets in Latin America is hampered by other and usually formidable obstacles that derive from external factors primarily connected with the instability, limited growth, and unsatisfactory conditions of foreign trade and external financing.

It is more useful, therefore, to identify the present obstacles to planning in Latin America and to suggest ways of overcoming them than to draw up a balance-sheet of planning accomplishments and limitations in the region.

Internal Problems

THE FUNCTIONS OF PLANNING

The need for planning as the mainspring of a coordinated development policy has been generally accepted by governments, but there has been no effective unity of aims as regards planning objectives and basic priorities. From the beginning, a number of different attitudes emerged. In some instances there was a tendency to regard planning primarily as an instrument for mobilizing external financial resources and as an additional requirement for international financial cooperation, thus emphasizing the urgent need for plans of some kind, and tending to highlight those aspects of the plan most directly related to foreign aid. In others, planning was seen from a professional and theoretical point of view as a tool for shaping the structural changes essential to Latin America's development and as the expression of a national program of action, encompassing the different economic sectors and aimed at achieving the economic and social goals which planning itself would help to define. Again, it was sometimes regarded as a means of attaining the limited goal of more rational administration. In one way or another, all these points of view were incorporated in the plans drawn up, but substantive aims of economic and social policy were not often reflected in specific decisions.

The problem is all the more important in that the structural changes essential to the development of Latin America confront planners with a different and more difficult task than planning in developed economies, where the changes required are usually less drastic and where there is a wider consensus on more issues.

Moreover, those different outlooks have given rise to a destructive and sterile controversy, based on much confused thinking, concerning the planning most suitable for Latin America. It has been argued that "over-all" or "macro-economic" planning should be abandoned and that efforts should be concentrated on building up a sufficient number of well-planned specific projects. On the other hand, where stress has been laid on planning as an instrument for formulating basic long-term policy, immediate problems have sometimes been neglected or deferred for future study. Instead of attempting to coordinate the efforts to define long-term policy, which are indispensable for effecting the far-reaching changes essential to Latin American development, with the machinery designed to implement that policy by immediate action, there has been a tendency to reject or underestimate one aspect and concentrate exclusively on the other.[5]

POLITICAL SUPPORT FOR PLANNING

The need for planning the economic and social changes essential to the development process raises the problem of the political viability of Latin American plans and the amount of effective support required by the planning effort. The plans generally encounter resistance from sectors which feel threatened by specific measures or are exerting pressure for a large share of national income. At the same time, the plans often encounter resistance from the traditional government administration, reluctant to institute changes and jealously guarding its policy-making power against any possible transfer of power which may imply reorganization of the administrative structure to facilitate the establishment of the policy-making machinery which planning requires.

Thus, plans inevitably suffer during the implementation stage from serious obstacles which cannot be overcome unless the governments provide ample and sustained support, a support which is not always forthcoming in Latin American experience.

Moreover, apart from substantive reasons, the difficulties of successful planning arise to some extent from the manner in which the plan takes shape. In some cases, there has been little or no communication between the technical planning officials and the government departments during the preparatory stages.

PARTICIPATION OF THE PRIVATE SECTOR

The problem of political support is even greater where the private sector is concerned. Resistance from some parts of the private sector

[5] These and other problems touched upon in this chapter were the subject of detailed study at a seminar organized by the Latin American Institute for Economic and Social Planning and held in June 1965. In this connection, see *Discusiones sobre Planificación*, Textos del Instituto, Editorial Siglo XXI (Mexico, 1966).

is inevitable whenever plans incorporate decisions to institute changes affecting specific situations or interests, but there seems to be a wide margin of potential support which has not been mobilized because of deficiencies in the planning process itself.

In general, there is a lack of communication between planning organs and the private sector. Rarely is any attempt made, during preparation of the plan, to consult representative national opinion groups (Parliament, political parties, trade unions, employers' associations, universities), or the sectors directly concerned (entrepreneurs, importers, exporters, and consumer associations).

This phenomenon, like others, arises partly because planning is not expressed in terms of specific economic policy measures which might induce the private sector to follow particular guidelines. The private sector regards the plan as an over-all review of the economic situation providing valuable information on the intentions of the public sector, but the plan does not guide its activity by furnishing incentives or disincentives in the form of credit, trade, or tax policy measures, for example.

OPERATION OF THE PLANNING MACHINERY

The varying degrees of political support for planning, the poor definition of its functions and its relationship with the decision-making centers, and the limited participation of the private sectors are not calculated to promote the more efficient operation of the planning machinery. Moreover, its operational flaws and weaknesses make still more remote the possibilities of forging closer links between the planning offices and the permanent decisions of the government authorities and other interested sectors.

The opposition which is bound to arise from the traditional policy-making organs, both among the political authorities and in the national administration as a whole, would seem to necessitate some sort of "strategy" for introducing planning machinery, which would obviate such friction as far as possible so that planning could be progressively built into the administrative structure and procedures.

In this respect, planning in Latin America has manifested serious shortcomings. Isolated as they usually are from the traditional channels of administration and decision-making, the planning offices have often been saddled with the responsibility of preparing a development plan with a minimum of guidance from the political authorities, or none at all. As a rule, contracts have continued to be sporadic and inadequate throughout the formulation stage, and the planning agencies have not been punctual in presenting the technical alternatives together with a justification and evaluation of implications, which would have required decisions at the political level. In the circumstances, the plan which has been drawn up has not been discussed in sufficient detail by the various government policy-making and executive organs, and therefore creates resistance in the ministries and decentralized agencies.

There have also been instances of an over-concentration of resources and activities in the central planning agency. While such a concentration was essential at the time, the result was that a high proportion of the planning experts—who are in any case few and far between—were grouped in this central office, and since the ministries and autonomous agencies have done very little in the way of planning, that office has tended to assume direct responsibility for the preparation of sectoral plans and projects.

While there would seem to be every justification for making the central planning office a division of the Office of the President of the Republic, since the support of the Chief of State and his Cabinet is a *sine qua non* for the satisfactory operation of the central agency, this has not automatically guaranteed the institution the stability and backing it needs, or the maintenance of easy channels of communication. In some instances, a change of government has halted planning processes that were making good headway, and in others it has pumped new life into efforts that seemed to be petering out. An attempt has been made to maintain communication through development councils or boards consisting of ministers, high-level officials, and technical experts. However, these organs have not always served their purpose. In other instances they have done useful work in coordinating development policy with the work of other departments of the national administration, but this coordination is apt to weaken at the operational level for lack of proper direction and supervision. The absence of efficient sectoral and intersectoral coordination machinery means that the coordination achieved at the core of the system weakens or disappears altogether at the lower levels as a result of organizational and procedural deficiencies.

The direct link between the head of the central planning office and the President of the Republic, which exists in some countries, seems to impart greater flexibility to the central planning agency by forestalling the difficulties inherent in the operation of pluripersonal bodies, which, in Latin America, have as a rule proved to be slow-moving and lacking in dynamism. It is observable, however, that when the technical director of the planning office does not have ministerial rank or a voice in the Cabinet, he finds himself at a definite disadvantage, and the central planning agency cannot discharge its functions efficiently, especially that of coordinating the public sector for purposes of implementing the plan. At the same time, the technical director in charge of the central agency is exposed to political pressures, and is often replaced when the government changes, since he is held responsible, whereas that responsibility would otherwise be assumed by the planning council or board.

The sectoral planning agencies are generally weak and faced with organizational and procedural problems. However, this is far from being the rule in the various ministries and decentralized agencies. They are often regarded merely as operational instruments for compiling statistical data; they are assigned routine duties which relegate programming activities to a secondary place, or they are used as agencies for the study of the most widely varying questions. They do not get the political support they need to carry out their functions and are usually cut off from the central planning agencies, the operational agencies of the ministry concerned, and the decentralized and autonomous agencies in their sector.

Similarly, regional planning has had to cope with innumerable obstacles, not the least of which is the fact that political divisions and economic areas are not the same. Since the regions suitable as a basis for planning often comprise different political divisions, each with its own interests and provincial, state, or local pressure groups, it is very difficult to reconcile opinions and advance toward common objectives. Furthermore, some provincial or state governments are riddled with administrative weaknesses or are not sufficiently active in promoting economic and social development.

In the last analysis, those problems are simply so many corollaries of the general rule that planning organs have been superimposed on an administrative structure which has not been adapted to the demands of planned development policy.

In recent years, some countries have established central organization and methods offices, which have assumed responsibility for administrative reform. In many cases, these central offices have had no connection with the agencies of the planning system, or with those in charge of staff and budget administration. Action taken to promote the reform has nothing whatever to do with national development activities. Thus, although general planning efforts have indirectly served to focus attention on administrative streamlining, this task has usually been undertaken independently of economic development policies.

"OPERABILITY" OF THE PLANS

In addition to the problems arising from administrative organization and the position of planning machinery within the administration, other factors help to widen the gulf between the planning organs and the policy-makers.

The crux of the problem is that the plans formulated thus far cover only a part of the planning process; in other words, the planning effort has not yet been carried through to a conclusion, as regards either the plans drawn up or the establishment and operation of effective machinery for the periodic revision of plans and for the supervision and evaluation of their practical application.

Many of the over-all plans embody forecasts based on an improvement—sometimes substantial—in previous trends and on the anticipation of potential limiting factors. As a result, the over-all plans leave a wide gap between macroeconomic considerations and general principles, on the one hand, and their implementation by means of specific policies (monetary, exchange, fiscal) and operational plans, on the other. At the other extreme, some plans for immediate action which have begun to be applied merely enumerate partial proposals and certain specific projects often without evaluating them in broader perspective.

The lack of an effective "bridge" between the two dimensions of the planning effort has been detrimental to both types of plan, in the first instance because it greatly detracts from their viability, and in the second, because the plans fail to come to grips with the fundamental obstacles to development. This absence of an organic relationship between the long-term general plan and the corresponding specific plans in terms of the use of the various economic policy instruments and the mobilization and allocation of resources, is still one of the principal shortcomings of planning efforts in Latin America.

It is as much the result of poorly conceived development policy as of failure to design and implement effective short-term planning schemes.

1. *Definition of development policy.* The lack of a clear definition of that policy is reflected in the fact that the growth targets of long-term plans are not usually expressed in terms of the employment, productivity, and training of human resources. Despite the significance and magnitude of the underemployment problem in Latin America, most plans do not deal with it specifically, and little attention is devoted to the occupational structure and educational pattern of the employed population. Similarly, too little attention is paid to the supply of and demand for labor, and the need to bring the economic development targets established in the plan into line with the supply of manpower available, particularly of skilled labor. The problem of sectoral differences in productivity and the assimilation of technology is hardly mentioned in the majority of the plans, and the relevant proposals are confined to the broadest generalizations, no attempt being made at analysis in depth.

Much the same may be said in connection with the continuing high degree of income concentration in Latin America, which is another factor exerting a marked influence on the region's development. The plans often allude to this problem in the diagnosis, and even go so far as to list certain general palliatives (absorption of unemployment, increases in productivity, and/or price and wage, tax, public expenditure, and education policies), but these statements of principle are not translated into specific terms, nor is due allowance made for the effects on income distribution of the targets established in the plan and of the proposals for attaining them.

From another standpoint, although a broad and integrated view of development, in which economic and social factors are closely interrelated, has been gaining wide acceptance in Latin America, there remains the specific practical problem of how to decide whether funds should be allocated to particular social services (education, housing, and public health), or used to enlarge the economic infrastructure and the immediately productive field of the economy. In the absence of objective guidelines, decisions are influenced in the end by circumstantial factors, such as the power of the authorities responsible in each field, or political considerations of the moment. Through force of circumstance rather than as a result of deliberate policy, social expenditure has been increasing proportionately in most Latin American countries, and this process has been encouraged by the tenor of foreign aid over the last few years. It is a matter of conjecture how far this concentration of effort can be maintained, unless a similar effort is made to broaden the economic base which must sustain it. Moreover, serious doubts are beginning to emerge as to the effectiveness of certain kinds of social action in favor of particular social groups, when they are intended to relieve shortages which really reflect more deeply rooted problems of economic and social marginality. All this places a very heavy burden on those responsible for planning, who have neither sufficient experience nor the necessary technical machinery for discharging their responsibilities, and who are further hampered by the failure of governments to adopt the political decisions to support them.

Finally, it should be pointed out that, with the exception of Central America, most Latin American development plans have not explicitly incorporated the regional economic integration prospects in their plans as a variable with a bearing on their development policies. Integration appears to be taking its own course, along channels relatively far removed from planning efforts. Although there are several fundamental reasons for this, it may reasonably be supposed that this separate development is also affected by the fact that economic integration would raise new problems and that technical planners do not have the necessary methodological instruments to cope with them.

2. *Short-term planning schemes.* The second problem arises from the fact that countries have not yet succeeded in developing and activating the essential technical machinery required to complete the various stages of planning so that general economic policy can be translated into effective and immediate action.

Despite considerable progress in improving procedures for allocating public-sector resources by means of medium-term public investment plans and the use of program and performance budgeting techniques for the annual government budget, there are still acute problems. No comparable progress has been made, for example, in working out annual operational plans and economic policy, or in standardizing annual economic budgets.

For example, in the application of public investment plans, there is a marked disparity between targets and financial estimates, either because the tax reforms on which they are based are not carried out to the extent or in the time anticipated, owing to delays in international financing or special problems of financing local cost, or because any unexpected shortage of financial resources in the public sector affects investment much more than current expenditure. The operational capacity of the public administration to undertake new or increased activities is often overestimated because there are no proper criteria for evaluating it objectively, although there has been some significant progress in that respect. On the other hand, there is a general tendency to underestimate the volume of projects under way and, consequently, to underestimate the lack of flexibility in the allocation of resources because priority, save in exceptional circumstances, must be given to partially executed projects.

The program and performance budget has been adopted as the model for annual public-sector budgets in most countries of the region, and Uruguay's new political constitution expressly stipulates that the Executive must present a breakdown of the national budget by programs. On the other hand, similar progress has not been made in the preparation of annual plans of operation, an exercise regularly carried out only by Venezuela. The formulation of experimental numerical models for the analysis of economic policy is being tried out chiefly in Venezuela and Chile. As regards national economic budgets, the only practical experiments thus far have been conducted in Argentina, where such a budget was drawn up. These comprised a series of quantitative estimates of the probable behavior of the chief macroeconomic variables—including private investment—and of the compatibility of public expenditure with the situation and needs of the national economy.

The wide disparity between the plans and the conduct of economic policy is usually most pronounced in countries suffering from acute and persistent inflationary pressures. Those countries are confronted not only with the practical problems associated with the level and system of prices, but with the fundamental difficulty of reconciling the plan's objectives with the requirements of stabilization policies. Growing concern with this problem has led to the preparation of plans specifically designed for that purpose. What happens, most often, is that two unrelated and frequently contradictory policies are superimposed on one another: the policy implicitly or explicitly related to development plans or based on them, and the policy intended primarily to stabilize prices.

3. *Procedures for controlling the implementation of plans.* The lack of progress in the formulation and implementation of operational plans is clearly demonstrated by the nonexistence of machinery for controlling the implementation of plans, evaluating the problems which arise, and insisting on the rectifications which are patently necessary.

Not only must administrative organs be established to assume those functions, but evaluation techniques must be developed which will be applicable to Latin American conditions.

SPECIFIC INVESTMENT PROJECTS

Without discussing the spurious distinction made between plans and projects, which unfortunately continues to be the subject of some controversy, there is no doubt that the lack of sufficient specific investment projects has proved a serious obstacle to the effective implementation of Latin American development plans.

This subject was examined in detail at a recent seminar at which a number of suggestions were put forward which might appropriately be summarized here.[6]

One suggestion referred to the need—particularly under present-day conditions in the Latin American economies—for a very broad interpretation of the "project" concept, covering every unit of activity capable of implementing a development plan.

The persistent shortage of projects, despite the progress achieved in certain immediate factors which are usually regarded as decisive, posits the existence of other root causes. It appears that the shortage of projects is merely another manifestation of the weakness of the decision-making and implementation machinery. The shortage of projects is no more acute than it was before, in absolute terms—quite the reverse. What seems to be happening is that, in one way or another, traditional policies of unplanned development provided incentives for public and private enterprise which led to the formulation of specific projects, some of them of considerable importance. There is still a continuous flow of investment decisions, some of which materialize in project form, but planning has imposed additional and much greater demands.

First, projects are now required to meet specific investment objectives and targets established in the plans and to fit into certain over-all strategies. Insofar as they are not clearly defined, the objectives and policy do not provide sufficient incentives for suitable projects, nor do they in themselves represent strategic projects. The economic integration of Latin America illustrates this point: until the political decisions have been taken and political agreements concluded at the appropriate levels, no public or private ventures in the form of specific projects can be launched.

Second, planning not only requires the initiation of a certain number of projects but also arranges them in the proper order of priority and determines the relationship between projects and groups of projects with due regard for their direct and indirect effects on the economy as a whole.

[6] The seminar in question was organized by the Latin American Institute for Economic and Social Planning and was held in Santiago, Chile, from July 6 to 14, 1965.

Viewed in this context, the problem of promoting, identifying, preparing, evaluating, and executing projects is closely linked with the establishment of an effective planning system and with the necessary administrative reforms. Naturally, the difficulties of rapidly translating a development strategy into operational plans cannot be disregarded, any more than the difficulties connected with the shortage of trained personnel, experience, and technological resources. When the first plans are drawn up, a high proportion of investment capacity—particularly in the public sector—is tied up in projects in progress, which can only occasionally be replaced by other projects better adapted to the new plans. In other words, the maturation period of projects of a certain magnitude tends to be longer, as suggested by the experience of the Bank, which found that a large power or transport project may take from three to five years or more, from the time it is decided to undertake the economic and engineering studies, to the time they are completed and the financing of the project can be approved and implementation started.

AVAILABILITY OF INFORMATION

Improvement of the planning process in Latin America is being hampered by problems of the availability and quality of the basic information on which it must be based. The information consists mainly, but not exclusively, of statistical data.

There are serious deficiencies in the quantity, quality, and timeliness of data that are basic to planning. Moreover, full justice has not been done to the statistical function within the planning effort. In general, national statistical offices occupy a very subordinate role in public administration as a whole; their employees are frequently ill-paid and their staff unqualified. Very few have adequate financial resources or mechanical equipment for the efficient collection and elaboration of data. Moreover, there are gaps in the legislation that make it compulsory to supply certain data and, above all, in the machinery for giving effect to that legislation. The various sectoral, regional, and local statistical services are not sufficiently coordinated, and national statistical programs have not been drawn up.

Problems have also cropped up in relations with the users, one being the underestimation of the information requirements of the public administration and private sector. Moreover, proper facilities have not been set up to enable the offices providing the data to use them as a guide in decision-making. Relations with the planning offices, in particular, are usually characterized by sporadic demands for data made when plans are already in course of preparation. These relations have never been systematized, let alone developed into a mechanism providing a permanent flow of up-to-date information that would facilitate the periodic revision and evaluation of plans.

The quality of data is uneven, varying in accordance with the sector to which they refer. Foreign trade statistics, followed by population data, are the most accurate, while data on domestic trade, services, construction, road transport, and unemployment are particularly poor. When censuses are used as a basis, there is a lack of continuity in the statistics, one of the results of this being the preparation of a new industrial directory every time an industrial census is taken, instead of updating an earlier edition. Delays are a common feature of the data-processing, but in some cases recently attempts have been made to overcome this problem by using sampling techniques. Another shortcoming is the lack of a systematic and continuous series of indicators for tracing short-term changes in the economy. Lastly, there is usually a long delay before the data are published.

External Problems

The limitations and obstacles cited have undoubtedly detracted from the effectiveness of planning. They can only be overcome by decisions taken in the countries themselves and by the progressive improvement of planning machinery. It should be noted, however, that the implementation of Latin America's development plans has been and is still hampered by serious obstacles deriving from the evolution of trade and financial transactions with countries outside the region.

These obstacles are known as exogenous factors, not only because they are largely beyond the country's control or because they arise from new circumstances which could not have been predicted when the plans were being formulated, but, in particular, because from without they alter the economic context in which the plans within the region must be implemented.

A review of recent trends makes this situation quite clear. In the short space of time that has elapsed since planning activities first began to gain ground, several important factors have assumed considerable significance: the insufficient and unstable growth of exports, external debt commitments, the need to replenish gold and foreign exchange reserves, and—as a result—the irregular trend of imports and the urgent need for a policy of import restriction.

EXPORT TRENDS

Exports have expanded irregularly, as shown by the fact that the annual growth rates in terms of volume fluctuated between a high of 9.2 per cent in 1962 and a low of 2.2 per cent in 1964, while the figure for 1966 was 4 per cent. These averages for the region as a whole reflect occasional violent fluctuations in certain countries, resulting in sharp reductions in absolute terms.

Export trends in terms of current prices have been somewhat steadier. Nevertheless, thus far in the sixties, Latin America has lost a substantial proportion of its share in world trade. The sharpest drop was in its contribution to total United States imports—from about 21 per cent in the three-year period 1960–1962 to less than 16 per cent in 1966—but there was also a marked reduction in its share of imports by the European Economic Community (from 6 to 5.5 per cent) and the European Free Trade Association (from 5.4 to 4.2 per cent). These decreases have not been offset by the sizable increase in intra-Latin American trade.

The recent trends were influenced by structural and institutional factors created by the preponderance of primary commodities in Latin American exports and their scant diversification, and by the limitations, obstacles, and adverse conditions which continue to affect world trade. Although the problem may arise in part from the shortcomings of national export promotion policies, serious imbalances are expected to develop, judging from projections of the future value of exports on the basis of trends over the past fifteen years, compared with the potential demand for imports. In the circumstances, by 1975 the trade deficit may well range from $4,600 to $5,500 million at 1960 prices. This huge deficit will be further inflated by the sums required to finance outflows in the form of amortization, interest, and profits, with the result that it will become impossible to obtain new inflows of foreign capital.

EXTERNAL DEBT

The gross inflow of foreign capital has reached high levels and increased rapidly in the present decade, as shown by the fact that Latin America's aggregate external public debt rose from $6,100 million in 1960 to over $12,000 million in 1966.

This is not reflected in an equally large net contribution to Latin American development financing. On the contrary, net external financing—defined here as the balance on current account—has fallen off considerably as a result of debt commitments: from $1,100 million in 1961 it rose to its peak ($1,230 million) in 1962, declined steeply to $500 million in 1965 and recovered only partially in 1966 ($950 million). Variables which are strategic in the implementation of plans have not only shown a negative trend but have fluctuated very widely.

The critical situation in some countries has prompted governments to renegotiate the cumulative debt, consolidating and reconverting loans to mitigate the immediate effects on the balance of payments. However, considerable progress has been made in extending the scope of external financing to other fields of economic activity and in obtaining more favorable terms, although the interest rates on some foreign loans have increased in the last two years.

In addition, loans generally have very short maturation periods. A balance sheet of the position at December 31, 1964 shows that in accordance with the original repayment periods the debt was made up as follows: 18 per cent repayable in less than five years, 28 per cent in five to ten years, and 54 per cent over more than ten years. But the repayment periods applicable at that time reflected a critical position: 47 per cent of the total debt had to be paid off in the next five years,

24 per cent in five to ten years, and 29 per cent over more than ten years.

OTHER FACTORS

Other factors have further weakened the already tenuous effect of the growth of exports on real import capacity, one of them being the need to build up international reserves to a reasonable level in the last few years. Latin America's gross gold and foreign exchange holdings in 1960 amounted to $3,000 million but dropped sharply to $2,200 million in 1962; a subsequent recovery brought them up to $3,200 million in 1965. In other words, $1,000 million were used to build up reserves during these three years. Moreover, monetary liabilities, including balance-of-payments loans, were cut by $500 million over the same period. In short, this meant a total reduction of $1,500 million in the purchasing power of exports between 1962 and 1965.

The evolution of the terms of trade has had a similar effect. Although the trend has not been particularly unfavorable during the sixties, the losses due to the deterioration in the terms of trade since 1960 amount to roughly $1,000 million for the region as a whole. Some countries have suffered more than others. Venezuela's losses amounted to $1,800 million and Brazil's to $500 million during the same period.

IMPORT TRENDS

The factors that have been described above are responsible for the irregular trend of imports and in some cases have made it necessary to introduce a policy of import restrictions. This has weakened the possibility of increasing the supplies urgently needed for the implementation of development policy and plans.

The value of imports of goods and services in 1960 was practically the same as the value of exports: about $8,600 million. Not until 1964 did Latin America regain its 1957 level of imports (some $9,300 million). It is even more significant that in recent years imports have expanded more slowly than exports, the trade surplus being as high as $1,200 million in 1966. Exports amounted to about $12,000 million, compared with $10,760 million for imports of goods and services.

Conclusions

Planning, like every other process, must be developed and improved. Thus far Latin America has gone through the first stage; it has established planning agencies, prepared a variety of plans, worked out consistent development policies with some success, allocated public resources more systematically, trained a large group of professionals in new techniques locally, and accumulated a fund of valuable experience. At the same time, it has encountered limitations and obstacles including a general lack of political support for planning, inadequate over-all development strategies, no effective coordination between policy and operational machinery, and other more specific drawbacks.

Measures to overcome those limitations and obstacles would represent the second stage of planning in Latin America, in which development plans would be better formulated and above all more efficiently carried out. Some conclusions from the analysis made here might usefully be analyzed by national agencies and the competent organs of foreign financial and technical cooperation.

National Planning Machinery

(*a*) The planning systems that have been developed should be completed by renewed efforts in many areas and, in particular, by:

(i) Establishing a closer relationship between over-all guidelines and short-term operational machinery, preferably by drawing up annual plans of operation incorporating decisions to mobilize and allocate resources and implementing detailed economic policy;

(ii) Supplementing the process of formulating and implementing plans by the periodic evaluation of results, and establishing appropriate organs for the purpose.

(*b*) Planning systems should be brought more closely into line with long- and short-term development priorities:

(i) Through the coordination of national planning with the aims of regional economic integration;

(ii) Through measures to relate planning to such questions as the assimilation of new techniques, employment, and training, income distribution, and the improvement of levels of living;

(iii) Through action to relate planning to anti-inflationary measures.

(*c*) Stronger coordination should be established between planning agencies and the political authorities, the national administration, and the private sector by:

(i) Carefully reviewing the relations between planning offices and top-level national authorities;

(ii) Ensuring that administrative reform programs allow for proper coordination between planning bodies and the general, sectoral, or regional decision-making centers;

(iii) Establishing or improving existing channels of communication with the various representative bodies of the private sector (political parties, trade unions, entrepreneurs' associations, etc.).

(*d*) Further research should be carried out to discover the most effective technical means of implementing the various planning activities. The following questions should be urgently considered:

(i) Methods and techniques for preparing annual plans (including such instruments as the national economic budget);

(ii) Methods and techniques for evaluating and supervising the implementation of plans;

(iii) Methods and techniques for formulating development policy with due regard to maximum utilization of human resources, the economic integration of Latin America, the redistribution of income, and a reasonable allocation of resources between social and economic objectives.

(*e*) It is imperative to improve data-gathering and data-processing so that reliable statistics will be readily available for the preparation of plans and the supervision of their execution. To that end:

(i) The offices which collect, tabulate, and publish information should be given greater autonomy and provided with additional staff and technical resources;

(ii) Basic programs of urgently needed information should be prepared for priority action, to ensure a steady flow of up-to-date data;

(iii) Machinery should be devised and put into operation for providing information on progress achieved in implementing plans.

External Technical and Financial Cooperation[7]

(*a*) Technical cooperation from international and other external sources in national planning activities should be encouraged. The need for such cooperation is greater than ever at the present stage, especially in the following areas:

(i) The study and dissemination of the methods and techniques referred to above;

(ii) The training of technical personnel to perform their present functions, and of those in line for promotion in the near future (annual plans, evaluation, and supervision, etc.);

(iii) The exchange of experience between planning agencies in the various countries of the region.

(*b*) The provision of technical information and specific projections concerning the following should be systematically coordinated:

(i) The economic growth of the various Latin American countries;

(ii) World market prospects, by groups of products and by specific products;

(iii) Estimates of the developing countries' external financing, resources, and needs.

(*c*) External financing has exerted a profound influence on national planning activities. It is therefore essential to continue the progress already achieved in the following ways:

(i) By financing programs of concerted action in many different fields, and, in particular, by replacing the old system of project financing by a new system, which will ensure the over-all financing of development plans, and supplementary and compensatory financing needs, on suitable terms.

(ii) By extending amortization periods and lowering interest rates on foreign loans;

(iii) By allocating resources more flexibly, so that they are not

7 The following conclusions contain no reference to foreign trade despite its importance in the execution of Latin America's development plans, in order to avoid raising issues of world economic policy.

made contingent upon the import content of investments and can cover local costs;

(iv) By more flexible use of external financing with a view to eliminating the conditions attached;

(v) By financial support for national and international planning agencies.

CHAPTER IV

REMARKS ON FINANCING AND FOREIGN INVESTMENT[1]

Desirability of Establishing a Target for Foreign Investment

Limited Volume and Inappropriate Composition of Foreign Investment

It is a matter of concern that so little foreign capital is being invested in Latin America. The object of this chapter is, first, to examine the factors influencing this situation and, second, to consider the possibilities for a greater absorption of such capital.

The limited amount of international public loans raises problems of considerable importance. Owing to the nature of such loans, they are used principally for social capital investment in transport, power, and other services that account for a major proportion of public investment.

During the nineteenth century and from the beginning of the present century until the First World War, the financing of economic development was entirely dependent on private capital, and consequently the foreign contribution to Latin American public investment was very high in relation to the tiny percentage which it currently represents.

1 From *International Co-operation in a Latin American Development Policy* (United Nations publication, September 1954, Sales No.: 1954.II.G.2), pp. 13–41.

This is the principal explanation for the lack of social capital that at present characterizes most of the Latin American countries. It has not been possible, as in the past, to resort to the private bond market in order to finance these requirements, and, as will be explained below, direct private investment would have been too costly. Social capital investment is essential in creating a favorable environment for private investment, and its inadequacy constitutes one of the major obstacles hindering the economic development of Latin America.

Moreover, during the earlier period referred to, most of the resources used for social capital investment came from bond issues on the financial markets, principally in London. In fact, over two-thirds of aggregate investment in social capital and for other purposes was the product of bond issues. As is well known, the international bond market is no longer accessible to Latin American countries, and it has fallen to the international credit institutions to fill the gap by lending public funds.

The contrast between the relatively small share of public resources in foreign investment and the considerable proportion which was previously derived from bond issues is another point that needs to be stressed. The interest paid on bonds is far below the rate of return on direct investment of foreign private capital. Since direct investment constituted less than one-third of total investment prior to the First World War, the cost of capital formation at that time was lower for debtor countries than in recent years, when the proportion represented by direct investment of foreign private capital has been very high.

What is now required is to encourage foreign capital investment, in order to accelerate Latin America's economic development. It is clear that to maintain so high a proportion of private capital would involve a substantial increase in the incidence of financial services on the balance of payments. This does not mean that the absolute amount of private investment will have to be reduced. On the contrary, its expansion is desirable for Latin America. But an even more intensive increase must take place in loans of public resources at a relatively low rate of interest. This follows from the two requirements already mentioned: first, the need to reduce the cost of foreign investment for Latin America; and second, the need to increase the participation of international public resources in financing the social capital investment necessary to provide an ample opportunity for domestic and foreign private investment.

Increased loans of public funds also mean that the role of international credit institutions will have to be strongly emphasized, at least until the private bond market is reopened. Should this occur, the Latin American countries would be the first to welcome such a development. Not only would an additional source of credit be available that could in certain cases advantageously take the place of the credit institutions, but also private investors in the United States and other countries would feel renewed interest in participating in the economic development of the Latin American countries.

From another point of view, larger-scale international loans for social capital investment would have favorable internal consequences in the Latin American countries. It is a well-known fact that the need to finance such investment without adequate domestic savings has frequently caused governments to resort to the expansion of bank credit. On the other hand, in those cases where it has been possible to use the genuine savings of the population for basic investment, this has generally been done at the expense of private investment, which in turn has been forced to utilize bank credit as a substitute. A larger contribution of foreign resources, covering at least 20 to 25 per cent of this basic capital investment, could therefore prove very useful in the application of an anti-inflationary policy.

With regard to investment of private foreign capital, one further observation may be made. In the first place, the greater part of such investment does not constitute new-capital inflows but rather represents reinvestment of profits accruing from capital already invested. It is, of course, desirable for profits to be reinvested rather than remitted abroad. If this reinvestment is deducted, however, the annual average inflow of new capital in the shape of foreign private investment is appreciably reduced.

Another indication of the limited amount of foreign capital invested in Latin America in recent years is the relationship between the amount invested and the financial remittances required to service and amortize the stock of capital. It is obvious that, in developing countries, the capital inflow should exceed the outflow of remittances. Nevertheless, a time comes when this is no longer necessary. As income increases, a higher domestic savings coefficient enables a country to carry the burden of remittances even if its balance-of-payments assets do not include new investment sufficing at least to cover the amount such remittances represent. Although the Latin American countries in general are, of course, still far from reaching this stage, the figures for remittances nevertheless exceed those for investment.

In this context, it should be remembered that approximately 30 per cent of private capital investment has been earmarked for developing export activities, principally mining and petroleum production. As a result, a part of the remittances has been covered by increased exports. Even so, this very fact is a striking comment on the insufficiency of foreign investment.

It does not stand alone, however. Still more eloquent testimony is provided by the small share of foreign investment in the total capital investment effected by the Latin American countries.

The Foreign Investment Target

Until the research that has been initiated is intensified and extended, it would be rash to specify, for practical purposes, the totals which foreign investment should reach if a given rate of growth is to be attained. It seems advisable, however, to establish a target for investment policy. Once this policy was mapped out, the activities of international credit institutions would be judged not only by the care with which they examined projects submitted for approval—a factor of vital importance—but also by the volume of their operations. If, within a reasonable time, a minimum figure had not been attained, it would have to be concluded that investment policy was not being satisfactorily implemented, and the determining factors of the situation would have to be reconsidered.

Moreover, the establishment of an investment target might have very positive effects upon the Latin American countries themselves, creating an atmosphere favorable to economic development programming both in government circles and among the leaders of political and economic life, as well as in the entrepreneurial and labor sectors.

The doubts and uncertainties as to the possibility of obtaining an adequate and reasonable degree of foreign financial cooperation have not exactly played an encouraging role in the formulation of development programs. This task entails considerable effort and heavy expenditure, and it is understandable that governments should be reluctant to assume such commitments if they cannot rely on obtaining the foreign capital required to supplement domestic savings.

It would be oversimplifying to assert that this explains why several countries still show no interest in programming and why others have not yet put into the task either the energy or the sense of continuity it demands. Obviously, however, the existence of a policy aimed at raising investment can greatly reinforce the authority of those who are endeavoring to follow the path of development programming in the various countries. The process signifies not only the formulation of a program but also the adoption of a series of measures to attract investment and to ensure that it bears fruit. Care must be taken not to lose sight of the real facts of the case. The establishment of an investment target might have the twofold virtue of focusing the efforts of credit institutions on its attainment and also of influencing the Latin American governments themselves. Interest in development policy is as yet in its initial stages—in some cases very confused initial stages—and it may be indispensable to add this external stimulus to domestic incentives, if certain aspirations toward economic development are to crystallize in a definite policy.

The Necessity of Continuity in Credit Policy

In addition to establishing certain investment goals for Latin America, it is desirable to analyze the possibilities of introducing those specific procedures which experience recommends. Hitherto, the general practice has been to grant loans gradually, as the corresponding projects are approved. A country drawing up an investment program, partially based on foreign resources, does not know beforehand whether it will or will not be able to count on those resources during the years in which the program is being implemented. Furthermore, in countries subject to great economic instability of external origin, the volume of domestic savings envisaged in the program might perceptibly diminish, thus seriously affecting the program unless credit institutions were to assume responsibility for a reasonable share of the investment which it was planned to make with these savings. If development policy is controlled, as is to be hoped, by wise and responsible agencies, they may harbor some doubts as to the desirability of involving their country in an investment program which in actual fact cannot be implemented; and these doubts may induce them to restrict the scope of the program, or simply to eliminate it, and to follow the more prudent course of approving the projects one by one, as and when the required resources become available.

It is clear that international credit institutions could not unconditionally approve their own participation in an investment program. There is no question of such a thing; they could simply approve in principle the investment to be financed in each year of the program, making final approval conditional upon the submission of a satisfactory project and upon fulfillment of the requisites held to be indispensable for its efficacious execution. At the same time, they might undertake to finance additional investment in the event that the country concerned, for external reasons beyond its control, found itself unable to mobilize the amount of domestic resources envisaged in the program.

Toward an Inter-American Investment Program

The starting point and keynote of this discussion has been that Latin America requires a development policy with ample international cooperation. Some of the elements of this policy already exist, and if it can be duly concerted, it will constitute the first step in a new experiment on whose present and future importance no further stress need be laid. This new experiment demands a search for new methods and instruments of action, which may properly be discussed here. Just as a national development policy finds expression in a program, so a program will also be needed for an inter-American development policy, and in that program, investment will naturally have to play a dominant role, for a period of years long enough to allow the Latin American countries to increase their own savings capacity. This inter-American program, however, can only be based on national programs, at any rate for the larger countries, and in this sphere a considerable effort, which has only just begun, will have to be made. Meanwhile, the establishment of a provisional investment target might in itself be of great importance if the governments decided to adopt it as a first step toward an inter-American program.

The governments of the inter-American system could have at their disposal the results of ECLA's work on analyses and projections of economic development, together with any other background material they might require in order to consider—at such periodic meetings as they might deem expedient—the establishment of new targets and eventually the formulation of an inter-American investment program.

This would not be a Marshall Plan for Latin America. The Marshall Plan, conceived to meet a very serious situation, had necessarily to be based on subsidies. The economic development of the Latin American countries can proceed at a rapid rate without recourse to subsidies, except in the case of a few countries where per capita income is extremely low. Latin America's need is for productive loans with long amortization periods and at rates of interest as low as those prevailing on the money markets. In this connection an essential distinction must be drawn. The Marshall Plan has disseminated a concept of aid which usually embraces ordinary loans. But in fact two entirely different operations are involved. A loan presupposes regular amortization and interest payments, while aid implies an act of donation pure and simple.

It is desirable to forestall the psychological and political effects of this confusion, not only in the United States, but also in the Latin American countries, lest the idea spread that their economic development depends upon such donations and that the primary aim of inter-American conferences is to obtain resources on that basis. Despite the extremely high per capita income levels in the United States, there are community needs which have not yet been satisfactorily met; for example, low-cost housing facilities in the larger towns leave much to be desired. Furthermore, the heavy taxes are not only a burden upon those in the higher-income brackets—so much so that in some respects the standard of living of this sector of the population is lower than that of corresponding groups in Latin America—but they have a considerable incidence on the earnings of the middle- and lower-income groups.

It is therefore a moot question whether the prestige and continuity of an inter-American economic development policy would be best served by basing it upon resources obtained through taxation, drawing upon private finances, or by savings, in competition with domestic productive investment.

Collaboration of Independent Experts in a Development Policy

There is yet another aspect of the problem of public investment of international resources in Latin America which requires extremely careful handling. A program is the concrete expression of a development policy, which consists not only in investment but also in the adoption of a series of measures designed to raise the savings coefficient, to encourage domestic investment, and also to create conditions in which such investment can produce the desired results. The degree and form of external cooperation will depend upon the wisdom and common sense of the policy pursued, and it is readily understandable that credit institutions, while prepared to cooperate in certain aspects of that policy, may at the same time wish to link their loan commitments to the fulfillment of specific conditions. It is indeed inconceivable that one of the parties should guarantee to contribute resources over a certain period of years without the other party's likewise accepting an obligation to observe certain basic conditions, previously agreed upon by both parties. Without this measure of reciprocity, it would be impossible to put into practice an effective international cooperation policy.

All international negotiations of this kind involve very delicate questions, and the possibility of finding more satisfactory formulas should be explored. The formulation of a program—especially if important economic and financial measures are necessary for its implementation—usually calls for the advice of experts who can speak impartially and with authority by virtue of their detachment from the environment and from the interests at stake. It is questionable whether credit institutions, precisely because they have a direct interest in the solution of the problem, are always best qualified to give such advice, still less to campaign for or against the adoption of given measures. Their zeal might often be interpreted as an intention to intervene in a country's domestic problems, or even as a device of the creditor to impose his terms on the debtor.

Here, experience can provide a guide to future action. If both a government and the credit-institution authorities were jointly to express their confidence in certain independent experts and were to request their views and recommendations, it would be less difficult to negotiate the contribution of foreign resources to a national development program, and there would be less risk of irritating understandable national susceptibilities. What is more, the experts in question, because of their impartial and neutral position, could advantageously mediate in the negotiations, seeking formulas which are sometimes difficult to find when the two parties are dealing with each other directly.

Obstacles Hindering the Investment of International Public Resources

Attention has already been drawn to the desirability of establishing a minimum foreign-investment target to be attained over a transition period. During this interim, it will have been possible to adopt a number of measures to mitigate—or eliminate, as the case may be—the principal hindrances to the Latin American operations of the two leading international credit institutions.[2]

The existing obstacles are varied in nature and have been divided here into two large groups: those pertaining to the Latin American countries themselves and those deriving from the policies of the abovementioned institutions.

Obstacles Pertaining to the Latin American Countries

LACK OF INVESTMENT PROGRAMS AND PROPERLY PRESENTED PROJECTS

The International Bank for Reconstruction and Development has emphasized the desirability of drawing up development programs that

[2] At that time, the International Bank for Reconstruction and Development (IBRD) and the Export-Import Bank (EXIMBANK).

encompass all public-sector projects and estimate the investment requirements of private economic activities. The task of programming was begun some time ago in several countries and is now being undertaken in some others. Unquestionably the presentation of well-prepared over-all programs will have very favorable effects on the policy of credit institutions. Nevertheless, as previously remarked, the preparation of such programs is a difficult and costly process; consequently, willingness on the part of these institutions to agree in principle to finance a program for its entire duration would constitute a powerful incentive to programming.

The preparation of specific investment projects also requires considerable technical and financial resources which governments are not always willing or able to stake, quite apart from the time it takes to formulate such projects. The risk that a project may fail in the end to obtain approval, after these resources have been used, sometimes acts as a deterrent. Nevertheless, experience has been gradually indicating satisfactory procedures. In several cases, IBRD has sanctioned certain undertakings in principle and has encouraged the submission of projects which were afterward approved. Furthermore, on occasion, it has even suggested the expansion of such projects with a view to increasing their economic efficiency. In this respect, larger-scale technical cooperation with governments on the part of the United Nations and its specialized agencies could help to remove the obstacles. Such cooperation in the preparation of projects has been given in specific cases, but there is also a need to train technical personnel in the various countries who would be capable of formulating projects or of evaluating those drawn up by other technical experts.

DEFECTIVE MANAGEMENT OF ENTERPRISES

There are certain badly managed public utilities which the credit institutions have suggested should be reorganized before loans are granted. It has happened that loans have been made for the purpose of importing equipment which rapidly deteriorated because it was not properly used. The elimination of such difficulties of course depends upon the governments themselves, although a commitment to grant the loan on condition that given requisites are fulfilled might facilitate the adoption of corrective measures.

OBSTACLES CREATED BY INFLATION

The inflation prevailing in several Latin American countries is a considerable obstacle to the investment of international resources, although in some cases sizable loans have been granted. Nevertheless, such resources can hardly be obtained for the purposes of a far-reaching investment program unless measures are taken to control inflation, at least in part. Conversely, it cannot be ignored that the success of an anti-inflationary program generally depends upon the availability of such resources on carefully concerted terms.

There are many recent examples which afford very useful lessons. If inflation is caused by the use of bank credit to finance private investment, the immediate consequence of suspending such investment in order to curb credit expansion is unemployment, first in the industries directly affected, and second in those which supplied consumer goods to persons employed in the first group, with all the attendant repercussions. A contraction of the economy ensues, with results that generally lead to a renewed inflationary expansion of credit. The only way to prevent this is to cover the inflationary excess of investment with foreign capital—whether the same investment as before is involved, or other new investment—and to continue in this manner until such time as it can be covered entirely from a higher domestic savings coefficient.

In such cases, an inflow of foreign capital makes it possible to obviate the distortions that accompany straightforward deflation. Although such an inflow alone cannot correct the disequilibrium underlying the inflationary process, it is equally true that stabilization becomes an easier task if the real supply of goods increases, or can be expanded by means of additional imports financed with foreign resources.

Hence it appears that the best way of combating this type of inflation is to adopt an investment program while simultaneously applying energetic anti-inflationary measures.

If inflation is due to public-sector investment, higher taxation is generally the most convenient formula, insofar as the reduction of such investment is inadvisable. But this increase in taxation takes time and very often it is necessary to find solutions for technical, administrative, and political problems. Foreign capital can facilitate the transitional process, enabling it to be carried out in a shorter time or reducing its negative effects on the level of income. Thus a temporary contribution of international resources becomes essential, just as when the aim is to obviate the effects of a contraction in investment expenditure.

The problem becomes much more difficult in the case of wage or cost inflation. Here, too, a substantial investment program is imperative. The program, together with other measures, will enable productivity and income to increase rapidly, without which inflationary pressure cannot be withstood.

It is no exaggeration to say that inflation, owing to its economic, social, moral, and political effects, is the most acute problem facing Latin America. It must, of course, be combated by domestic measures, applied with firmness and conviction. Nevertheless, if such action is to be taken, the contribution of international resources is indispensable. Otherwise, anti-inflationary measures would be incompatible not only with development but even with the stability of the domestic economy at the level of employment reached in inflationary conditions. Once such a pooling of effort is achieved, the capacity for absorption of international resources would substantially increase.

OBSTACLES CREATED BY THE DIFFICULTY OF MEETING EXTERNAL PAYMENTS

Apart from inflation, the difficulty which a country may experience in the financial servicing of foreign loans is among the factors that have most seriously limited the capacity for absorption of foreign capital. As a general rule, the Latin American countries have to face periodic foreign exchange difficulties which could be appreciably reduced—and perhaps obviated altogether—if farsighted measures were adopted to encourage exports and to promote import substitution, thus altering the composition of imports. It has already been stated that one of the most significant aspects of a development program consists precisely in effecting the investment required to introduce such structural changes in the economy. Consequently, a country's capacity to pay for financial services—and therefore the ceiling for the foreign loans which could be raised—should not be judged in the light of such foreign exchange crises, but should be assessed with due regard to the possibilities of structural readjustment. Thus it might often happen that foreign exchange difficulties, instead of discouraging the investment of international resources, could become an incentive thereto, helping to expand the capacity for capital absorption.

Obstacles Deriving from the Policy of Credit Institutions

LIMITING INVESTMENT TO IMPORTS OF FOREIGN EQUIPMENT

The international credit institutions' practice of limiting the financing they grant to the amount needed to pay for imports of capital goods has a reasonable basis, if each loan is considered separately on its own merits. It appears logical that the recipient of a loan should draw upon domestic savings to cover the proportion of his investment represented by local expenditure. A reservation should be made, however. There are cases where a rise in production also entails an increase in the working capital represented by semifinished goods imported from abroad. There would be no valid grounds for restricting investment to goods constituting fixed capital alone.

If the economic process is considered as a whole, however, some doubts arise which call for comment. The following example may be taken. Supposing that at a given moment a country has net savings, equivalent to 10 per cent of its national income, which are entirely used for investment, and that additional investment is planned which would raise the total investment coefficient to 12 per cent of income. Half of this additional investment corresponds to capital goods which will have to be imported and for which appropriate international resources will be available, in accordance with the current practice under discussion. The other half, however, equivalent to 1 per cent of income, will represent domestic expenditure. If spontaneous savings stand at only 10 per cent, there will be no means of covering this additional sum, unless the State—if it is involved—resorts to higher taxes for this purpose, which might be a reasonable solution in favorable circumstances. In contrast, the only expedient open to the private entrepreneur is recourse to the banking system, with ensuing inflationary effects both in the internal economy and on the balance of payments.

A closer analysis of this example is warranted by the lessons it offers. The persons for whom employment is provided by that half of the additional investment which must be covered locally will mainly come from the increase in the active population plus the population displaced from primary production and from low-productivity activities. Of the net income earned by these new employees out of funds supplied by the banking system, part will be spent locally and part on imports. Consequently, if a balance-of-payments deficit is to be avoided, it will be necessary to cover at least the latter part with resources from abroad. As regards the share of domestic demand, an inflationary pressure on supply will occur, as at best supply will take some time to increase, whereas the income increment is usually quickly spent. Hence, from this direction also imports will receive a stimulus, owing to the additional pressure generated by the inflationary expansion of trade.

If it is not additional employment that is involved, but simply the transfer of persons already employed in production of consumer goods to production of capital goods, the inflationary impact will be greater, since the volume of income will remain the same, while production for consumption will diminish.

In the example under consideration, the only way in which the share of local expenditure in the increase in investment could be covered—without inflationary consequences—would be to leave unused an equivalent proportion of the savings representing 10 per cent of income.

Obviously, therefore, if the economic process is viewed as a whole, the practice followed in this respect limits the possibilities of productive absorption of international resources, or leads to inflationary consequences. The problem lies, however, not only in the lack of savings but also in the difficulties of transferring them abroad in order to purchase capital goods. It may happen that all the savings required are available and yet their transfer abroad may cause a balance-of-payments disequilibrium. Such a situation is of course inconceivable in countries which manufacture their own capital goods and have no need to import them.

In this as in other aspects of international investment, the practices followed by the London financial market before the First World War displayed very interesting features in the matter of adaptability to real requirements. The bonds that were floated when a British railway was being built abroad covered not only the materials and equipment that had to be exported but also the amount of sterling required for transfer to the country receiving the investment, to cover wages and other local expenses. It would be inadvisable to adopt the same procedure today, but its lesson can be profitably applied in searching for a more satisfactory solution to this aspect of the problem.

It must be acknowledged that such a solution would be difficult to find for an individual project. Under a development program, on the other hand, if it is calculated that a country's spontaneous domestic saving cannot exceed a given proportion of its income, and if an investment plan involving a larger amount is drawn up, the excess must be covered with international resources, whatever the projects for which it is to be used. In this connection it is interesting to note that for the economic development program for southern Italy, IBRD loaned funds to cover the additional imports brought about by the increase in income.

PRIORITY FOR PRIVATE INVESTMENT

As previously noted, current opinion in the Latin American countries is in favor of encouraging private enterprise and there could therefore be no fundamental objection to the principle of giving priority to private investment. Accordingly, the investment of public international resources is generally regarded as justifiable only if no private foreign capital is available for the purpose. But there are two points which must be considered in working toward a satisfactory and practical application of such a policy. The Latin American countries are traditionally in favor of the State's assuming responsibility for certain types of public investment which in some other countries have been undertaken by private enterprise. The fact that this has been compatible with substantial private investment in other public services shows that such an attitude was not dictated by ideological considerations but simply grew up because in this way economic development was more satisfactorily served.

Nevertheless, it is evident that there is now a tendency to place some undertakings formerly left to private enterprise in the hands of the state. This again must not be ascribed to the influence of ideological considerations. One significant example is sufficient to make the position clear. For the state to exercise control over public utility tariffs is an established practice. In the United States, rates which provide a yield of 6 per cent of the capital invested are considered reasonable. Although a somewhat higher ceiling may be justifiable in the Latin American countries, private capital could hardly be attracted into new public utility enterprises with yields at that level. To achieve this goal, it would be necessary to raise the rate of return substantially, and that would not in fact be warranted, in view of the nature of such enterprises. It is no longer, as in the past, a matter of introducing new techniques, but of utilizing those already familiar. Consequently, there is no reason whatever to pay foreign investors a considerable premium for technical know-how which has now become common property.

It is therefore understandable that in these circumstances governments should prefer to effect such basic investment on their own, and that they should have to resort to public international loans at a relatively low rate of interest until the private bond market has been re-established in the large financial centers. Again because of the low rate of return, the alternative of interesting Latin American private investors in such undertakings is rarely feasible.

Existing public utilities in the hands of foreign private investors are not in the same position. Any additional capital required can be obtained at suitable rates of interest, either in the financial market or from EXIMBANK and IBRD. The usual problem in this case is of a different nature. Tariffs have frequently not been adjusted to the rise in operational costs caused by inflation, and in some cases enterprises have reached the point where they can no longer make reasonable profits, or indeed where capital is actually being lost.

This is also a frequent occurrence in the case of State-owned public utilities, where the situation derives more from the damaging results of inflation than from a specific policy of opposition to foreign investment. When, as often happens, there is a time lag in the adjustment of wages and salaries to the rise in prices, the profits of entrepreneurs generally increase, while in order to prevent a further upswing in the cost of living, public utility rates are not raised. There is thus a transfer of real income to the entrepreneurial sector, not only from the broad masses of the population, but also from public utility enterprises, whether they are private or State-owned. On the other hand, if it is difficult to increase tariffs when public utilities are State property, it is much more so when they belong to private interests, and particularly when, in addition, they are foreign-owned.

In other cases, there has been reluctance to accept foreign capital when, for one reason or another, it is to be used to establish a monopoly or with the open intention of limiting competition. This fact need only be touched upon here, as it will be discussed at a later stage. Lastly, the actual size of a foreign enterprise, and the disproportionate weight it may come to carry in a country's internal economic life, has at times given rise to feelings of mistrust. This situation, although hampering the access of private capital to ownership of enterprises, leaves open other opportunities for cooperation both on the part of private investors and of the international credit institutions, as will also be shown in due course.

In cases where well-founded misgivings exist, it would be desirable for the government to demarcate and define the field of action which it has reserved for itself and to give adequate guarantees to private entrepreneurs in all other activities not affected by the policy in question, in order to prevent any withdrawal on the part of private enterprise. The viability of such a policy has been demonstrated in recent years in Mexico, where agrarian reform and the expropriation of petroleum and the railways have not prevented private entrepreneurs, both national and foreign, from investing in manufacturing industry and other activities.

From another point of view, in cases where it is justifiable to give priority to private capital rather than to facilitate public investment, it is essential that the Latin American entrepreneur should be afforded ready access to international sources of capital and technical know-how in order that he may compete with foreign entrepreneurs on a reasonably equal footing. Herein lies one of the weakest points in the international loan systems, and this important aspect of the problem will be discussed later.

DIFFERENCES OF OPINION AS TO THE EXPEDIENCY OF A PROJECT

It sometimes happens that although there are no technical objections to a project, doubts may arise as to whether it is in the best interest of a country's economic development. It would not be difficult to settle the question if the two parties concerned had the same criteria for judging a project from this point of view. A case in point is the report of the Currie Mission on the economic development of Colombia. Although this mission was sent by the International Bank for Reconstruction and Development, the report expresses opinions for which its authors alone are responsible. They were not in favor of the establishment of steelworks at Paz del Rio, because, *inter alia*, domestic production costs were higher than the prices of imported iron and steel. It must be reiterated that if this criterion had carried the day throughout Latin America, industrial development would never have gained momentum. Even if costs are higher than foreign prices, an industry can be a sound economic proposition if the net increase in the product derived from the factors employed therein is greater than that obtainable in other activities, as was explained in the context of foreign trade problems. No judgment could therefore be passed on this specific point without reviewing the other investment alternatives and discussing the possibilities for import-substitution activities that a country will have to undertake by virtue of its own growth. It is in such instances that the need for a development program becomes most apparent.

RELUCTANCE TO INVEST IN CERTAIN TYPES OF PUBLIC SERVICES

Up to the time of the World Depression of the nineteen-thirties the Latin American governments had obtained loans in London and other European cities, and later in New York, for public-sector activities such as the provision of health services, schools, and public buildings. Their own productivity is not always high, but they do make a notable contribution to the over-all increase in productivity. As a rule these were long-term loans which were serviced out of general public funds and in some cases by means of special levies. The private capital market abroad continues to be practically inaccessible to Latin American countries and no other way of satisfying this need has yet appeared. There can be no doubt that a decision to grant loans for this purpose out of international public resources would considerably stimulate the absorption of such resources in Latin America.

NEED FOR A GOVERNMENT GUARANTEE FOR LOANS

This prerequisite also tends to impose serious limitations on the capacity for absorption of international resources in the field of private enterprise. On the one hand, there are governments which prefer, as is only natural, to satisfy their own needs before those of private entrepreneurs. On the other hand, private entrepreneurs are often deterred by the possibility that a State guarantee of a loan for which they are applying may entail direct intervention in their enterprise, although there might be no other reason for this. All this explains why international public resources have only rarely subsidized private undertakings, and these have generally been on a very large scale. Credit has been inaccessible to the small and medium-sized enterprises which carry so much weight in industrial development.

Access to International Public Resources for Latin American Entrepreneurs

The chief obstacles to the investment of international public resources having been set forth in the foregoing pages, and the possibilities of removing them having been reviewed in general terms, the time has now come to enlarge upon one such possibility in particular, whose vital importance must not be overlooked: that of using such resources to encourage enterprise and private investment on the part of entrepreneurs established in Latin America.

Economically and technically, the situation of these entrepreneurs is unquestionably inferior to that of their foreign counterparts, and any effort to bridge the gap will have marked effects on economic development and on the operation of the free-enterprise system.

It is a well-known fact that in Latin America the need for medium- and long-term credits for industry can be adequately satisfied only in very few cases, which is one of the factors which retards development. The banking system is well prepared to provide the usual short-term loans to supplement a lack of working capital, and such loans are often made with inflationary consequences. The basic organization for loans to industry is therefore available, but not the necessary resources for loans on sufficiently long terms. Banking legislation itself often prohibits the freezing of an unduly large proportion of current deposits in operations of this kind.

In some countries, besides commercial banks, there are special institutions for furthering industrial development, but they are almost always hampered by a shortage of resources. The solution therefore consists in using the best establishments existing in each country—without prejudice to the creation of others if it should seem advisable—so that through them international credit may reach entrepreneurs in Latin America.

Possible Solutions of the Problem

An examination of the difficulties leading to the failure of certain operations reveals no intrinsic obstacles to their elimination. If the most reliable and respected banks or other institutions were chosen in each country, there would be no reason not to provide them with aggregate sums, proportionate to their capital and reserves, to be earmarked for direct loans to industry on certain prearranged terms. The "prior approval" requirement could be waived, except when the sums involved exceeded a certain limit, which would not be difficult to establish.

Consideration may now be given to the concrete possibilities for carrying out such operations on the broad scale which they could attain in all Latin America under an adequately organized system. There are three such possibilities: to organize an industrial credit system under the direction of the International Bank for Reconstruction and Development; to do so within the framework of the Export-Import Bank; and to establish a special fund.

Let us glance at the first two solutions and then give separate consideration to the special fund question. As regards IBRD, it would be desirable, for reasons already given, that these operations should not require a government guarantee, although the central bank in each country would have to approve the aggregate sums to be lent in order to cover the exchange risk. While it is true that the statutes of IBRD demand such a guarantee, these operations could be conducted by means of an affiliated organization, such as the International Finance Corporation, for which the Bank itself drew up a project in 1951 at the request of the United Nations Economic and Social Council. This Corporation is authorized to carry out operations of the type advocated here, although the end pursued is different. The aim of the Corporation is primarily to attract foreign private investment to the less-developed countries, and also to promote domestic investment, either through loan operations or by underwriting shares which it later sells on the domestic or foreign market. The Corporation's fundamental objectives and the idea of industrial loans are not incompatible. In fact, they are complementary.

The fact that the Export-Import Bank has begun successfully to carry out industrial credit transactions of this type indicates that it is fully qualified to do so. Moreover, its available resources are much bigger than the Corporation's. Since it is not obliged to obtain funds by issuing bonds on financial markets, it can act with a freedom that it perhaps might not enjoy if it were compelled to take account of certain doubts or reservations with which operations unfamiliar to foreign financial centers might be received.

Establishment of a Special Fund within the Inter-American System

An objection to this idea might be raised at the outset: namely, that a new body is being planned when two institutions already exist that could fill the same role. Recommendations as to the most appropriate solution are beyond the scope of the present analysis. It should be pointed out, however, that if such an industrial credit system is to be broad enough, a special instrument will need to be established, either in combination with the agency projected by IBRD or as a new department of EXIMBANK. The operations involved are of a different type from those normally carried out by these two banks, and they necessitate appropriate experience. In this connection, it would perhaps be necessary to establish agencies or branches in the principal countries in order to maintain closer contact with the banking system and gain direct knowledge of industrial needs. It is obvious that such an objective would entail the training of specialized personnel, most of whom might be drawn from the Latin American banks themselves, if due importance is to be attached to firsthand knowledge of the operational environment.

On all these grounds, a third possibility is presented here, the choice of which might be influenced by other considerations also.

If the proposal should materialize, all the countries would have to contribute capital; but of course only a comparatively small proportion of the credit resources could come from Latin America, since the whole point of the idea is to attract international resources to the region. It would therefore be essential to endow this institution with an adequate amount of special resources, while the capital, although it could be used for credit operations, would be mainly earmarked for underwriting possible losses in the application of the resources in question.

In the present circumstances, it would be very difficult to find any solution other than the endowment by the United States of a special fund for credit operations. Given this source, the form taken by the contribution does not seem to matter. However, there is one source of financing that, on account of its special character, might be considered the most suitable. It is calculated that the United States Government receives about $100 million annually from the tax imposed on the yield of capital invested in Latin America by United States companies. This revenue thus accrues from Latin American sources, and—although discussion of the legal aspects of the question would be out of place here—there is an argument for its remaining in Latin America and contributing to the acceleration of the region's rate of growth. Indeed, the United States Treasury itself has demonstrated its willingness to consider a reduction in the receipts from this tax, as a means of encouraging the investment of private United States capital in the Latin American countries. The possibility of abolishing the tax altogether has frequently been discussed, but objections to this idea have been raised, not so much on account of the reduction in public revenue (which would be negligible), as because of the discriminatory treatment which would thereby be introduced into the United States tax system. This stumbling block prevents United States investment in Latin America from receiving maximum tax incentives, but, on the other hand, the possibilities of using these funds to encourage private enterprise in the Latin American countries themselves might well be examined.

Unfortunately, in present circumstances the Latin American countries could not utilize the United States money market to obtain resources for a development fund of this nature; but if the United States could undertake to endow the fund with the revenue accruing from the above-mentioned tax for an appropriate number of years, these resources could serve as the basis for the issue of a loan on the United States money market, on terms similar to those usual in Treasury operations. This would be a means of providing the fund, as its operations gradually expanded, with much more substantial resources than could be obtained through the direct contribution of tax proceeds. Such a formula would offer the advantage of helping to renew the interest of private investors in Latin American development, while a financial market which has remained practically closed to Latin America since the World Depression would be reopened, even if only in this special form.

The exact amount of resources which Latin America could absorb each year in these industrial-credit operations cannot be estimated. It would mainly depend on the skill with which the system is organized and managed. But, given the considerable potential needs of the Latin American countries, it may safely be assumed that from $50 to $100 million at least could be absorbed annually once the system had been organized.

Investment of Foreign Private Capital

Brief Review of the Present Situation

Investment in Latin America of private capital both from the United States and from other sources has been primarily channeled into export activities. This traditional characteristic continues to prevail. Except in special cases, investment in internal activities has not aroused the same degree of interest. It is determined by other criteria, requires knowledge of a local market which is usually limited in size, and is subject to transfer difficulties in service payments which do not usually affect investment aimed at promoting exports. It is customary to cite as an instructive example the great attraction of Canada's domestic development for the entrepreneur in the United States. But Canada constitutes a special case on which generalizations cannot legitimately be based.

Apart from this, the returns on capital in the United States have been high; and it is only natural that the foreign private investor should try to obtain a yield at least equal to what he would receive at home. There are, of course, types of investment in Latin America on which the yield is much larger. But if, in such circumstances, investment of this kind were to spread and expand substantially, the burden of financial services might become a very serious factor in the balance-of-payments positions of the Latin American countries.

All this leads to the conclusion that even under highly favorable conditions such investment in Latin America cannot reasonably be expected to increase enough to make a substantial contribution to the acceleration of the region's rate of development. And even if that should at any time occur, the burden of service payments would restrict the capacity for capital absorption. Suffice it to bear in mind that even if the rate of return on private capital were only 10 per cent, two and a half times more capital in the shape of international public resources could be absorbed with the same service payments, given the relation between interest rates.

Obstacles, and the Possibilities of Removing Them

This is far from implying that the present state of affairs may be considered satisfactory. There is a general desire to receive more foreign private capital, particularly in those frequent cases in which it is accompanied by new production, organization, and market development techniques. But it cannot be denied that there are real difficulties which sometimes hamper the inflow of this capital to several Latin American countries. The chief problems are reviewed below.

TRANSFER DIFFICULTIES

Emphasis has been laid elsewhere upon the need for a farsighted policy of encouraging exports and promoting import substitution in order to reduce or eliminate the foreign exchange crises which recur at such frequent intervals in Latin America. A policy of this kind would, of course, alleviate the transfer difficulties in many countries.

Inflation is also one of the major causes of these difficulties. Unless it is merely a cost inflation that is involved, the profits and interest to be transferred abroad increase, and if the currency has not depreciated externally to the same degree as internally, the pressure of such transfers on the balance of payments may give rise to serious distortions. This is what happened in those unquestionably significant cases in which dollar quotations long remained steady while domestic prices were rising sharply.

Such effects are often aggravated by a practice current among foreign firms which operate in Latin America with comparatively liberal credit granted by the banking system of the country concerned. They are in the habit of taking account of their responsibilities abroad rather than of the real capital allocated to their local operations. Thus the foreign concern is working on the basis of a substantial amount of domestic capital, yet transfers its profits abroad as if they were the proceeds of the foreign capital invested.

Provisions which ensure the remittance of service payments on the capital invested, up to a specified maximum, and of a given proportion of amortization payments are an improvement upon previous conditions, in which remittances of service payments were subject to severe restrictions. Only a free-exchange market, however, allows absolutely unlimited transfers, although the relief this implies is often partly offset by the instability that is generally produced in such cases, or by the fact that the devaluation of the currency is greater in the market in question than in the internal economy. Be this as it may, herein lies one of the characteristic evils of inflation. On the one hand it causes an excessive increase in company profits, and on the other it leads to restrictive measures or to unfavorable situations which, although they may be justified by circumstances, are considered to militate against the interests of private capital. In fact, satisfactory solutions are quite impossible to find when an inflationary movement of this type is under way; and this provides still further evidence of the adverse effects on economic development which, sooner or later, inflation is bound to produce.

RESTRICTIONS ON CERTAIN TYPES OF INVESTMENT

Sometimes a selective criterion is established for the types of investment which a country wishes to admit or to which it is prepared to grant special exchange treatment on the lines referred to. Such a policy represents favoring investments of a particular type and discouraging other undertakings for which, in the opinion of the authorities, domestic firms could be responsible. The latter include all those activities whose techniques are easily accessible and in which the investment of foreign capital and the consequent remittance of profits abroad would be unjustifiable, so long as such funds could be used elsewhere to the positive advantage of the country concerned.

The motives underlying this attitude are understandable, and so are the misgivings it arouses in capital-exporting countries. The idea of discrimination always gives rise to uneasiness, and it may well be asked whether the adverse effects on foreign investment caused by this form of discouragement are or are not, in practice, offset by tangible benefits.

The organization of a system of international credit for the Latin American entrepreneur might modify the atmosphere that has bred restrictions of this kind, since he would no longer feel at a disadvantage vis-à-vis his foreign counterpart on account of capital shortages. If, in addition, he were to be given easier access to up-to-date techniques as a means of increasing productivity, most of the economic arguments in favor of a system of selective approval of foreign private investment would be invalidated.

OPPOSITION TO CERTAIN TYPES OF INVESTMENT

There is one controversial and therefore delicate question which cannot be bypassed if the aim of making an objective survey of the obstacles to foreign private investment is to be fulfilled. Even in those cases where there has been a tendency toward selective control of investment, Latin America has not really afforded any striking instances of animosity toward foreign capital invested in freely competitive conditions. When a hostile feeling toward foreign capital has arisen, it has generally been because the very nature of the concession—as in the case of public utilities—or the organization or size of the company itself has in practice led to the establishment of a monopoly or to open restriction of competition. In contrast to such cases, which have been much in the public eye, countless others could be cited of foreign commercial and industrial enterprises which, besides having earned general recognition of their technical and economic efficiency, have never been the object of demonstrations of hostility of any kind, although in the course of their operations they may have encountered transfer problems or administrative difficulties with the authorities.

There is no reason to suppose that the attitude of the Latin American public in this respect is any different from that of the public in the United States. The fact that a company is an example of free enterprise is not enough to incline the general public in its favor. Free enterprise must go hand-in-hand with free and fair competition, and on this point public opinion holds a theoretical position which is unassailable. In the United States the pressure of public opinion has won two fundamental victories. The first is reflected in legislation protecting the general interests of the community, coupled with machinery for applying the law and supervising its implementation; and the second is represented by the development of a sense of collective responsibility, together with the practice of giving publicity to their operations, adopted by those large corporations which, on account of their size or the nature of the market, are faced only with limited competition.

An assurance that United States companies operating in Latin America are not in general exempt from the same legislation protecting the community in which they operate might help to clear the air in this connection. Such an interpretation may be placed upon the decision of the United States Department of Justice to inquire into the working methods of a large United States corporation operating in Central America.

In some cases, the application of antimonopolistic measures might break up an operational complex to the detriment of the efficiency of an organization. This does not imply that the problem cannot be satisfactorily solved. There are effective possibilities for international cooperation in this respect. Intergovernmental agreements could be envisaged, aimed at ensuring that the business methods of enterprises should be subject to appropriate regulations which, without affecting the companies' freedom of action in their own field, would safeguard the interests of the community and would also enable Latin American countries to ascertain the real amount of profits earned in their own territory and to apply reasonable taxes.

The complexity of economic life makes it impossible to establish a single formula to solve the serious and varied problems which this type of enterprise brings in its train. But once a policy of cooperation with common aims has been established, it will first permit the gradual elimination of disruptive factors, and later progressively facilitate the creation of favorable conditions for effective investment in Latin America's economic development.

It is understandable that in cases such as those just mentioned, the State may consider the alternative of making the investment itself, in order to obviate the complications which a limited degree or total lack of competition involves. It could not be said that by acting thus a Latin American country would be tampering with the principle of free enterprise. This principle has already been violated, once free competition ceases to exist or is severely restricted. From this point of view, there can be no reason why a government should not resort to public international loans.

Even if this obstacle to a government's access to international loans were to be overcome, however, others might arise in connection with the loan operation itself. Credit institutions are naturally obliged to see that their resources are advantageously applied in projects with sound economic bases; and they must also make sure that the management of the companies concerned is reasonably efficient. No question of principle is involved, but one of practical judgment.

In this connection, possibilities are opened up which perhaps have not yet been fully exploited. There are cases where, even though private enterprise cannot operate satisfactorily for the above-mentioned reasons, it can do so very effectively in the realm of management or service contracts, whichever term is preferred. For example, the State may sign an agreement with a private firm for the building of a given plant and entrust the management of the concern to the same firm or to another long enough to amortize the whole or a considerable part of the loan. Such firms may also wish to contribute a share of the capital, on either a temporary or a permanent basis. There are various possibilities, both in these respects and in cases where special elements of risk exist. At all events, a general characteristic of such contracts might be a commitment on the part of the foreign private firm to train local technical and administrative personnel so that in the course of time they could assume responsibility for the entire operation of the enterprise.

Final Considerations

Nothing has hitherto been said about the nationalization of foreign enterprises. In capital-exporting countries, however, this possibility is usually mentioned as one of the deterrents to the foreign investor. Although there have been very few instances of nationalization in Latin America, and those with a backwash of troublesome indemnization problems have been even rarer, it is undeniable that their psychological repercussions have often been far-reaching. While a discussion of this problem and of the merits of any legal formulas are outside the scope of the present volume, there can be no doubt that in this and other aspects of the foreign investment problem a satisfactory and lasting solution can be reached only on the basis of a policy of international cooperation in the economic development of Latin America. A well-planned policy, which is complemented by essential internal measures, and which, besides speeding up the rate of economic growth, may help to remedy certain ills such as those indicated above, will give a better understanding of the objectives pursued through investment of foreign capital; and that will be the surest guarantee that such capital will receive favorable treatment.

Latin America's political instability is also frequently mentioned as a source of discouragement to investment of foreign private capital. Undoubtedly, certain political changes which have taken place through irregular channels may also have significant psychological repercussions abroad. But such events must be viewed in their proper perspective. Latin America is subject not only to the vicissitudes of its internal politics but also to the impact of political and economic changes which occur within the large industrial centers and which in one way or another are usually far-reaching in their effects. All this affects Latin America's balance of payments, its development potential, its capacity to import and its ability to service foreign capital. On the other hand, it cannot be said that the governments which have come to power in Latin America as a result of irregular political changes have, as a general rule, been any less well disposed toward foreign capital than those that have assumed office through the regular constitutional processes. In any case, the favorable attitude of the type of government will not depend upon the merits of any given formula, but upon the creation of the propitious climate to which reference has been made, through an appropriate combination of national and international measures.

CHAPTER V

ECONOMIC INTEGRATION IN RELATION TO THE DEVELOPMENT OF LATIN AMERICA[1]

The Tardiness of Latin America's Development

In the twenty years or so that have elapsed since the end of the Second World War, Latin America's rate of development has been slow and fluctuating, and in vast areas of the region has so greatly slackened that average per capita income has increased only by 50 per cent, rising from a minimal figure of $280 to its present modest level of $430. Unless the trends that have thus evolved in the first half of the sixties are modified, the average per capita income of the 600 million inhabitants that Latin America will have at the end of the present century will be only about $650, and even if the growth rate registered in the last fifteen years is outstripped in the future, would not exceed $850.[2]

This slow rate of development, which entails such unsatisfactory

[1] "A Contribution to Economic Integration Policy in Latin America" (E/CN.-12/728, April 20, 1967), pp. 3–31.

[2] Data expressed in terms of 1960 prices. During the first four years of the present decade, average per capita income in the region as a whole increased at a cumulative annual rate of 1 per cent. In the interval between 1950 and 1964 the corresponding growth rate was 1.5 per cent.

material and cultural living conditions for the broad masses of the Latin American population, is thrown into sharp relief when it is borne in mind that such an average income—which, in default of radical reforms, could be expected to materialize only by the end of the century—represents no more than one-fifth of that currently enjoyed in the United States and little more than half the corresponding levels in Western Europe and in the USSR, while it is also lower than the figure registered in many other private-enterprise countries and centrally planned economies. These gaps are bound to widen considerably, for while the Latin American countries in the aggregate have attained an annual growth rate of barely 1 per cent, the other regions mentioned are developing two or three times as dynamically, quite apart from such examples of exceptionally rapid expansion as afforded by Japan and some of the centrally planned economies. Thus, while Latin America took twenty years to raise its average per capita income by 50 per cent, the members of the European Economic Community achieved the same relative increase in under ten years, while the other areas referred to did so in even less time, after having already completed an arduous phase of post-war reconstruction.

Moreover, in its cultural and material living conditions Latin America will continue to lag still farther behind on account of the wide disparities currently existing between its income levels and those of other areas. A 4 per cent increase in income in the United States enables its 192 million inhabitants to expand their consumption, on an average, by $55 per capita; in Latin America, when incomes rises by 5 per cent, the per capita increment in the consumption of the region's 230 million inhabitants averages only $5.

These various data testify to the slowness and inadequacy of Latin America's development, and to the region's failure to participate in the economic expansion that is taking place in vast geographical areas of the world.

While it is true that particular characteristics, such as the high rate of population growth, help to retard per capita development, and that special circumstances which have arisen in the past and still persist in some countries at times permit more rapid spurts, it is equally undeniable that the experience of the past twenty years affords plenty of evidence of the difficulties attending Latin America's development, and that the foregoing comparisons of national income indices reflect the truth of this picture of the region's backwardness in relation to the world at large, which becomes yet more marked when future development prospects are considered.

The contemplation of these problems, and the comparison of Latin America's experience with that of other countries, make it very clear that the region has not succeeded in establishing the economic and social conditions required for the development of a mode of economic growth whose sources of dynamic energy are permanent and powerful enough for the desired objectives to be attained. A great deal is being done of late at both the national and the international level; but, at the same time, the limitations imposed upon Latin America's development by the policy of the industrial countries with which the region has trade and financial links have been and still are stringent. Nevertheless, the question may well be asked whether it does not lie with the Latin American countries themselves to adopt the strategic decisions that may help, again at both the national and the international level, to prevent a delay of thirty or thirty-five years before the region can attain that modest per capita income of $650, which will still be accompanied by its train of unemployment, underproductive jobs, and minimal levels of living for 50 per cent of the Latin American population.

In secretariat documents and at the sessions of the Commission, ECLA has repeatedly discussed the problems of Latin America's economic development and the essential features of the policies that should be pursued. But it will not be superfluous to analyze a few points in the present document, which once again points toward regional economic integration as the only possible path for Latin America to take at this stage of its development.

The Present Stage of Development and the Need for Regional Economic Integration

The problem of Latin America's development could be summed up by compressing the reciprocal economic and social relationships involved in its mechanics into the following terms. The low average income in Latin America is determined by the failure of the national economies to develop as dynamically as needed, not only for full utilization of their available manpower and material resources, but also for the assimilation of technical progress, which is an indispensable requisite for the improvement of productivity. Many obstacles which the region has not had the skill or the power to circumvent have hitherto prevented the establishment of the conditions required for such a process.

The World Depression of the thirties and the policy applied by the industrialized countries disrupted the pattern of development that the Latin American economies had been following. Some countries were severely affected, while others were able to cushion the depressive impact by measures which later came to shape a new economic policy. Provisions which, to begin with, were primarily directed toward correcting the balance-of-payments deficits, mitigating the effects of the fall in world market prices and the contraction in exports of primary commodities, spurred on an import-substitution process which acquired major importance as time went by, and in many countries became one of the objectives of a deliberate industrialization policy. In practice, this process constituted the dynamic factor in a new growth pattern, and its repercussions made themselves felt in the economic and social changes that characterized one phase of Latin America's development.

The economic variables representative of this growth pattern are well known: a long-term downward trend in the ratios between foreign trade and the domestic product, an expansion of the industrial sector's share in the formation of that product, and a striking change in the composition of imports. If the existing situation is compared with that prevailing in 1928–1929, the statistics for the region as a whole show that the import coefficient has plummeted from 30 to 9 per cent and the export coefficient from 31 to 14 per cent, while industry's contribution to the domestic product has risen from 13 to 23 per cent. Furthermore, the proportion of imports represented by consumer goods has dwindled from 46 to 18 per cent, while the share of intermediate products, fuels, and capital goods has climbed from 54 to 82 per cent.

The industrialization process has not taken place in all the Latin American countries simultaneously, or at the same pace. The geographically or economically smaller countries (the majority) were slower to adopt this policy, and in many of them exports have continued to play the leading dynamic role in the growth process and in determining the economic situation. At the present stage of the region's development, the various countries display such marked disparities that they can be classified in accordance with those economic ratios that indicate differences of structure, income levels, and degrees of industrialization. At one end of the scale, a relatively advanced stage of industrial development and low import coefficients are found in Argentina, Brazil, and Mexico, especially in the first two. Close to them, although with special characteristics of their own, come Chile and Colombia. At the other end are the less developed countries such as Bolivia, Ecuador, Paraguay, and most of the Central American countries, where as a rule export and import coefficients are still high. Venezuela exemplifies a different type of economy, one that developed quickly on the basis of petroleum exports and has been undergoing a rapid metamorphosis in recent years.

Despite these differences, all the countries have pursued a very similar policy as regards the conduct of the import-substitution process, and all have continued to export primary products. In effect, the Latin American countries that are smaller in size or relatively less developed are embarking upon industrialization or proceeding from one stage to another through the same channels used by the more developed countries some time ago. Only recently have certain changes begun to creep in, with the initial integration efforts of the ALALC countries and the more vigorous decisions that are being adopted in the integration movement of the five Central American countries.

The purpose of the present chapter is to discuss some essential aspects of over-all development policy, especially those relating to the evolution of the external sector, in order to see how far that sector is contributing to the establishment of the basic prerequisites for an acceleration of the Latin American countries' economic growth rates which will enable them to make up their lag. It is a matter of evaluating the possible alternatives that may present themselves, given existing conditions in the national economies and of international policy, with the aim of defining the role that integration will have to play as an instrument of Latin America's development.

While it is no easy matter to make such an evaluation for the region as a whole, because of the marked differences among the Latin American countries, the experience of recent years unquestionably provides adequate grounds for certain basic inferences in the light of which Latin America's current development problem can be stated in reasonably accurate terms.

The countries that made most progress in import substitution, reducing their import and export coefficients, witnessed a slackening of their growth rate as time went by and have found themselves faced with serious difficulties as they approach later stages of development. This state of affairs has arisen in Argentina, Brazil, Chile, and Colombia, although in different circumstances and periods. Mexico is the only one of this more advanced group of countries in which industrialization has continued intensively in recent years, thanks to peculiarly favorable conditions, but here, too, potential limitations exist, of the same type as those hindering the continuance of the process in the other countries.

The decline in the growth rate also affected the group of countries at less advanced stages of industrial development, whose economic development patterns were still comparatively open to the outside world. In their case, the fluctuations of external demand or purchasing power were reflected in the marked instability of the rate of development, which decreased from the mid fifties onward. The improvement registered in the economic situation of many Latin American countries in the last two years is attributable to the rise in export prices for primary products—which in turn must be largely ascribed to factors that may alter over the very short term or are already undergoing modification—rather than to changes in the basic conditions upon which development traditionally depends.

Within the complex of factors and events that have been particularly influential in weakening and slowing down the rate of economic growth, attention must be drawn to those relating to the conduct of the import-substitution process and those which have maintained and aggravated the external bottleneck in the Latin American economies.

Although the import-substitution process was a fundamental dynamic factor in the development of what are now the most advanced countries, and is playing a similar role, in conjunction with external demand, in those that are relatively less developed, it has had virtually no influence on the diversification of Latin American exports. The countries of the region have continued to rely on their exports of primary products, while the industrialization process, under the aegis of a strongly protectionist regime, has been confined within the narrow bounds of domestic markets.

In these circumstances, the Latin American countries have been unable to solve the problem of their balance-of-payments deficits. On the one hand, there has been a substantial drop in exports through the deterioration of the terms of trade, and external purchasing power has remained stationary or increased very slowly. On the other, the substitution process has altered the composition of imports but has not reduced the aggregate volume of external supply requirements, which, on the contrary, has tended to expand with the growth of income and of demand for the items not replaced by domestic production. External financing has covered balance-of-payments disequilibria, for given periods, and played an active part in the import-substitution process, but the terms have tightened increasingly, so that the rate of economic growth and the further continuance of the substitution process itself have become unduly vulnerable to the vicissitudes of the balance of payments.

Two other features of this policy are of great significance for the region's development problem. They concern the economic productivity of the substitution process and the implications of dependence upon exports of primary products.

The economic yields of import-substitution activities have fallen short of the levels they might have reached had a national industrialization policy been applied. The process has been carried on at relatively high costs, to some extent imputable to excessive and indiscriminate tariff protection, and through an industrial organization which has failed to attain normal standards of efficiency, partly because the markets are too small for advantage to be taken of economies of scale and specialization in important branches of industry. At the same time, as exports have continued to depend upon primary commodities, foreign trade has not transmitted to the Latin American countries all the dynamic impetus that might have been expected of the intensive economic expansion registered in the industrialized countries. In short, the assimilation of technical progress has been held up and the improvement of over-all productivity impeded.

Obviously, if the region is to regain this lost ground, some means of rapidly expanding domestic production and increasing the efficiency of Latin America's economic organization must be devised. To that end, institutional reforms must be introduced, and the technical progress and high productivity indices of contemporary industry must be assimilated. This is impracticable, as is being demonstrated, if the policy of industrialization within the narrow confines of individual country markets is persistently adhered to, and if foreign trade is restricted to primary products. It is indispensable, therefore, to expand trade flows and to establish gradually a diversified structure of production, demand for which will transcend the bounds of the national markets and, in addition, will mean that imports can be increased.

A solution of this kind is hardly conceivable if each individual Latin American country—including the most advanced within the region—has no defense against the powerful industrialized countries and the still more powerful regional and political groupings they have formed. The developing countries have neither the resources nor the technical ability to compete with others even in the developing areas, and much less in the industrialized regions. And insofar as they might be able to do so, experience is showing that they would encounter very strong opposition.

The only solution, therefore, is to establish a gradual integration process conducive to the economic union of the Latin American countries. By this means, the national economies could take advantage of each region's resources and potential, and organize their activities, at much higher levels of productivity than at present, on the basis of a market of 230 million inhabitants, increasing at one of the highest population growth rates in the world. They would thus have found the remedy for the present bottleneck in their foreign trade, which is due to the fact that their development possibilities are tied to the fluctuations and poor sales prospects encountered by their primary products on the markets of the industrialized countries.

Given the existing position of production techniques and international economic policy, regional integration appears to be the only efficacious formula for the creation of new dynamic stimuli and a new national growth structure, more flexible and more productive than that afforded by the substitution process. This thesis must not be interpreted as the expression of an alternative policy or of a policy sufficient in itself, since the integration process cannot be put into effect unless, at the same time, national development programs are carried out, trade with other regions reaches specific levels, and adequate technical and financial cooperation is forthcoming from abroad.

It will be useful, therefore, to analyze the arguments in favor of integration more thoroughly, demarcating more precisely its place within the framework of integrated national development policies.

Development Problems and the Role of Foreign Trade

It has been shown that the bottleneck in the external sector has been a very important cause of the low productivity and the lack of dynamic force displayed by the Latin American economies. It must not be inferred, however, that the only aim of economic policy is to surmount this obstacle. Latin America's development problem is much more complex, since other economic and social factors and conditions, which have not yet been studied, or in any event not thoroughly enough, have combined with external difficulties to perpetuate the backwardness of the Latin American countries. Although these factors are all too well known, it is worthwhile to restate them here in order to show the reciprocal relationships that link them with foreign trade and with the approaches to regional integration that are formulated in the present document.

In the first place, attention may be drawn to the general limiting factors relating to the efficiency of economic and social organization, which still subsist because of the slowness with which the structural and institutional reforms required by an up-to-date and progressive society are being introduced. This state of affairs is reflected in the lack of social mobility and the extreme inequity of property and income distribution; these factors in turn determine the rigidity of the social structure in many countries, low levels of living, deficient training and organization of human resources, and the constant frustration of incipient economic growth incentives.

Second, there are other limiting factors more closely linked to economic policy and market size. Thus, the want of internal and external competition in national economic activities has led to monopolies and restrictive practices, which in turn have had repercussions in the shape of the concentration of ownership, ill-advised allocation of resources, under-utilization of production capacity, and higher costs. At the same time, the small size of the individual country market, which may not have been a serious obstacle in the early phases of industrialization, has made it impossible to reap the benefits of economies of scale and of particular degrees of specialization, and affords no incentive to the continuance of a dynamic investment process, especially in the relatively less developed countries of the region. Furthermore, the slow progress that has been made in organizing planning procedures precludes a sufficiently rapid implementation of efficacious policies, execution of plans, and formation of investment absorption capacity.

Third, something must be said of the more specifically economic factors. These are numerous, but the following may be singled out as severely retarding the development of the Latin American countries: the underdevelopment and stagnation of the rural economy, especially in the sectors producing for domestic consumption; and the public sector's lack of funds—resulting from inefficient tax systems and, in most countries, from the absence of proper financial machinery and institutions—which hinders the execution of the basic investment projects needed to encourage private investment in productive activities. In this context, reference must also be made to the financial and monetary disequilibria manifested in the dizzy inflationary spirals whose harmful effects on the allocation of resources and the formation of savings finally culminate in the disruption of the conditions required for economic growth.

Fourth, and last, mention must be made of the limiting factors connected with the external sector. These derive from the inadequacy of external purchasing power, the deterioration of the terms of trade, the heavy burden represented by service payments on external loans and investment, the low levels of gold and foreign exchange reserves, the absence of a genuine policy of international financial cooperation, and the Latin American countries' insufficient bargaining power for the purpose of obtaining satisfactory trade and financial terms from the industrialized countries.

The various socioeconomic conditions cited here as obstacles to development, and the limiting factors of a more specifically economic character, combine with the external bottleneck to slow the rate of economic growth.

In several important respects, it would be difficult to draw a line between the facts that represent primary causes and the phenomena that might be regarded as their manifestations or effects. The operation of all these obstacles and limiting factors is interrelated. Thus, a policy which succeeded in removing internal obstacles would make for the improvement of external conditions, but a more flexible and easier balance-of-payments position would be needed to facilitate the implementation of reforms and the execution of over-all development programs.

In these reciprocal relationships, the influence of the external sector is far-reaching, and its operation, up to a point, autonomous, since its movements depend upon international market forces and on the policy of the industrialized countries, fields in which the Latin American governments can exercise little control and take little action.

Moreover, the situation is unfortunate in that, as long as the external obstacles subsist, it is difficult to make a clean sweep of the limiting factors of an internal nature. The reason is that the development of Latin America is largely dependent on imports of essential goods, on the application of the technical improvements that originate in the industrialized countries, and on financial cooperation from abroad.

It is worthwhile to cite a few aspects of development which will illustrate the strategic importance of the external sector. For example, even if the countries carried out the necessary reforms to promote an increase in domestic savings with the aim of augmenting real investment, these reforms could not be put into effect unless at the same time enough external purchasing power was acquired to cover the imports entailed by such investment. Progress in planning will unquestionably increase investment absorption capacity, but again, investment projects could not be executed without the corresponding imports of capital goods that some countries are not now, and may never be, in a position to produce, because of the small size of their market, or for want of technical know-how. In short, the implementation of a policy designed to improve the living conditions of the lower-income sectors will encounter serious obstacles, if it proves impossible to expand imports, even in the case of actual consumer goods whose domestic production cannot immediately be developed.

To sum up, when the restrictive effects of the various factors are more thoroughly analyzed, it will not seem surprising if, in many countries, the obstacles deriving from the external sector should prove to be as serious as others, or even more formidable—in the sense that unless they are removed it will be impossible to surmount the rest.

Finally, this study leaves no room for doubt on one point. Development policy must attack on several internal and external fronts at the same time. Everything need not be done at once, for that will often be physically impossible. What is wanted is a strategy that will immediately tackle the more vulnerable points, among which the external bottleneck, alongside the need for internal basic reforms, has been plainly shown to constitute one of the most significant.

Long-term Limitations of a Policy of Import Substitution and External Borrowing

CHRONIC BALANCE-OF-PAYMENTS DEFICITS

The countries of the region have tried to get rid of the external bottleneck and stimulate economic growth by resorting more or less intensively to three basic measures: import controls and import substitution, external financing, and the promotion of traditional exports or of new export lines.

For a number of reasons, both external and internal—among which a lack of planned policies or an excess of caution have been common —little has been achieved in the diversification of exports, and the Latin American countries have continued to depend in this respect on their primary products. Policy has concentrated mainly on the restriction of imports and their replacement by domestic production, and on the utilization of external financing. It is here that the larger countries have found the dynamic growth factors for which they had previously relied on exports. In the smaller countries, these factors have been combined, to a greater or lesser extent, with export movements, and as a result more stable development conditions have been promoted.

As time goes by, however, such a policy tends to lose its efficacy. Once the import-substitution process and external borrowing reach a certain saturation point, extremely inflexible conditions are created that ultimately bring about a decline in the rate of growth. In the following pages the mechanics of this phenomenon will be analyzed. The first step will be to study import-substitution policy, with particular reference to the experience of the countries that have advanced farthest in their industrialization process, in order to draw generally applicable conclusions.

IMPORT SUBSTITUTION, ECONOMIC GROWTH, AND BALANCE-OF-PAYMENTS EQUILIBRIUM

The evolution of the import-substitution process may conveniently be mapped out in several stages, although some rather arbitrary divisions are involved. An analysis of this kind is useful in clarifying the effect of the process on the rate of growth and on balance-of-payments trends.

In an initial phase, import substitution develops in the sector producing nondurable consumer goods, where the production techniques employed are relatively simple and capital intensity is low. It is comparatively easy to make the necessary investment and launch these activities. By their means, the growth of the domestic product and of internal income is directly and indirectly promoted, and employment levels are raised. External resources may help to finance investment. And the foreign exchange released or transferred by the restriction of imports of nonessential goods, and often of capital goods for other sectors, makes it possible for this phase of the substitution process to develop. The import coefficient decreases, and the dynamic effects on the domestic product and internal income are accentuated insofar as substitution activities are based on the use of domestic raw materials. It was precisely because a high proportion of their direct raw-material inputs was available that this stage was facilitated in many Latin American countries.

The process continues in what may be demarcated as a second phase, when it extends to import substitution of other consumer goods, including even certain types of consumer durables, branches of intermediate products, and specific capital goods. The most highly industrialized countries of the region have completed this second phase, and several of the others are embarking upon it.

These new industrial activities use more complex techniques and require higher levels of technical know-how and more efficient organizing capacity. The ratio of fixed capital to output and the amount of investment per plant are higher, and economies of scale, or cost reductions in accordance with production levels, also acquire considerable importance.

The dynamic impetus of these activities is so considerable that they come to dominate the economic and financial process—as has been shown by the experience of Argentina and Brazil, in recent years—especially when the stage of installing the motor-vehicle industry is reached. Alongside these quantitative effects, there are others, no less significant, which influence development. This phase of industrialization involves the absorption of technical know-how and production techniques which raise the general level of training, organization, and modernization in national economic structures.

But serious difficulties set limits to the economic soundness and hamper the operation of this process and the conditions attending it in Latin America. In the first place, its effects on the balance of payments must be considered.

This phase is characterized by a marked substitution effort in the case of intermediate products, although there is an initial increase in requirements of imports of parts or spares not manufactured in the country, but these are later gradually replaced by domestic production. In any event, as the volume of production in import-substitution activities is usually greater than that of the former external purchases concerned, demand for imported parts and spares may very soon exceed the value of the goods that once were imported. If the high import content of industrial plant is also taken into consideration, together with the additional demand for imported goods generated by the increase in the product and in income, it will be seen that the volume of imports tends to exceed the original import-substitution output.

Consequently, if there has been no expansion of exports, the balance of payments will tend to become unfavorable or the previous deficit will increase. Efforts to restrict imports of other items are then redoubled, but little is gained in terms of foreign exchange, as the restrictions that have long been in operation have gradually limited imports to essential goods. In all likelihood, these new import-substitutional investments will affect investment plans in other public or private activities through the shortage of external resources.

If, in Latin America's experience, these effects did not immediately make themselves felt, it was because the countries concerned resorted to external financing, or because an important part was played in the substitution process by direct foreign investment, as was the case in Argentina, Brazil, and Mexico. But the foreign exchange commitments under the heads of service payments and remittances of profits to which this external financing gave rise soon began to aggravate the balance-of-payments deficits.

In a third phase—upon which the most advanced countries of the region are now venturing—the import-substitution process would have to cover basic intermediate products and various types of capital goods. The activities concerned are mainly of the type needing large-scale plant and heavy investment, and operating on the basis of complex technologies and high degrees of specialization, especially in the capital-goods industries.

The development of these activities under adequate productivity and cost conditions and in line with up-to-date techniques will be difficult unless the policy of producing solely for the domestic market is drastically changed. A certain level of specialization and plant size is essential, and it can be achieved only through the expansion of trade. Moreover, the bottleneck in the external sector creates serious obstacles to the channeling of real resources toward the investment need for this purpose. There are no nonessential imports that can be restricted in order to divert foreign exchange into the new activities, the critical financial situation does nothing to encourage direct foreign investment, and new loans are increasingly spent on servicing the accumulated debts.

To sum up, the following conclusions may be drawn from the experience gained in Latin America's import-substitution process:

(*a*) Import substitution, at each separate stage, has generated a strong, dynamic impetus which has raised the national income and has decisively influenced economic and social development;

(*b*) The productivity and general efficiency of import substitution have fallen below the levels that might have been expected, because import substitution has been carried out indiscriminately under conditions of widespread *de facto* monopoly, aimed at a relatively small and unduly protected domestic market;

(*c*) In spite of the advances made in import substitution, the external imbalance has been aggravated and the economies have become more vulnerable to the vicissitudes of the balance of payments; and

(*d*) The rigidity to which the process has led explains the present decline in the rate of development and the frequent economic recessions suffered by the more industrialized countries of the region, particularly Argentina and Brazil. By contrast, industrialization has been able to forge ahead in those countries that have contrived to raise their current foreign exchange earnings during the last few years, as is the case in Mexico.

However, many of the Latin American countries are still in the early stages of industrialization and have fairly high import coefficients. There are practical possibilities open to them for reducing the coefficients and making some headway in import substitution, as they are already doing. But it must be borne in mind that, in general, their domestic markets are far smaller in absolute terms, and the obstacles to import substitution will arise at an earlier stage of industrial development. That is, even at different levels of industrialization these countries are now finding, or will soon find, that the dynamic potential of import substitution has been exhausted. In other words, the economics of import-substitution activities, the obstacles to their subsequent development, and the decline in their dynamic impetus are determined in these countries by conditions far more restrictive than those obtaining in the more advanced countries, because their domestic markets are much smaller and other impediments to development are more serious.

EXTERNAL FINANCING, RATE OF GROWTH, AND BALANCE-OF-PAYMENTS EQUILIBRIUM

Foreign capital, in its various forms, is the additional source of funds to which the developing countries have access for the increased investment needed to step up their rate of growth.

As these external resources fulfill their dynamic role in the growth process, the conditions governing foreign investment, the movement of funds, and the development of the economy making use of them are clearly defined. Inflows should be sufficiently flexible and, in principle, should follow a given steadily rising trend. They should suffice to cover the mounting debt-service payments and returns on foreign investment, and possibly to provide a balance, over a given period, to finance the excess of imports over exports, which the country needs in order to increase the real resources upon which it can draw.

Moreover, there must be a rise in domestic income and savings as well as exports, so that, after a certain stage has been reached, the external accounts will produce a surplus with which to cover, in some measure, the transfer payments deriving from debt servicing and returns on investments.

While it is true that, in practice, economic and financial factors are not as flexible as might be required, there is no doubt that this must be the pattern, if external financing is to operate satisfactorily. In this respect, Latin America's experience in the last few years is very enlightening, since the critical financial situation affecting many countries of the region has been due precisely to the fact that those essential conditions were not met.

External sources of funds often lack the flexibility needed to feed a flow of capital that will meet the aforementioned aims. In practice, capital flows tend to dry up when a country's borrowing increases, and much more so should the outlook for the balance-of-payments position be bleak. The short amortization periods and high interest payable on the large volume of external financing to which the Latin American countries have recourse merely aggravate the position. In addition, the decisions adopted by financing centers may be affected by political factors, while at the same time national policy imposes limits on foreign participation in production activities.

In brief, if capital inflow fails to increase because of one of these factors, the time will inevitably come when transfer payments for servicing and returns will tend to exceed new inflows. The higher the rates of amortization, interest, and returns, the sooner will this come about. If capital flows are reduced and export earnings fail to increase sufficiently, the rate of economic growth will decline to the point of an actual recession, unless refinancing is secured on suitable terms.

This, broadly speaking, describes Latin America's experience in recent years. The increase in its foreign exchange liabilities under the head of service payments and returns have gradually absorbed increasing proportions of the new-capital inflows, and current foreign exchange earnings from exports have either remained at a standstill or have gone up all too slowly. In other words, the necessary financial and economic conditions were lacking for a sustained dynamic evolution of the process of absorbing external loans and investment. This is obviously what happened, for example, in Argentina, Brazil, and Chile.

Two factors added to the rigidity of the process: the restriction of imports to essential items, leaving no room for further retrenchment, and the effect of the deterioration in the terms of trade for primary products. The impact of the latter was so heavy that Latin America's losses exceeded the whole of the net external financing used by the region since the mid fifties.

It may be inferred, therefore, that a policy which emphasizes external financing and import substitution but fails to expand exports tends to lose its efficacy, often within a relatively brief period. Nothing can be done to put matters right beyond a certain point, except at the expense of the growth rate.

There are two reasons for this: in the first place, import substitution in the Latin American countries has failed to reduce the over-all demand for imports; secondly, debt servicing follows a rigid pattern, being only partly dependent on the evolution of export earnings. Amortization and interest payments constitute fixed-term outflows while returns on foreign investment in local production of import-substitution activities are comparatively high and depend upon domestic market trends. Export trends can only affect returns on investment in export activities.

Thus the balance of payments of those countries which have made most headway in import substitution and in the use of external financing have acquired a highly rigid real and financial structure. It was only when export earnings increased to some extent that the process could develop along fairly satisfactory lines.

Latin America's Foreign Trade Deficit

In the present analysis of general development problems and the shortcomings of the policies applied in Latin America, the expansion and diversification of exports emerges as one of the most important aims. Accordingly, it would be useful to examine the practical possibilities open to the Latin American countries, taken individually, of achieving the aim of expanding foreign trade, under existing conditions, based on the expected trends in the world economy.[3]

From the technical projections made in relation to exports of primary products over the long term, it does not appear that the Latin American countries can achieve the external purchasing capacity needed to meet the cost of imports and the servicing of the external financing required by a faster economic growth than at present. It is useful to remember that only in the early postwar years has Latin America attained a growth of 3 per cent per capita, thanks to highly

[3] This point was studied by the ECLA secretariat in "Latin America and the United Nations Conference on Trade and Development" (E/CN.12/693) and "The United Nations Conference on Trade and Development: Analysis of the Results and Prospects for Latin America" (E/CN.12/712).

favorable export conditions which in some degree recurred during the hostilities in Korea. On the other hand, notwithstanding the exceptional economic growth of the industrialized countries to which the region is linked, the last ten years have marked a gradual decline in Latin America's foreign trade, either because of the deterioration of the terms of trade or the slow growth of the volume of sales.

The improvement noted in the last two years has been due mainly to the higher prices caused by supply restrictions, which are now being largely adjusted, and not to an expansion in the volume of regional sales. Only a few Latin American exports—such as minerals—are expected to do better. Be that as it may, it is to be hoped that the concerted action adopted by the Latin American countries can bring about a change in the attitude of the industrialized countries which will prevent existing conditions from worsening and may result in brighter prospects.

It is obvious, however, that not even under the most favorable conditions can the Latin American countries proceed with industrialization and ensure their future growth if they continue to be dependent on exports of primary products. If they propose to speed up their growth rate, the size of the gap between their export earnings and their liabilities for imports and service payments will be such that it will be hard to fill by means of additional external borrowing.

The Latin American countries will therefore have to find a way of pressing on with the process of economic and social change by creating an up-to-date industry to produce for both home and export market. There may be some question as to whether the Latin American countries would be capable, individually, of making the necessary investments and of competing with the industrialized countries on their home ground and in other parts of the world. While some encouraging experience exists in this respect, it is difficult to imagine that it can be done on the scale and within the span required by the acceleration of development. There are two implications of the difficulty and, in certain respects, the physical impossibility of rapidly attaining such a target. First, the high production costs prevailing in Latin America, and second, the industrialized countries' reluctance to import manufactures from the developing countries.

It does not seem reasonable, therefore, to expect the Latin American countries to achieve those new forms of growth if they have to rely only on what the industrialized countries are prepared to grant them, in respect either to trade or to financing.

On the other hand, if the Latin American countries form an economic union they will have created the economic and political conditions they require to achieve their objectives of industrialization and trade expansion and will have a powerful instrument for securing better terms from the industrialized countries.

Regional Economic Integration as an Instrument of National Development

THE CONTRIBUTION OF INTEGRATION TOWARD ELIMINATING THE FOREIGN TRADE DEFICIT

Regional economic integration will contribute directly, and in two ways, to eliminating the foreign trade deficit which is preventing the more rapid growth of the Latin American countries. On the one hand, it will expand intraregional trade through new flows of manufactured products and increased trade in traditional products and, on the other hand, it will facilitate the continuation of import substitution in purchases from third countries.

During the course of this evolution, the coefficient of imports from the rest of the world can be reduced as required by the balances of payments, while that of imports from the integrated countries will soar. In fact, as the national economies forge ahead in the integration process, trade will be stimulated by the coordination of policies, the reduction of customs duties, and the elimination of other stumbling blocks or obstacles, and the preferences agreed upon or agreements entered into with a view to reserving the domestic market to investment from the integrated area will tend to displace trade with third countries.

It should be borne in mind, however, that under existing conditions in Latin America the benefits deriving from integration will, particularly in the early stages, depend primarily on the extent to which it enables each country to expand over and above the level it could attain without the help of integration. This must, of course, be an overall evaluation, since many items now imported from third countries will gradually be imported from other Latin American countries. But integration should, at the same time, generate additional exports from those countries which changed the source of their supplies. Obviously, however, a unilateral shift in imports would not be harmful if the Latin American countries could secure equal or better terms in the integrated area than those obtainable from third countries. In any case, the important fact is that Latin American integration must bring about the expansion and diversification of trade in every country of the region.

While, in all probability, a conspicuous change will take place in the composition of extraregional imports, their volume will tend to increase, and there are indeed good grounds for desiring this, especially in the early stages of integration. The experience of the European Common Market is a fine illustration of this advantage. Extra-area imports by the countries of the Community went up by more than 50 per cent between 1958 and 1963, that is, in the same proportion as the product. In spite of this, area imports increased at a still faster pace: 130 per cent, over the same period, according to the values expressed in current dollars. In other words, these highly industrialized countries, in spite of having increased their reciprocal trade to a level representing 40 per cent of their total trade, nevertheless continued to import from the rest of the world without reducing the product-growth coefficient, which reached an annual average of 6.5 per cent.[4]

MARKET SIZE, PRODUCTIVITY, AND EFFICIENT USE OF REGIONAL RESOURCES

Most of the Latin American countries have extremely small markets. This is clear from a few comparisons using population and average per capita income as approximate indices of market size, which is tantamount to considering the product or total income of each country. On this basis, Brazil, Argentina, and Mexico, in that order,

[4] The domestic product is expressed in constant prices, and imports in current dollars.

possess the largest domestic markets in the region. Brazil's market, for instance, is five times the size of Colombia's, and eight times larger than that of all members of the Central American integration scheme put together. The ratios of Mexico's market to the same areas is apparently three to one and nearly five to one, respectively. Argentina stands midway between Brazil and Mexico. Some thought should be given to the huge disparities there must be with respect to other countries of the region with smaller populations and income.

The Brazilian, Argentine, and Mexican markets, large though they may be when compared with the rest of Latin America, also seem very small when measured against the markets of the industrialized countries. Thus, for example, the comparative indices reveal that France, with its 47 million inhabitants, has a market four to five times larger than that of each of the three leading Latin American countries, and that their combined product is scarcely 65 per cent that of France. The gap would be even greater if they were compared with the Federal Republic of West Germany. In these rough comparisons, the volume of production in Sweden is only slightly smaller than in Brazil and a little larger than in Argentina.

In actual fact, Latin America's domestic markets are even smaller, relatively speaking, than would appear from the indices, particularly in regard to manufactures. A more accurate analysis should take into account such individual factors as the integration of the national economies, income distribution, the structures of demand, and the level of industrial development, which adversely affect the position of the Latin American countries.

The small size of the domestic markets prevents the Latin American countries from going ahead with industrialization on the basis of productivity levels and production costs similar to those in the industrialized countries, since they cannot establish industrial plants of the size and degree of specialization required to enable them to take advantage of economies of scale. Investments to develop certain key industries can only be made if strong protection is received from the State, and then only at the expense of productivity and of efficiency in the utilization of resources.

In most Latin American countries the domestic market is so small that there are a great many industrial activities in which investment is not justified on technical grounds and, consequently, it is practically impossible for import substitution to proceed any farther. Prospects are more favorable in the larger countries, Argentina, Brazil, and Mexico, and their market potential, combined with ample resources, largely explains their faster and more advanced stage of development.

The economies of scale which cannot be turned to account because of market limitations are of significant proportions in important industries producing durable consumer goods, capital goods, and basic intermediate products. Such economies depend on a number of factors, such as the indivisible nature of investment, the disproportion between the increase in a plant's production capacity and the cost of equipment, and the possibility of introducing up-to-date techniques and a certain degree of specialization when operating on an extensive scale of production.

Regional integration will play a direct part in solving all these development problems deriving from the size of the market. As the integration process advances, production activities in each country will be able to count on the potential demand of the whole integrated area. It will therefore be possible to establish up-to-date plants of optimum size, with an adequate level of specialization, and to carry on with industrialization in other sectors where nothing can be done today within the limitations on the domestic markets.

Concurrently with the broadening of the market, integration will provide the enormous advantages deriving from the optimum location of new investment, in terms of the cheapest sources of raw materials, energy, fuels, and other inputs with an important influence on production costs. Some highly illustrative examples of economies in investment and reduction in costs to be achieved through optimum regional location and through the establishment of plants that are up-to-date as regards specialization, techniques, and size, are to be found in the chapter dealing with regional investment policy.

The potential expansion of the market will assume exceptional proportions in the Latin American countries that are of small or medium geographic or economic size. For example, on the basis of the aforementioned approximate indices, it can be stated that the five countries of the Central American economic community would have a potential additional market twenty-five times larger than that of their integration area itself; as regards Colombia, the rest of Latin America would represent a market fourteen times larger, and Chile, twenty-two times larger.

The broader market will also play a very important part in the major countries of the region. Thus it may be estimated that, compared with Brazil, the rest of Latin America represents a population of 150 million, and a market two and a half times larger than the local market; compared with Argentina, the population is 205 million, and the market four times larger; and in the case of Mexico, 190 million inhabitants, and a market five times the size of the Mexican market. Here it should be stressed that these comparisons give only an approximate idea of the potential market expansion. In practice, it cannot be taken for granted that a given industry of a country can count on the whole economic space of the region as a market, since the advantages inherent in location, transport costs, and other general factors will tend to limit the scope of the market within the integrated area, a limitation which is all the more important because of the geographical size of the region. That is why this document places such stress on the need for embarking forthwith on a study of transport facilities with a view to the adoption of a coordinated policy for promoting integration. Whatever the difficulties, however, the huge disparities noted between the size of the domestic markets and the potential size of the regional market convey some idea of the force that would be gathered by the incentives to trade expansion. As progress is made in the establishment of a regional transport network and in the reduction of transport costs, the geographical size of Latin America will become an advantage, since, concurrently with enlarging the real market, advantage can be taken of the region's resources in consideration of the most suitable locations in the diversification and specialization of economic activities.

A matter of some concern—and rightly so—is that the reduction in customs duties and the removal of obstacles to trade might give rise to an investment race aimed at the expansion of existing activities and the replacement of equipment. Such action might well have adverse repercussions were it to deflect resources from other higher-priority investments and undermine the economic activity of the less-industrialized countries or those which cannot at once promote a process of modernization. These and other problems which will have to be provided for in establishing the instruments for an integration policy are dealt with later on in this book. In the meantime, it should be stated here that integration will have to come about gradually, so that the countries concerned will have time to introduce the necessary adjustments and reforms, as and when domestic output and income increase. In the first few years, action would be focused primarily on the integration of dynamic industries which have a strategic part to play in development, and in which, moreover, the economies of scale are usually considerable.

ASSIMILATION OF NEW TECHNIQUES

Technical progress has been the basic factor in the economic growth of the industrialized countries. According to the extensive research which has been done on the subject it has as great or greater dynamic influence than the human effort and the actual volume of capital invested in the production process.

Nevertheless, the Latin American countries are not taking advantage of the potential offered by technical advances in order to step up their development. A whole set of factors prevents them from doing so, preeminent among them being, because of their bearing on integration, the narrowness of the market, the lack of dynamism in foreign trade, and the limited resources allocated to manpower training and to scientific and technical research.

As mentioned previously, the limitations of the market and the slowness of income growth preclude the establishment of industrial plants with up-to-date production techniques in a broad range of activities. Even if this were feasible, the Latin American countries feel obliged to adopt a cautious policy, because it would not increase employment. Regional integration will break this vicious circle, since, by facilitating a more rapid increase in production and income, it will aid in the pursuit of the two objectives: the raising of productivity and employment levels—which today are incompatible.

In the analyses of production in specific activities and of the economy as a whole, an effort is made to explain the part played in the expansion of production by each of the above-mentioned factors: technical progress, human effort, and capital. In actual fact, however, technical progress does not act entirely on its own, but through better training and organization of the human factor and more efficient use of the new capital goods used in the new production techniques. Therefore, as long as the Latin American countries continue to rely on exports of primary products and fail to increase their external purchasing power, owing to the deterioration of the terms of trade or the lack of external demand, they will be unable to take full advantage of this powerful factor for development.

By removing the external bottleneck, integration will permit the countries of the region to use their export earnings more efficiently for the acquisition of capital goods and for the establishment of up-to-date plants to promote autonomous scientific and technical progress for Latin America. Clearly, foreign scientific and technical cooperation and coordinated action in regional education, training, and research programs will be needed here.

REGIONAL INTEGRATION AND INTERNATIONAL POLICY AIMS

As shown above, regional integration is essential if the Latin American countries are to speed up their economic and social development and emerge from the stagnation in which they find themselves at present. However, integration does not represent an alternative to the aims of expansion and diversification of trade with other regions, particularly with the industrialized countries.

The Latin American countries must take decisive steps toward integration and, at the same time, press on with their international economic policy aims. No other course is open to them, as 90 per cent of their present trade is with areas outside the region; they rely on the industrialized countries for supplies of essential goods and require foreign financial and technical cooperation if they are to make any headway in integration itself. Furthermore, it should be made plain right from the start that in the early stages of integration, requirements of imports from other areas will increase considerably, and at a later stage their structure will change, though they will not diminish in absolute terms. On the contrary, it would be more logical for them to continue expanding, although on a lesser scale than the domestic product.

Two experiences which occurred under very dissimilar conditions in the Central American countries and in the European Economic Community (European Common Market) illustrate these relationships between the evolution of trade and economic growth in an integrated area. The five Central American countries which are making steady progress in integration increased their reciprocal trade by a total of 150 per cent between 1961 and 1964. At the same time, their extra-area imports grew by 40 per cent. Undoubtedly the integration process has been helped in the last two or three years by the improvement in the export sector of the countries concerned, which enabled external supplies to be increased on the scale indicated above. The countries of the European Common Market, with a combined population of 175 million inhabitants, a market probably three times the size of Latin America's, and a level of industrial development which cannot be compared with the average for Latin America, increased their imports from third countries, as previously indicated, by more than 50 per cent between 1958 and 1963, notwithstanding the tremendous growth of their reciprocal trade.

All these considerations point to the need for an over-all coordination of integration aims with trade policy and international financing objectives. The Latin American countries will have to pool their efforts and work out a common policy vis-à-vis the industrialized countries; their economic union would give them the negotiating power they lack individually and place them on a better competitive footing. Coordinated action with the industrialized countries and international financing agencies is at once urgent and imperative, because radical changes must be brought about in the present situation so that the industrialized countries will facilitate the expansion of trade in primary products on the basis of adequate terms of trade, permit the entry of exports of manufactures from the developing countries, and increase their technical and financial cooperation in line with new systems that would be less onerous for the recipient countries.

CHAPTER VI

INFLATION AND GROWTH IN LATIN AMERICA

Economic Development or Monetary Stability: The False Dilemma[1]

Introduction and Summary

Inflation and Monetary Orthodoxy

The economists of ECLA are often thought of as having a certain leaning toward inflation, as being prompted by the belief that this phenomenon is inevitable in the economic development of Latin America. Nothing could be farther from our thoughts. This erroneous interpretation arises perhaps partly from the fact that the problem of inflation has not yet been systematically dealt with in our studies.

Two facts largely explain why our thinking is wrongly judged. We reject the theory, which is so current, that inflation is caused solely by the financial disorder and lack of monetary restraint of the Latin American countries, not because we deny the existence of these patent aberrations but because there are extremely powerful structural

[1] See Raúl Prebisch, "Economic Development or Monetary Stability: The False Dilemma," *Economic Bulletin for Latin America*, VI, no. 1 (March 1961), 1–9.

factors in Latin America which lead to inflation and against which monetary policy is powerless. This is the first fact.

The second is the critical position we have adopted toward certain measures aimed at monetary stabilization. We all agree that a supreme effort must be made to arrest inflation and to achieve stability on sound bases. But we are seriously worried about achieving this at the expense of a decline in over-all income, of its stagnation, or of a slowing-down in its rate of development.

Those who advocate this type of anti-inflationary policy—both those who suggest it from outside and those who live in the midst of this harsh and hazardous reality of Latin America—sometimes entertain the odd notion that the region's monetary sins must be redeemed by sacrifice. The evil of inflation must be atoned for by retrenchment. But very often the classic form of punishment does not fall upon those who unleashed inflation or who thrived on it, but on the broad masses of the people who were suffering its consequences.

The general mistake persists of considering inflation as a purely monetary phenomenon, to be combated as such. Inflation cannot be explained as something divorced from the economic and social maladjustments and stresses to which the economic development of our countries gives rise. Nor can serious thought be given to an autonomous anti-inflationary policy, as if only monetary considerations were involved; it must be an integral part of development policy.

Economic development calls for constant changes in production methods in the economic and social structure and in patterns of income distribution. Not to make these changes in time, or to undertake them partially and incompletely, leads to the maladjustments and stresses which release the ever-latent and extremely powerful inflationary forces in the Latin American economy.

This should not be construed as meaning that inflation is inevitable in our countries. Far from it. To avoid inflation, however, there must be a rational and far-sighted policy of economic development and social betterment; in other words, an essentially new approach in which an answer other than inflation is sought to these maladjustments and stresses arising from development.

This is not merely a technical problem; it is essentially a political one in which the paramount task for economists is to clarify and to persuade. We have often seen politicians who, imbued with the genuine desire measurably to improve the well-being of the masses, are frequently blinded by the corrosive illusion of inflation. Have we offered them any other alternative? Have we come to them with a coherent and feasible set of principles which would have enabled them to escape from the dilemma of choosing between inflation and an over-simplified and perplexing monetary orthodoxy? Latin American economists are indebted to the politicians of our countries. It would be well, in this book, to requite them as far as is fitting.

The object of these pages is to demonstrate that there is a solution to the problem of monetary stabilization that is different from the one so often recommended by the orthodox school. Before going into this any further, however, the structural factors usually leading to inflation should be examined. Perhaps a general picture should be presented here which will allow us, from the very outset, to grasp the nature and trend of our argument, even at the risk of indulging later in possible repetitions.

The Why and Wherefore of the Dilemma

It is common knowledge that the economic development of a peripheral country is very closely linked to the trend followed by its exports. On the one hand, the rate of growth of its exports sets a limit to spontaneous economic development. On the other hand, continuous fluctuation in this rate contributes to serious internal instability. When there is a cyclic increase in exports, income in the aggregate expands with relative ease, and this calls for a volume of imports easily paid for by exports. But when exports fall off, these imports cannot be maintained and, as a result, neither can the level of income formerly attained. Under an orthodox system of monetary stability, the external and internal disequilibrium thus produced necessarily leads to a contraction of economic activity, and the balance tends to be restored at a lower income level.

This contraction usually arouses the ever-latent inflationary forces lurking within the Latin American economy, that is, if they are not already at work. Recourse is then had to the expansion of credit, and this, while counteracting the downward trend of income, also impedes the readjustment of imports and, consequently, restoration of the internal balance.

Disequilibrium is one of the factors which renders it very difficult for our countries to apply an anticyclic policy that does not compromise monetary stability. Hence, the solution does not lie in counteracting the effects of contraction but in preventing them by means of effective structural changes. The purpose of these changes is twofold: to allow the rate of development to exceed the limit imposed by exports; and, at the same time, to keep internal activity operating at the highest level of employment without being affected by export fluctuations.

Structural rather than cyclic measures should be resorted to in order to overcome the external vulnerability of our economies, although some anticyclic measures are also helpful as a complement to the structural solutions.

Another—and perhaps the most significant—factor hampering an anticyclic policy is the inadequacy of savings, which becomes more acute when exports decline. Any attempt then made to maintain the level of investment previously achieved is usually one of the chief causes of the inflationary expansion of credit.

The savings coefficient is relatively low in our countries, not only because average per capita income is also low but, in addition, because of the form in which this income is distributed and of the prevailing patterns of consumption. An increase in this coefficient calls for work on distribution and consumption—in other words, on the social structure—and, at the same time, for a change in the structure of production and imports so that the increased savings can be converted into capital goods. In order to do this and to facilitate a rise in the savings coefficient to a level which would accelerate the rate of economic development, an additional contribution in the form of international funds is usually needed.

Resistance to these structural changes, which are essential to a rise in the savings coefficient, often leads to inflation in our countries. Inflation not only makes it possible to raise the level of public and private expenditure and investment but, by enlarging the profits of entrepreneurs and, through them, of other high-income groups, it also causes them to increase their consumption, generally on a much higher scale than that of investments. It is therefore a socially costly and regressive method of raising the savings coefficient.

Since the inadequacy of savings becomes more acute during the period of contraction, it is extremely difficult, if not impossible, for monetary authorities to oppose an expansion of credit to cover expenditure and investments which tend to shrink. It should not be concluded, however, that this type of inflation of expenditure and investments—different from inflation of costs—is attributable solely to the structural vulnerability of the economy. The effects of inflationary forces are usually also felt in periods of prosperity, when increased economic activity stimulates expenditure and creates new investment opportunities.

These forces tend to burst forth whenever a marked change takes place. When the change is favorable, however, inflationary expansion cannot be attributed to vulnerability of the economy—as it can when the change is unfavorable—but to the powerlessness of the central banks to arrest these inflationary forces; indeed they may well be operating within the banks themselves.

It is therefore an expression of the aforementioned lack of financial and monetary restraint which, while it may not explain our inflationary phenomena in all their great complexity, is nevertheless a very important element thereof.

The simple orthodox formula of credit containment—perfectly correct when rising exports stimulate domestic activity—completely ignores the phenomena of structural vulnerability and, once the decline sets in, exposes the economy ineluctably to the inflationary forces.

All this relates to the inflation of expenditure and investments, where the inflationary pressure of demand first causes prices to rise and then brings about an increase in wages and salaries, in order—very rightly—to restore the real income of the workers. This is the traditional type of inflation in our countries, although there are new aspects to structural vulnerability.

However, inflationary phenomena of another type emerge as the process of development continues. Either because of the form in which the structural changes required by development are carried out, or because they are undertaken only partially or inadequately, regressive movements come into operation in income distribution. Efforts to compensate for their effects lead to higher wages and salaries and their inevitable impact on prices.

There are three main elements in these regressive movements which derive from economic development itself: the cost of import substitution; the higher cost of agricultural products; and the rise in taxes and duties which affect mass consumption in one way or another.

Import-substitution policy, while reflecting an inevitable structural change, has been carried out with very serious flaws. Very often considerations of economic feasibility have not been given their due, and it was not until recently that an attempt was made to break the confining bonds of national markets by means of the gradual economic integration of our countries. First and foremost, this policy has been applied in a discriminatory way, without promoting a corresponding expansion in exports, and thus it has been carried farther than it might have been under other circumstances.

The cost of substitution has thus been exaggerated to the detriment of mass consumption, particularly when the increase in productivity has been small in the rest of the economy.

This is particularly true of the productivity of the land and it constitutes one of the chief obstacles to economic development. Antiquated systems of land tenure have contributed to the relative rise in the cost of food in some Latin American countries as demand increased with population growth.

If to this is added the greater cost of some elements or inputs of agricultural production as a result of substitution policy and agricultural wage increases arising from higher productivity in other branches of the economy, the answer may be found to why, in some countries, costs and prices relative to agricultural production have risen with a marked effect on mass consumption.

To raise wages and salaries is a very understandable reaction. However, it fails to solve the problem either in the present or in the previous case; it is merely reflected in the aforementioned inflationary spiral. Nor does the solution lie in the policy of credit containment; if central banks do not increase the amount of currency in circulation when salaries and wages rise, they cause a contraction in economic activity. Hence, the contraction may be due not only to the external vulnerability of the economy but also to the endeavor to use monetary instruments to deal with the consequences of its structural flaws.

In the case of an inflation of expenditure and investments, and not of costs, the inflationary rise in prices likewise involves a corresponding readjustment of salaries and wages. Unlike the previous case, however, this increase is not inflationary but is the correction of an inflationary phenomenon. Nevertheless, what happens very often is that the entrepreneurs, instead of absorbing it at the expense of their inflation-swollen profits, resort to credit expansion and transfer it to prices, thus generating the inflationary spiral.

Inflation is asymmetrical insofar as its distributive effects are concerned. It is used by entrepreneurs to modify distribution to their advantage and to the detriment chiefly of the workers. Yet, if avoided, it does not help the workers to achieve the opposite effect and increase their relative share.

Hence, inflation is not an effective means of redistributing income from the point of view of the broad masses. In those cases where positive results are achieved at the expense of social groups other than the entrepreneurs, there is no doubt that taxation, if judiciously applied, is a more efficacious and less disruptive method. In fact, taxation is the income redistribution instrument *par excellence*, and the Latin American masses must learn to wield their growing political power so that it can be used for economic and social purposes. Likewise they must learn to wield their trade union power—already very substantial in some countries—to effect sizable increases in productivity and thus raise their real income, instead of wasting their energy on securing salary and wage increases which are soon cancelled out by the inflationary spiral. What is needed, therefore, is a salary and wage policy which leads to this goal and at the same time ensures the growing participation of the broad masses in the process of national capital formation.

All these considerations allow us to approach the problem of inflation in our countries in all its vast complexity. In actual fact, it merges with the problem of development. There is inflation because the economy is structurally vulnerable, because there are regressive income-distribution factors, because there are not enough savings to expedite investment within a given economic and social structure. The resulting maladjustments and tensions encourage latent inflationary forces to burst forth. By means of regular and intensive economic development the maximum resistance can be offered to these inflationary forces and the policy of monetary stability can thus be upheld on sound bases (which do not exist today) as an integral part of economic development policy.

Structural Vulnerability of the Economy and Inflationary Forces

Growth and Vulnerability

STRUCTURAL CHARACTER OF THE SOLUTION

This section attempts to explain how the growth of income at a more rapid rate than exports permit, and continual fluctuation of exports, release inflationary forces that upset monetary stability in Latin American countries.

The solution of this problem is fundamental because it calls for structural changes that will allow the economy to grow beyond the limit imposed by exports, while at the same time giving it the strength it must have to prevent, rather than correct, the internal consequences of these export fluctuations.

In the absence of such structural changes, these countries will inevitably be faced with the dilemma of choosing between a policy of monetary stability that subordinates economic development to the tempo and fluctuation of exports, on the one hand, and an attempt to counterbalance the effects of these factors through inflation on the other. In our countries, a corrective policy of a compensatory nature is difficult to apply for reasons that will be explained in due course.

We will begin by explaining the nature of the structural phenomenon, summarizing briefly what we have been expounding for some time in ECLA.

EXPORTS AS A FACTOR LIMITING GROWTH

The growth of exports places an upper limit on the rate of development in a peripheral country. This limit is set by the intensity with which the demand for imports expands with the growth of per capita income. A simple example will serve to illustrate this point. Let us suppose that primary exports grow at an annual rate of 2 per cent per capita. Per capita income can rise at the same rate only if the demand for imports also increases at 2 per cent, that is, if the income-elasticity is 1. But if imports expand at a higher rate, it will not be possible for per capita income to rise spontaneously at the same rate as exports. If imports tend to expand by 1.50 for each 1 per cent of increase in per capita income, the latter cannot rise by as much as 2 per cent, since in that case the demand for imports would go up by 3 per cent, thus exceeding the rate of 2 per cent at which exports increase. Obviously an external imbalance of this kind could not continue for long.[2] If development is to be accompanied by external balance, the annual growth of per capita income must not exceed 1.33, since this rate, given the income-elasticity of demand for imports, will result in a growth of 2 per cent in imports, that is, the same rate as for exports.

Consequently, if per capita income is to rise more rapidly, import substitution is essential. In the example given above, an annual per capita import-substitution rate of 1 per cent is required if income is to grow by 2 per cent. A 3 per cent rise in income would require an expansion of 4.5 per cent in import demand, of which 2.5 per cent would have to be met from domestic production in order to maintain this rate of growth in conjunction with a dynamic equilibrium.

The rate of growth of exports in Latin American countries has in fact generally been much lower than that in the above illustration, and in some cases exports have declined instead of grown. Hence the great proportions which the substitution process has had to assume.

This disparity in the trends of external trade is a consequence of the well-known fact that, as per capita income grows, the demand for industrial goods tends to expand more rapidly than the demand for

[2] In the interest of simplification, a balance of payments consisting only of imports and exports is assumed; at this juncture it would be pointless to include other balance-of-payments components.

primary commodities. Peripheral countries import the former and export the latter, whereas the position of the major industrial countries is exactly the reverse. In the industrial countries, import substitution can in no way be justified on the grounds of growth; if it takes place for other reasons, income-elasticity of demand for primary commodities tends to become weaker still, with the result that the peripheral countries which export those commodities have to intensify their substitution policy in order to maintain the same rate of income growth.

It follows from the above arguments that, even with the same population increase, a peripheral country cannot attain the same rate of spontaneous growth as the industrial centers with which it trades, because of differences of elasticity, which are generally rendered even greater by the protectionist policies applied by these centers. Hence import substitution (and the development of industrial exports to the centers) is a *sine qua non* for rectifying these differences. Since the peripheral countries of Latin America have a much more rapid population growth than the industrial centers, the process has to be proportionately more vigorous.

The substitution process has to be steadily maintained so long as income continues to grow more than exports, even when the coefficient of elasticity of demand for imports is not constant, as was assumed for the sake of simplification in the illustrative example. This depends on the rate of growth of per capita income, on the changes in import demand arising from technical developments and consumer preferences, on changes in the composition of imports caused by substitution policy, and on the cost of the substitutions.

IMPROVISION OF SUBSTITUTION POLICY

If there were in practice a regular and constant increase in exports, it would be comparatively easy to determine the extent of the substitution effort required annually. Unfortunately this is not so, since exports are subject to a continuous undulating movement which makes the systematic application of this policy difficult.

When exports increase comparatively rapidly during the favorable phase of this cyclical movement, the domestic economy can obtain all the imports required for its development and there is no apparent need for substitution. All is well so long as exports continue to rise or are maintained at a high level, and provided that a prudent monetary policy has been pursued. This latter aspect will be dealt with below. But as soon as exports fall off, the country finds that its income in the aggregate has grown to such an extent that the volume of imports required is higher than what can be paid for by its declining exports. An import-substitution policy therefore has to be improvised. It is generally applied not as a prudent measure that anticipates the demands of development, but as a step imposed by critical circumstances when there is already an external disequilibrium.

The frequent result of this has been that considerations of economic feasibility and of anticyclic flexibility are left out of account. Moreover, the inescapable need to protect substitution activities, and the various extreme forms which such protection usually assumes, create conditions unfavorable to export development and thus increase the tendency to disequilibrium. All this points to the need for a review of substitution policy.

Above all, it is essential to adopt substitution measures in advance without waiting until external disequilibrium imposes them as an unavoidable necessity. It is precisely in the ascending phase, when savings are mounting and there are greater resources for importing capital goods, that special emphasis should be laid on substitution policy.

How can substitutions be planned in advance? How can the pressure of future events be forestalled? This is a problem to which the secretariat of ECLA has long been devoting attention, and it was with this in mind that the first analyses and projections of economic development were attempted. Sufficient progress has now been made to enable us to determine the requirements of an important substitution policy.

THE ECONOMIC FEASIBILITY OF IMPORT SUBSTITUTION

Much less progress has been made in elucidating the problem of the economic feasibility of substitution activities. Generally speaking, it has been undertaken in the light of considerations of circumstance rather than on the basis of a selective criterion. When external disequilibrium arises, the reaction often is to restrict imports of finished consumer goods by measures which, albeit unintentionally, involve the promotion of substitution production, regardless of the type of goods concerned.

The laudable aim of thus facilitating imports essential to economic activity at the expense of finished consumer goods has led to increasing rigidity in the composition of imports, with serious consequences for some countries. These consequences may also be felt in other countries if a rational and farsighted substitution policy is not followed.

What has happened is that the structure of imports has become so distorted that the imports are limited to raw materials, intermediate goods vital to the maintenance of economic activity, and a few capital goods, together with essential items for direct consumption. As a result, any subsequent appreciable contraction in the capacity to import has a depressive effect on the economy, because it becomes difficult to obtain these essential and urgently needed goods from abroad. It remains a paradox that industrialization, instead of helping greatly to soften the internal impact of external fluctuations, is bringing us to a new and unknown type of external vulnerability.

All this is of great importance not only for the proper functioning of monetary policy but also for economic development policy itself, and consequently it is essential to formulate a substitution policy whereby the requirements of economic feasibility and the aim of endowing the economy with the strongest possible structural resistance to external fluctuations are combined.

Reasons of economic feasibility should induce us again to create a situation in which it would be possible to import a wide range of finished consumer goods for which substitution production would be less economic than that of other goods. By this means the reducible margin of imports could be restored in whole or in part, an essential condition of anticyclic flexibility.

DISCRIMINATION AGAINST EXPORTS

Obviously the development of new exports, in addition to traditional lines, would help considerably to achieve this aim. This brings us to the other fundamental error: an asymmetrical development policy. The need for import substitution and for the consequent protection of substitution activities has been unavoidable. But there has been a failure to boost exports to the same extent. There has been discrimination in favor of industrial substitution and against exports, mainly industrial exports. The ideal policy would have been to promote exports in order to place them once more on an equal footing with substitution activities, which does not necessarily mean equal incentives.

This aspect is sufficiently important to merit examination as follows. Limitation of external demand for primary exports makes it necessary to devote part of the *increase* in the factors of production to substitution activities. As their productivity is lower than in the industrial centers, they need to be given a certain subsidy in the form of tariff protection. Yet there would be possibilities of using a smaller subsidy to develop new industrial export activities, whereby a greater quantity of industrial goods could be obtained through trade than those that could be manufactured by substitution production.

By subsidizing substitution production rather than production intended for new exports (industrial or primary), export opportunities have been lost which, had they been properly used, would have reduced the scope of substitution policy or made more rapid economic growth possible.

This is admittedly a problem for which there is no simple practical solution, but it is unquestionably true that the lack of subsidy policy, especially for new exports and, even more, the negative subsidy that monetary overvaluation sometimes constitutes, have caused the Latin American countries to miss export opportunities, to the detriment of their economic development.

However, it should be recalled that some countries, conscious of this need to encourage exports, have resorted to multiple rates of exchange. It is open to question whether this is the best formula. At all events, multiple rates of exchange have been rejected by the school of monetary orthodoxy, without the application in their stead of any rational subsidy policy, which, it might be added, might come up against other forms of doctrinaire opposition. All these questions should be thoroughly debated, and it is to be hoped that, when countries review their policies of economic cooperation with Latin America, this subject will receive the attention it deserves.

In the matter of new exports, there is one thing that is self-evident: if external demand makes it possible to employ the whole of the increase in the active population and other factors of production on customary exports, it would be absurd to embark on substitution activities that would yield a lower net product. This is, in essence, the classic argument of an essentially static character.

However, it can happen that, by increasing exports beyond a certain point, prices fall both for the increment and for those that already existed, and the resultant net product is often lower than that which could be obtained by substitution activities, and may even be negative. This is the basic argument in favor of protection in developing countries whose exports have a much lower income-elasticity of demand in the rest of the world than industrial imports have in the Latin American countries.

The Internal Impact of External Fluctuations

THE INTERNAL CYCLIC UPSWING

In the preceding section it was explained how, when exports underwent a cyclic decline, the economy's over-all income—as a result of its previous growth—required a volume of imports larger than exports permitted. Income would thus have to contract until the consequent reduction of imports restored the export-import balance. This is the requirement of an orthodox policy of monetary stability.

Thus, through successive expansions and contractions, the spontaneous growth of the internal economy follows the tempo imposed by exports, if no substitution policy has been followed. The country is then faced with the dilemma, referred to above, of choosing between monetary stability, which requires domestic activity to contract until over-all income has been reduced to a level consistent with exports, and inflationary credit expansion to counteract the contraction in the economy, to the detriment of monetary stability. Before analyzing this question, however, it is advisable to consider the course followed by the internal economy during this undulating movement of exports.

This movement is generally accompanied by a change in the terms of trade, which improve during the ascending phase and deteriorate when exports decline, with a consequent change in the profits and other returns from this branch of production. Thus there is heavier demand for goods and services in internal activities, and production increases, both because of a greater use of productive capacity and because that capacity is expanded by new investment.

Entrepreneurs in internal activities also get a higher return on these new investments, because of the fall in costs that accompanies the better utilization of capacity and because of the rise in domestic prices. The extent to which this occurs depends mainly on the form and methods adopted for limiting imports in order to protect domestic production. If this is done by customs duties that merely compensate for differences in productivity between domestic and foreign output, without providing any excessive margin of profit for the entrepreneur, the rise in domestic prices tends to be moderate, as foreign competition makes itself felt instantly. If, on the other hand, the protective margin is large, or if imports are limited by bans or direct restrictive measures, domestic prices may rise considerably, even without the stimulus of an inflationary credit expansion.

However this may be, the general rise in profits facilitates further investment, with a consequent increase in employment, although generally not at the expense of consumer activities. Employment shows an upward trend in both forms of activity, but more especially in investment activities, because of the growth of the active population. Public investment and expenditure also tend to increase, as a result of higher tax returns, especially when these are closely linked with foreign trade.

When the over-all income of the economy is thus expanded, there tends to be a stronger general upward movement in the growth rate of imports—that is, there is a cyclic increase in their coefficient—owing to changes in income distribution in favor of entrepreneurs and other social groups high on the income distribution scale.

In this ascending phase, easy credit and new opportunities for expenditure and investment stimulate the expansion of credit beyond the point required by the increment in business activity. This expansion tends to speed up utilization of the economy's idle capacity and to broaden it, so that imports proceed at a brisker pace. In general terms, it can be stated that inflationary credit expansion tends to increase imports to a corresponding extent.

THE CYCLIC DOWNSWING

A decline in exports and a deterioration in the terms of trade naturally lead to phenomena of an opposite kind. First, over-all demand falls off as a result of contracting demand in the export sector; this, coupled with the decrease in revenue, discourages investment, thereby reducing employment in export activities, with further depressive effects on over-all employment, income, and imports.

The State, of course, suffers from the same depressive effects as a result of falling tax revenue; and the endeavor to maintain the level of its expenditure and investment generally leads to a deficit, with its inevitable inflationary effects. These effects tend to relieve the contraction of the economy and to give private investment further encouragement, and for this purpose recourse is usually had to credit expansion, also, which leads to further compensatory effects on over-all economic activity.

However, if the impact of a contraction in exports on over-all income is counteracted in this way, the decline in imports is prevented or attenuated, thereby intensifying external disequilibrium. The continuation of such a policy makes monetary depreciation inevitable.

THE IMPORT LAG

For a better understanding of the nature and magnitude of this external disequilibrium, attention must be given to the way in which a growth in exports entails an increase in imports as part of the undulating movement. This phenomenon could be explained in the following way. When there is no inflationary pressure, imports always lag behind exports; but while, during the upswing, this lag indicates a surplus of exports over imports and accordingly an accumulation of foreign currency, during the downswing the exact opposite occurs, because the previously accumulated foreign currency reserves are used up. These reserves will not be completely exhausted if exports stop declining at a level higher than their starting point, which is customary in their growth process.

If inflationary pressure makes itself felt—that is, if part of public or private investment is financed with bank credit instead of genuine savings—imports will tend to rise with greater rapidity and approach or even exceed exports during the upward phase. At all events, inflationary investment—or inflationary expenditure covered by bank credit—by accentuating the growth of imports will tend to bring about external disequilibrium proportionate to the magnitude of such investment. For these reasons, monetary reserves tend to shrink more than they otherwise would, and if inflationary pressure is very strong, monetary reserves may not only lose all the ground they have gained but may even fall below their previous level. This phenomenon usually occurs in an acute form during the downswing when inflationary pressure originating in the previous phase, added to the pressure that continues to develop later, intensifies the external disequilibrium characteristic of this phase of the cycle.

COMPENSATORY EFFECTS OF INFLATION

The decline in exports is evidenced both by the inadequacy of internal demand and by excess demand for imports until the contraction in income reestablishes external equilibrium. Thus, if exports decrease by 1,000 and the import coefficient is 0.20—we shall suppose it to be constant for purposes of simplification—the first impact of the reduction will be a fall of 800 in internal demand and of only 200 in imports, compared with the drop of 1,000 in exports.

The fall in internal demand will bring over-all income down with it until the latter is sufficiently low to bring about a decrease in imports to the same extent as exports. On the basis of the foregoing example, this will occur when over-all income falls to 5,000.

The credit expansion which usually occurs then is not always a spontaneous consequence of economic contraction, for it is sometimes the expression of an anticyclic policy. At all events, expansion tends to correct the inadequacy of demand. At the same time, however, it prevents a decline in imports and thus runs counter to the re-establishment of external equilibrium. In our example, an expansion of 1,000 will offset the fall in exports and the gap of 800 in internal demand. But imports will fail to decline and external disequilibrium will be equivalent to the amount of the drop in exports. Naturally, disequilibrium leads to a monetary devaluation which, in its turn, tends to bring about external equilibrium by restricting imports and promoting exports.

But this policy of an inflationary nature has very serious defects, since its positive effects depend essentially on the regressive redistribution of income. In fact, devaluation leads to price rises—if this has not already occurred—with the resultant redistribution of income in favor of entrepreneurs and high-income groups in general.

Such income redistribution generates certain changes in the composition of demand: it reduces the demand of the broad masses and boosts that of the high-income groups. Apart from its social effects, this would have no adverse effect on the total volume of internal demand if the investment coefficients of demand of the broad masses and of the high-income groups were the same. But this does not happen in practice; the coefficient of the latter is usually higher.

Thus a new problem arises. A reduction of the import coefficient is essential to correct external disequilibrium. But, as the demand for imports of the high-income groups tends to remain at the same level, or to rise, depending on the intensity of inflationary pressure, the contraction necessarily makes itself felt on the rest of the imports. The very decrease in consumption suffered by the mass of the population has depressive effects on internal activity and thereby makes for a regressive readjustment of imports.

As a result, the inflationary redistribution produces two opposite effects. By expanding investment, it tends to maintain internal economic activity at a level higher than is justified by exports. At the same time, however, the increased imports of the groups favored by the redistribution tend to limit the scope of this process.

It is therefore not strange that intensive credit inflation may be accompanied by inadequate use of productive capacity or may result in a slow rate of income growth, if no direct measures are taken to modify the composition of imports.

POSSIBILITIES OF AN ANTICYCLIC POLICY

Inflationary expansion is far from being a satisfactory anticyclic instrument. Would it be possible to pursue a policy of expansion without inflationary consequences? Can a fiscal deficit possibly be used in our countries to counteract external contraction without inflation ensuing?

It should be remembered that, even if inflationary credit expansion counterbalances the inadequacy of internal demand, such expansion constitutes an obstacle to the reestablishment of external equilibrium by preventing a readjustment of imports. An apparently simple problem thus arises: to divert excess demand for imports toward internal demand, to compensate in a noninflationary way for the shortage resulting from the fall in exports. In practice such an operation involves serious difficulties. Let us examine the chief of these.

For it to be possible to divert the excess demand for imports, it is essential that there should be an easily reducible margin. The most favorable case is when this margin consists of imports which can be cut or abolished without lowering the level of employment or affecting mass consumption unfavorably.

Let us suppose that the articles concerned are for the high-income groups. Part of the excess demand can be absorbed by import taxes. These taxes must be high enough to divert the rest of the excess demand toward the internal market. This diversion will be converted into inflationary demand pressure to the extent that there is no idle capacity in the economy. And the only way to avoid this is by absorbing the excess demand by means of new taxes of an internal nature.

In this way all the excess demand—except that part which has been covered by the aforesaid idle capacity and the resultant rise in employment—will have been collected by the State in the form of taxes. The resources accumulated in this way enable the State to cover the investments which formerly were made in an inflationary manner and thereby to ensure employment for that part of the labor force not absorbed by fuller utilization of the available capacity referred to above.

The operation consists essentially in shifting excess demand for imports to internal demand for the factors occupied in investment activities. This is, however, a simple case. Let us now examine the complications, first those arising from the composition of the reducible margin and then those resulting from the inadequacy of that margin.

Let us suppose that, in order to restore external equilibrium, the import share of the high-income groups is insufficient and it is essential to replace the imports that form a direct part of mass consumption. To carry out an operation similar to the previous one would be tantamount to placing a direct burden on mass consumption; but if this burden is eschewed, inflationary pressure will emerge which will, in any event, make prices rise in the same way as if the burden had been applied. In both cases there is the danger of setting off the spiral already referred to. There is no alternative but to obtain financial aid from international sources to cover investments to an extent equivalent to the inflationary pressure. And this is even more cogent if the reducible margin is insufficient or if resources are lacking to cover all the imports essential to the maintenance of the level of economic activity. The only solution is international aid.

Careful examination of the problem reveals that the policy we are considering consists of maintaining the volume of investment which was previously made in an inflationary way, but covering it with savings provided by taxes and with international financial assistance. Such international aid is essential when imports vital to mass consumption or economic activity cannot be reduced. It is conceivable that a higher level of internal savings might be achieved which would cover all investment, but this would not solve the problem, because the lack of resources for essential imports would make it necessary to restrict mass consumption—or lower the level of economic activity—which would also have unfavorable effects for the population at large.

This is not all, however. Covering essential imports in this way is a temporary device until structural transformations are introduced to restore dynamic external equilibrium on a more lasting basis. It is therefore essential to invest capital in import substitution and export industries. Insofar as the absence of internal savings or the extent or composition of the reducible margin leaves no room for corresponding imports of capital goods, international financial assistance will also be required.

All this follows a logical line of reasoning. In practice, however, it would run into two serious difficulties. First, a greater internal savings effort through taxes or the floating of loans is required when a drop in exports has already weakened saving capacity. Second, recourse is had to international aid as a normal part of an anticyclic policy.

INTERNATIONAL FINANCIAL ASSISTANCE

The difficulty does not lie solely in the deep-rooted reluctance of international credit institutions to cover internal investments, which would seem to have no very serious basis, but rather in a consideration far more deserving of attention. The amount of international assistance that a country requires must correspond to the rate of growth it wishes to maintain, or attain, and to the savings effort it can make. But if considerations connected with anticyclic policy enter into the picture, the amount of international resources required could easily be exaggerated.

Again, a compensatory policy might require a type of internal investment—public works and construction, for example—which would exceed the level proper to a rational distribution of available resources among the various investment requirements. In other words, as a result of this type of anticyclic policy, excessive resources might be used for such investments to the detriment, to cite one example, of the production or importation of machinery and equipment.

International financial assistance can be justified as a means of supplementing the scant savings in our countries but not as a normal part of anticyclic policy to cover the imports required for the maintenance of economic activity. The solution does not lie there, but in a farsighted policy of import substitution that anticipates the cyclic decline of exports so as to obviate—or at least mitigate—its effect on the internal economy.

These considerations are relevant to anticyclic policy but not to means for stemming inflation. Contributions from national resources to cover external disequilibrium while the above-mentioned measures are being taken to deal with it fundamentally are usually a *sine qua non*.

Structural Equilibrium

CURRENCY DEVALUATION AS AN AGENT OF STRUCTURAL EQUILIBRIUM

Are direct measures likely to be necessary to deal effectively with structural disequilibrium or is devaluation sufficient? The school of monetary orthodoxy usually advocates devaluation in all cases, whether the phenomenon is basically structural or merely a temporary departure from structural equilibrium. Neither the nature nor the effects of devaluation are the same in the two cases.

A departure from structural equilibrium usually occurs in our countries in the event of currency overvaluation. A rise in internal prices unaccompanied by a similar movement in import and export prices leads to disequilibrium by encouraging the former and discouraging the latter. This disparity may originate in inflationary pressure on prices or in an upward movement of wages and salaries to a figure unjustified by the level of productivity.

So long as there are no obstacles to an increase in imports, the rise in internal prices will be confined to those goods and services which are not linked to external trade, so that external disequilibrium is merely a direct consequence of inflationary pressure. If direct restrictive measures are applied to lessen or correct disequilibrium, the rise in prices will spread to the whole economy and occasion a readjustment in salaries and wages.

Such a readjustment will cause the cost of exports to rise but not their prices, owing to monetary overvaluation; and likewise it will affect those branches of production that compete with imports of articles which, for one reason or another, are free of restrictions. The damage which exports and the other aforementioned branches of production suffer makes devaluation indispensable if competitive conditions are to be reestablished and the flow of external trade restored on a balanced basis. The same occurs when the increase in prices is caused by a rise in wages and salaries unjustified by productivity.

The case is very different when disequilibrium results from growth of income beyond the level justified by exports. This is the structural disequilibrium which occurs when exports fall off, as we saw earlier. If, in order to maintain or raise the level of internal activity, recourse is had to credit expansion, with resulting devaluation, this will tend to reestablish equilibrium even though accompanied by the regressive effects mentioned earlier.

In this case, devaluation acts in a different way. The prices of exports and imports rise and, as costs are not adjusted simultaneously, an extraordinarily large margin of profit is generated which, while encouraging traditional exports and promoting the development of new lines, brings into being hitherto nonexistent import-substitution activities and offers an incentive to those already in operation.

But, as wages and salaries mount, these effects gradually diminish; and, in order to keep productive activity at the higher level achieved, it becomes necessary either to resort to further devaluation or to take steps to place direct restrictions on imports or subsidize specific exports.

It might be argued that the rise in remuneration need not keep pace with devaluation, since competition will prevent prices from moving up, except in the case of new activities which may have cost more to develop. It is possible to think along these lines, although practices restricting competition frequently combine to push up prices to the extent permitted by the greater margin of protection afforded by devaluation.

When this fact sooner or later entails an adjustment in wages and salaries correlative to devaluation, the latter loses its effectiveness. In other words, devaluation acts in this case solely as a stabilizing factor so long as it has regressive effects on income distribution.

It is true that import prices may be prevented from rising—except for imports to be replaced by nationally produced items—if devaluation is accompanied by a proportional cut in customs duties for all existing industries, so as to avoid double protection. The protection provided by tariffs would thus be wholly or partly replaced by the protection resulting from devaluation. Consequently, the rise in prices would be confined to items produced by the new substitution activities, whose cost is higher than that of the articles previously imported.

An adjustment in wages and salaries, which is justifiable when there are extraordinary profits, would not be an adequate solution in this case, since there would be no such profits, and it would lead to an inflationary spiral. Other measures should therefore be adopted to prevent the rise in prices from affecting the consumption of the population at large.

From the point of view of exports, the incentive given by devaluation to traditional items might bring about a deterioration in the terms of trade, if one country's products constituted a substantial proportion of the international supply. Steps would then have to be taken to restrict exports, either by taxes and duties which would absorb all, or part, of the extraordinary profit, or by direct controls. The incentive to devaluation would thus be confined to new exports.

Measures of this kind imply deliberate intervention in the economy and lessen the prestige which devaluation normally enjoys as an automatic method of restoring equilibrium "by allowing money to find its own level." Moreover, such action is very seldom taken, because the amount of devaluation is usually determined by the particular effect that it is desired to produce.

The question is therefore one of economic policy, and the advantages and disadvantages of such a method have to be compared in practice with those of other measures, such as direct export subsidies, import substitution, and protective tariffs.

THE GOLD STANDARD AND STRUCTURAL EQUILIBRIUM

Those who uphold the theory of monetary orthodoxy usually fail to see the problem of Latin American structural equilibrium as clearly as they might, despite the constant prompting of a reality which they prefer to ignore. They have inherited the fundamental principles of the gold standard and apply them to the policy of monetary stability. The adherents of the classic theory did not notice the structural problem, nor had they any reason to notice it in the golden age of the gold standard under British hegemony.

The operation of the gold standard did not jeopardize in any way the structural equilibrium of the world economy, since the British center, with its individual structure, had found in the peripheral countries and the dynamic centers a structural adaptability which facilitated the movement of gold in either direction. It is not surprising, therefore, that equilibrium was believed to be inherent in the operation of the gold standard. But, at the end of the last century and in the early 1900's, the main dynamic center began to feel the consequences of certain structural changes in the rest of the world which were accompanied by constant signs of instability. I refer in particular to the repercussions of the process taking place in the other dynamic centers (for example, Germany) and of protectionism, and to certain monetary procedures that tended to keep gold in the leading countries.

One result of this was of great importance: the British center began to lose its knack of drawing back the gold that it sent out. Clear proof of the perplexity and distress which this caused the monetary authorities is to be found in Sir John Clapham's book on the Bank of England, the first written by an author with access to that institution's confidential files. An interpretation of those structural phenomena was, of course, still very premature in those days. But ideas were beginning to emerge for mitigating the consequences of the centrifugal tendency of gold. Thus, long before Keynes and earlier than the First World War, it was already thought desirable for the holdings of the world's central banks to be concentrated in the British center.

It is not surprising therefore that similar events now occurring in the main dynamic center—the United States—which superseded the British center after the First World War, should be reflected in measures whose objectives are basically analogous. It is undeniable that the new dynamic center has operated in structural conditions very different from those that prevailed in earlier times and which made it difficult for the gold standard to operate. These conditions became much less favorable when, during the great world Depression, the dynamic center reduced its import coefficient while continuous increases in productivity and technical innovations stimulated the expansiveness of its exports. It was impossible for the gold standard —monetary stability—to be maintained, and in the rest of the world, the other dynamic centers and the peripheral countries were obliged to adapt their structure to the structural changes in the focal dynamic center.

The process of adaptation had lasted nearly a quarter of a century, and, as soon as it was completed, contrary phenomena affecting the main dynamic center and posing a grave problem emerged in the other dynamic centers. These other centers either must liberalize their policy as regards imports from the rest of the world, including the principal dynamic center, without prejudice to other measures of readjustment or, by *force majeure*, they will be instrumental in inducing the principal center to seek equilibrium to the detriment of international trade.

Latin American countries could not fail to take an interest in the solution of this problem, since the more active development of world trade, by enhancing their export and import opportunities, is a factor of prime importance for the acceleration of their economic growth.

A Summary of the Relation between Growth and Inflation, 1929 to 1959[3]

The Position in 1929

During the nineteenth century, the economy of every country in the region had become organized very largely around its export industries. By the time of the First World War, the main features of economic structure could be summarized as follows. A substantial part of the proceeds of exports was earned by plantations, large cattle farms, or mines. Much of this income flowed straight out again. Some of it was remitted as profits to foreign companies or absentee landowners; the rent and profits received by local property-owners were mostly spent on imports. The remainder entered the local economy by two main channels, namely, taxes on foreign trade and profits of export and import merchants. These sustained civil service bureaucracies and commercial life in the large cities, where some manufacturing activities could be found, such as food processing and the clothing industry. A considerable fraction of the population, often those of Indian or Negro stock, worked on estates, plantations, or small holdings, or on

[3] See "Inflation and Growth: A Summary of Experience in Latin America," *Economic Bulletin for Latin America*, VII, no. 1 (1962), 28–45.

communal land, for little or no remuneration, so they hardly counted as part of the consumer market. They were also cut off from the city labor markets, not merely by distance and bad transport, but also by illiteracy, lack of technical skill, and quasi-feudal obligations to their employers and landlords.

It must not be inferred from these generalizations that all economies were at the same level in the early decades of this century. The scale of manufacturing, the extent of commercial agriculture, and the degree of urbanization varied greatly. Broadly speaking, they were all much more in evidence in the southern part of Latin America, where the original pattern of colonization had been modified by the extensive immigration of artisans, entrepreneurs, and farmers. In Argentina, particularly, the economy had become quite highly unified geographically and socially, at least by comparison with that of other countries in the region.

Where the process of industrialization had already got under way, it received a vigorous impulse from the conditions produced by the war of 1914–1918. Imports became hard to obtain. Shipping grew scarce; blockades were maintained by the belligerent powers; and both European and, eventually, North American industries were diverted to the manufacture of armaments and munitions. By the nineteen-twenties, Chile, Mexico, Uruguay, and Brazil (especially the south) were well on the same road as had been taken earlier by Argentina. Substantial proportions of the population were living in urban areas, and local industries could by now satisfy a significant part of local demand. The same signs of progress were also appearing in Colombia, Cuba, Peru, and Venezuela, although the degree of self-sufficiency they showed was lower, and typical of an earlier stage of development. Meanwhile, Argentine industry was expanding into new fields, such as engineering.

Yet all the Latin American economies were still vulnerable to fluctuations in foreign trade. Their exports, which provided a high proportion of income, consisted of a few important products, perhaps only a single item, and were sold to a limited number of buyer countries. The sectors producing for export had, except in the cases of Argentina and Uruguay, very limited possibilities of selling their output inside the economy. Even those countries which were becoming industrialized, and were thus growing less dependent on the income generated by exports, were vulnerable to the vicissitudes of external trade, though in a different way. Certain types of goods, not only the more highly processed consumer goods but also nearly all capital goods and intermediate products, had to be imported. The more advanced economies were coming to rely heavily on receipts of foreign exchange to provide the materials and equipment for their industrial sectors.

Despite the progress that had been made, internal developments continued to be hampered by the lack of economic integration. Some improvement had been made in the cultivation of export crops, but little technical progress could be seen in agricultural production for the home market. While owners of large estates still used the major part of their land, even when arable, for unorganized cattle grazing, the peasants on small holdings or communal land were employing techniques which were decades or even centuries out of date. Industrial firms, lacking the domestic market they needed for large-scale production, were often inefficient and/or monopolistic.

Nevertheless, as long as world trade was buoyant, as it was in most of the nineteen-twenties, economies did continue to grow. Exports expanded, private investment by foreigners was heavy, and governments could raise considerable finance overseas for public works. Incomes rose, and with them consumption and tax revenues. The cities were able to absorb a continuous flow of migrants from the country districts, attracted not merely by higher incomes, but also by amenities and services such as electricity, water supply, and schools, and in some cases by greater security.

These physical changes in the Latin American economies had been accompanied by others of a financial nature. In the nineteenth century, a number of countries had still used dollars for local currency, while those with their own money had kept it tied to gold; foreign banks had provided most of the financial services. The countries of the southern zone, which had made most progress economically, had begun to show greater financial independence. In an attempt to alleviate the consequences of slumps in world trade, they devalued their currencies, on occasion, and often suspended convertibility into gold. In addition, locally owned commercial banks played a growing part in the financial life of the more industrialized countries, and during the nineteen-twenties several central banks were established.

These moves toward monetary independence had, however, met with setbacks from time to time. There had already been bouts with inflation, especially in Chile, and on occasion local banks had been forced to close their doors. Sometimes devaluation could be ascribed to plain mismanagement of national finance. After the severe financial crises of 1921, when commodity markets had collapsed, there was a general attempt to return to the gold standard. Latin America was in this matter following the example of European countries which were trying to reestablish the international monetary system that had broken down in the First World War.

One of the consequences was that economic policy, in its present form and scope, was not applied in 1929 in any part of the region. Observance of the rules of the gold standard meant that certain problems never arose. A shortage of foreign reserves could hardly occur, and any incipient price inflation would be braked by shortage of money before it could gather momentum. Among the virtues of the gold standard was that it achieved these ends almost automatically, and problems requiring political decision and administrative action were less acute.

Few instruments for policy had as yet been created. Taxation was relatively low, being based mainly on import duties, and since a chronic budget deficit would have been hard to finance, expenditure was also limited. Despite the moves toward financial independence, monetary systems were still hardly developed enough to give much scope for deliberate policy. Exchange controls and multiple rates were as yet unknown. In any case, the material basis for a more active and independent policy hardly existed in most countries, if the lack of local capacity for producing manufactures is taken into account. Monetary expansion would have led quickly to an increase in imports and an unacceptable loss of foreign reserves. Furthermore, the political pressures for such policies were limited, since power was effectively in the hands of those not entirely dissatisfied with developments, and even the discontented could still find some scope for the improvement of their conditions so long as the national product continued to rise and it was possible for them to move out of backward sectors of the economy.

But the almost complete absence of a deliberate economic strategy proved a serious handicap in the years that followed. Administrations were not gaining experience in formulating policy and carrying it out; statistics were not being demanded because they were not needed, so they remained almost nonexistent; and political leaders had become accustomed to thinking that economic developments were, broadly speaking, outside their control and therefore not their responsibility.

The Consequences of the Depression: New Alternatives for Economic Policy Emerge

Great though its merits were, in retrospect it is hard to believe that the major economies of the region would have been prepared, or indeed able, to maintain the rules of the gold standard indefinitely, even if fluctuations in foreign trade had been avoided. These rules implied an overriding priority for balancing payments and for stabilizing the domestic price level. Income and employment could grow and recessions could be avoided, but only if foreign trade continued to expand. Thus the rate of expansion depended in the last resort on the pace at which the national product was growing in the leading industrial countries of North America and Western Europe, a pace which might prove too slow for an area with low per capita incomes and a fast rate of population increase.

However, the question was never put to the test. The Depression which started in 1929 was so deep that the gold standard was discarded as unworkable by the whole world, including the industrial countries themselves. World trade plunged sharply, and speculative movements of capital were heavy. The leading industrial countries one after another abandoned convertibility into gold and devalued their currencies. Those that retained the gold standard, as France did, found their exports more and more difficult to market; they had to bring imports down by inducing a fall in activity, and therefore in employment, of a magnitude that in the end proved to be intolerable. The abandonment of the gold standard was the necessary condition for the adoption of anticyclical programs such as public works schemes, which became increasingly necessary.

The slump came as a particularly severe shock to Latin America. Public revenues depended heavily on the taxation of foreign trade; and investment was being largely financed by foreign companies in export industries or in sectors which were linked with them. So the decline in exports, which was in any case relatively much sharper than in the industrial countries, meant reductions in income throughout the economy. At the same time, the foreign exchange shortage was aggravated by the drying up of the inflow of short-term capital, even in some cases by its reversal. Countries which were accustomed to relying on foreign sources for a large proportion of their supplies found it hard to make the necessary cut in their imports.

Governments discarded convertibility, not only into gold, but also into foreign currencies. This led to the appearance of free markets in which exchange rates were at a discount compared with official quotations and fluctuated from day to day. These were not the only breaches that occurred in the old economic order. Like many other countries, industrial or primary producer, those in Latin America introduced import quotas in an attempt to correct the deficit in foreign payments and increased duties on imports. (The United States had raised its tariff walls in 1930, under the Smoot-Hawley Act.) Many of them also defaulted on foreign debts, as a number of European countries were doing. Furthermore, several attempts were made, not very successfully, to stabilize commodity prices by international measures to control output.

Apart from these steps, which were common to almost the whole region, one group of countries took additional measures, whereas the remainder did not, and there has been a clear distinction between these two groups ever since. The additional measures can be summed up as autonomous monetary expansion, autonomous in the sense that it was much greater than would have been justified by movements in reserves. This was accompanied by legal and institutional changes such as the establishment of new central banks, or an increase in the power of those that already existed.

The countries which did take such autonomous action were, broadly speaking, the largest and those already partially industrialized—Argentina, Brazil, Chile, Colombia, and Mexico. They had the greatest incentive to attempt some form of compensation. Unemployment was a severe problem for their large city populations, which were not by any means powerless politically, and domestic bankers were threatened by the inability to meet current obligations. These countries had, moreover, the greatest scope for action: they had industries which could supply some at least of the needs of the local consumer and absorb some of the unemployment.

It must not be thought that compensatory action was in all cases deliberately chosen as an economic strategy and that exchange control was imposed to stop the consequent loss of reserves. The crisis developed so quickly that administrations improvised as best they could. Budget deficits appeared because revenues were falling fast, and the expansion of credit was often decided on at a few hours' notice to save banks from having to close their doors.

Although it was some time before the gold standard was consciously and finally rejected, each step represented a further break with conventional monetary standards. Backing for the currency fell; further devaluation occurred vis-à-vis not merely gold, but also the United States dollar; and more controls were imposed on purchases of foreign exchange. But the Depression was gradually changing attitudes as to what constituted permissible policy. Overseas, both professional and political opinion were swinging round in favor of the conscious use of fiscal and monetary policy, backed where necessary by direct controls, to prevent or cure cyclical depressions. The practical example of the New Deal in the United States was a particularly powerful stimulus to those Latin Americans who were urging a different and more autonomous approach.

Although a number of Latin American economies had already been in some degree diversified by the end of the previous decade, the Depression demonstrated how far this process was from being complete by revealing how much they still depended on imports. Because of the shortage of foreign exchange, the imports of Argentina, Brazil, and Mexico shrank in volume by more than one-half between 1929 and 1932, and those of Chile fell by more than three-quarters. Indeed, according to the League of Nations *World Economic Report, 1932–33*, Chilean exports fell more than those of any other of the thirty-eight countries covered. The problem of maintaining living standards and limiting unemployment was in part one of adapting financial policy to the new circumstances, but in real terms it was a question of replacing imports—particularly manufactures—with domestic products on a big scale and in a short period of time.

A strong impetus was given to industrialization by the measures taken to protect reserves of foreign exchange. Devaluation, import quotas, higher tariffs—all these had the incidental effect of opening new markets for the domestic producer, or strengthening his position against foreign competition. The sudden expansion of manufacturing was not, however, easy. One obstacle was the difficulty of financing it. Investment by foreigners was now small; private savings had been depressed by the decline in incomes; and equipment had become expensive to import, because of devaluation. There were also more deeply rooted handicaps to be overcome. The labor force lacked the range of skills needed; the landowning class was often unwilling to invest time and energy in new tasks to which, whatever their economic rationale, the traditional social prestige of agricultural activity did not attach; and those in trade and commerce usually preferred to follow in their customary family business, rather than undertake the risky and exacting work of founding industrial enterprises.

As regards physical inputs, the new industries' needs for fuel, materials, and semi-manufactures were heavy. Moreover, industrialization induced an increased demand for foodstuffs in the cities. What was required, and what was indeed imposed by the circumstances, was a wholesale transformation of the economy. This placed novel demands on a transport system which had been designed mainly as ancillary to foreign trade.

The official bureaucracy was also hardly capable of meeting the administrative requirements of the new situation. There was, as in many other parts of the world, a severe shortage of civil servants capable of framing economic strategy and administering import controls in such a way as to minimize the tensions of the process. Statistics were still, in any case, of such a low quality that policy was inevitably based on "hunches" or biased information.

Although the industrial sector did, in general, grow, in response to this stimulus, the products of the new industries were usually expensive. New factories, like the old, were often very small and inefficient and competition was still far from perfect. The response of agriculture to the demands of the new situation was even more inadequate. If allowance is made for the imported fuel and equipment needed by the new industries and for heavy consumer demand, in part stimulated by excessively expansionist policies, it is not surprising that the demand for foreign exchange did not abate; exchange rates were under continuous pressure.

In Brazil, Chile, and Mexico, price levels tended to rise after 1932. This was not true of Argentina and Uruguay. One reason was that the failure of their export markets released foodstuffs which could be consumed at home. Second, Argentina had made some progress in industrialization previously: a sizable industrial sector was already in existence at the start of the slump, with some surplus capacity, so substitution for imports involved a less radical departure from previous economic patterns. Third, both countries were reasonably supplied with basic social capital, such as transport and electricity, which facilitated the establishment of new industries; and the social environment itself made it easier than elsewhere to find entrepreneurs and suitable workers. Fourth, Argentina's fiscal and monetary policy was managed in such a way as to offset the effects of fluctuations in foreign trade; and, finally, industrialization there was relatively well balanced.

This experience is an interesting illustration of the relative significance of monetary and real factors, which was discussed above. It is possible to attribute currency devaluation and price rises to the laxness of the authorities, who expanded the supply of money, thus permitting government deficits to occur contemporaneously with the extension of more credit to the private sector. If this monetary expansion had not occurred, prices and exchange rates would probably have changed very little over the whole decade. But we must take into account the context of monetary policy. Faced with a catastrophic fall in exports, which was the original cause of the trouble, those responsible for policy had to make a series of choices between unpleasant alternatives. When revenue fell off, for example, governments were presented with a dilemma. On the one hand, they could make equally drastic reductions in expenditure and face the social implications of this, at a time when unemployment was already rising to dangerous levels. Alternatively, they could resort to deficit financing. Similarly, the monetary authorities had to decide whether to contract credit when their foreign reserves declined, and they had to make this decision at a time when commercial banks and business houses were already under severe financial stress. In many cases, the strain on the balance of payments and price inflation would have been much less if policy had been carefully framed, but the authorities ran risks either way, whether their policy was expansionist or restrictive. In several large economies, they chose rising prices and devaluation rather than falling incomes and unemployment.

In view of the political circumstances of the times in these countries, which included civil disturbance, it is doubtful whether any other choice was possible. Authorities who tried to adhere to strictly orthodox policies were usually removed from office.

Most of the remaining countries of the region either refrained from carrying out autonomous monetary policies, or at any rate did less in this direction, and gave up sooner. In the small economies of Central America and the Caribbean area the need and the opportunity for such policies were both limited. For one thing, urban proletariats were relatively smaller. While the Depression meant severe hardship, a great part of the population worked in subsistence sectors only remotely affected by fluctuations in the commercial part of the economy. Political pressure from this quarter to maintain incomes was therefore not very strong. The banking systems were, moreover, largely in foreign hands and there was opposition to measures which might lead to devaluation of the currency.

In any event, the scope for expansionist policies was quite limited in economics which were still essentially dependent on exports and with relatively small manufacturing sectors. A country at an incipient stage of industrialization is particularly deficient in the economic, social, and political conditions for further progress in this direction.

The countries of the region are usually divided into two groups. Exchange rates of countries in the Caribbean area and Central America which had suffered *de facto* devaluation nearly all regained the former parity with the United States dollar, or something close to it, as the Depression came to an end, making their currencies once more convertible into dollars. They were in effect now on a dollar standard and they continued to maintain orthodox financial practices in the following decades as well. These countries have experienced only moderate price rises over the past three decades. Nicaragua has reverted to more conservative practices in the past decade and price rises have slowed down there; Ecuador can also be included in the group, taking the period as a whole.

Venezuela falls into this class too. It possessed in petroleum an export which, until quite recently, has proved easy to market, and earnings of foreign exchange have climbed very rapidly. Even in the Depression, the upward trend was halted rather than reversed. The need for compensatory policy did not, therefore, arise in the nineteen-thirties, and the Venezuelan bolivar was so strong that it appreciated vis-à-vis the United States dollar.

There are therefore eleven countries which have followed, in general, orthodox policies in the matter of reserves for most of the past thirty years and which have, on the whole, experienced only moderate increases in prices. These countries will be known as Group O. They are mostly small economies, unindustrialized and heavily dependent on foreign trade. Even Cuba and Venezuela, although much larger, had in 1950 only narrow manufacturing sectors by comparison with their export industries. This type of economic structure tended to be preserved, as in certain other countries, by reciprocal trade agreements with the United States, which offered special marketing advantages for sugar and petroleum, in return for undertaking to restrict the protection of local industries.

The other nine countries of Latin America (Group U) have mostly followed less orthodox financial policies and have experienced, particularly in the past decade, steady-to-fast price inflation and a series of devaluations. Seven of these are the more industrialized economies of the region, and most of them are also large and highly urbanized. As a general rule, exports account for a smaller proportion of output. Bolivia and Paraguay are the other two countries which have followed unorthodox financial policies. Paraguay began to do so after the war. Structurally and in size they belong to the former group; but precisely because they lacked the industrial capacity needed for an expansionist policy, they experienced particularly violent bouts of inflation. They thus form a special class.

The Common Problems of the War Years

The fundamental contrast between these types of economy was for a time not very obvious. When the world pulled out of the Depression, Latin American imports rose, and local price inflation slowed to a halt. Accordingly, by the end of the nineteen-thirties, movements in prices appeared to be once more in step. During the war they accelerated again in almost every country.

This even occurred in economies of Group O. Their exports rose in nearly every case. The entire crops of the sugar-producing countries were purchased, usually by the United States; and firm contracts were offered by the same country for supplies of certain minerals, cereals, and agricultural materials. Some countries, for example, Haiti, were provided with financial and technical assistance for the development of new products. Even nonessentials like cacao and coffee profited from high prices. An exception was banana exports, which fell to very low levels; because of the need for special shipping facilities, bananas did not have much priority in the supply programs of belligerent countries.

But imports were prevented from rising in step with exports. Goods from Western Europe became increasingly difficult to obtain. These could largely be replaced by purchases from the United States, up to the time of the attack on Pearl Harbor; thenceforth the conversion of industry to war purposes in the United States, the shortage of shipping space, and submarine warfare in the Caribbean area severely limited supplies to Latin America. In some cases, the landed cost of imports rose, but the rise was limited because of price controls in the United States.

The expansion of incomes in export industries was therefore much bigger than the rise in the value of imports, and the automatic brake on inflation in dollar-standard countries ceased to function. Increases in foreign reserves induced an expansion of credit and thus stimulated investment in other sectors, so that the total expansion in demand was big. But these economies were quite unable to satisfy certain types of demand themselves. The net result was a moderate-to-fast rise in prices.

The situation was not, in broad outline, very different in the countries which had been following more expansive monetary policies in the nineteen-thirties. Heavy exports were expanding demand, and internal activity was stimulated, not only by an export surplus, but also by a great increase in the liquidity of some banking systems, and an influx of foreign capital from investors seeking refuge from the war. In some cases, the authorities tried to dampen the effect on credit of the growth of reserves. In Colombia, increases in deposits had to be invested in nonnegotiable bonds, which businesses were also compelled to buy, and in Mexico the authorities sold gold to absorb currency, besides taking measures to limit credit. Authorities in other countries, however, followed less stringent policies: now that the rules of the gold standard had been abandoned, there was no generally accepted set of principles for guiding policy.

A further fillip was given to import substitution, although the reason was no longer the shortage of foreign exchange. The nine countries in Group U were beset not merely by the same supply problems as the other group, but also, excepting Mexico and Colombia, with the additional difficulty of long hauls from the United States to their ports. Yet the very circumstances that made it difficult to import finished products also discouraged purchases of the machinery, materials, and fuel needed to manufacture them domestically.

Demand for the products of local secondary industry was so high that it stretched capacity to the limit. And the war revealed weaknesses in other sectors. In Peru, for example, food imports were cut by five-sixths between 1940 and 1942; and while local production was stimulated, areas of chronic shortage emerged, because of the poor communications inside the country. In Brazil, fuel was a serious problem. Wood and coffee were widely used as sources of energy; coal and gasoline were rationed; gasoline was increasingly adulterated with alcohol, and by 1942 cars and trucks were running on gas generated from alcohol and lignite. In Argentina, too, there was an acute shortage of energy supplies. In 1943 alone, 1.7 million tons of wheat, 1.5 million tons of flax and linseed, and 0.1 million tons of maize were burned as fuel. Another general weakness in the region was in basic metals; great efforts were made to develop local resources of iron ore, and such furnaces that existed were used intensively. The shortage of equipment was possibly most severe in transport. The railway from São Paulo to Rio de Janeiro, for example, was at times only allowed to carry foodstuffs and fuels.

These weaknesses did not check the rate of growth. Despite difficulties, important investments were made. For example, construction of the Volta Redonda steel plant was started in Brazil, and industries for making simple types of capital goods were established there. The consequence in many countries was a tendency toward rising prices, rather than stagnation. In the effort to avoid the dangers of inflation, governments once more followed the example of the industrial countries. Although some excess demand was considered inevitable in the United Kingdom and the United States because of the heavy burden of financing the war, a serious attempt was made to control prices in both these countries on the grounds that inflation would hamper the war effort. Price-control plans were also drawn up in Latin America, in some cases with the assistance of United States experts. In a number of countries, these were highly detailed: local price committees were set up in every Paraguayan town, for example; the Peruvian Government controlled food distribution; and in Brazil and Colombia, price controls were backed by elaborate systems of checking inventories and licensing production and imports. In practice, Latin American schemes seem to have had very much less success, judging by price indices, than those of the developed countries.

The smallest price increases for this group occurred once again in Argentina. Rents were frozen there, but the main explanation, as in the Depression, was that the structure of supply was more attuned to that of demand than in the other countries. Supplies of foodstuffs that could not be sold to overseas customers were diverted into the home market, and government controls were used to prevent food prices from falling too sharply. Industry was better placed to cope with the situation. It was able, for example, to keep much of the existing equipment in service by repairing or reconditioning it locally.

The degree of inflation in various countries could again be explained by referring to changes in the means of payment; but this is not particularly enlightening. The origin of the problem was that imports were being reduced while exports were rising. It was this that led to a general expansion of credit and incomes in the countries wherever special steps were not taken to prevent it. Moreover, the shortage of imports was simultaneously creating supply bottlenecks which could not be relieved until more food, fuel, materials, and equipment could be ordered from overseas. Consequently, price increases in particular commodities, notably food, led to wage demands. A purely monetary approach might lead to the conclusion that financial policy could have dealt with the whole problem successfully; certainly a firmer fiscal and monetary policy in many countries would have checked the general excess demand and reduced the pace of inflation. But supply problems in certain sectors could hardly be eased by global policies.

The Immediate Postwar Period: The Reemergence of Economic Policy Alternatives

The years following the cessation of hostilities were, like the middle of the nineteen-twenties, a period of prosperity in primary-producing countries. Reserves were high and exports rose rapidly as transport difficulties were eased. The industrial countries required big increases in supplies of primary commodities to enable them to reconvert their industries to peacetime needs and to build up their inventories of all goods from intermediate to final products.

Banking systems in Latin America were characterized by the liquidity of their assets, and segments of the public held big bank deposits, so demand was buoyant. All types of imports rose rapidly. The rise in imports of fuel and materials eased the restraints on domestic production. It took, however, a certain time to make up for the years in which investment had lagged, when no equipment had been bought for transport, or electric power, or to reequip local industries—for one reason because there were such long delays before orders for capital goods could be filled. Therefore, certain shortages still lingered on.

Price structures were quite distorted by the time the war came to an end. As international trade was resumed, it became clear that many Latin American currencies were overvalued, and shortages and controls had produced internal price relationships which were not likely to endure. It is theoretically possible for such distortions to be corrected by rises in some prices and falls in others. But under the booming conditions of trade, with rising export and import prices and some persistent shortages, the general movement was upward.

In different parts of the region, experience once again started to diverge. In the countries of Group O, currencies remained fully convertible, and these countries, together with Canada and the United States, became known as the "dollar area," or the "hard currency area." Here the rise in prices was limited. As imports climbed and reserves declined—if not in absolute terms, at least in relation to the national product—the conventional monetary machinery for stabilizing the balance of payments and checking price inflation was gradually reestablished. The price rises which did occur in these countries after the war were mainly the reflection of developments abroad. Because many of them import not merely manufactures but also staple foods, materials, and fuels, increases in import prices spread throughout the whole economy. Moreover, since export prices were also climbing and volumes increasing, the money supply could be expanded sufficiently to accommodate a general rise in the price level. This was a pure case of "imported inflation."

The countries in this group, which had experienced the biggest price rise during the war, remained at the end of the war with rather less liquidity in their banking system and with exchange rates that were obviously overvalued. So the operation of the dollar-standard mechanism was quicker and more drastic. Thus, in Nicaragua, where prices trebled between 1940 and 1945, they subsequently became stabilized at a lower level, and in Cuba the more gradual rise continued until 1948 before tapering off. For most members of the group, the trend in prices was always upward, but it slowed after the middle of 1948. This reflected the deceleration of price increases in the United States, which went through a brief recession in 1949.

In the group of countries which were following more flexible monetary policies, developments were different. The exchange position at the end of the war gave a rather illusory impression of strength, since part of the reserves represented an inflow of capital which had been removed from the risks of war and would now be repatriated. Moreover, the rise in world prices was steadily reducing the real value of these reserves. Nevertheless, for some years, the external balance did not appear a very urgent matter in most of these countries. Consequently, there was some room for choice in policy. The growing acceptance of Keynesian doctrines overseas was having an impression on Latin American authorities, although these ideas were often improperly used to justify inflation. The measures adopted in Western Europe to redistribute income, such as the "welfare state" in the United Kingdom were also having some impact. In the generally expansionist atmosphere, budget deficits and rapidly rising imports were common, while the possibilities of expanding export industries and seeking new ones were not widely explored.

The most vivid example of this was the case of Argentina. We have seen that since this country exports staple foods, it can absorb what it cannot sell abroad. For the same reason, the level of exports depends to a considerable degree on how much is left over from domestic consumption. Price and wage policies after 1945 had the effect of raising the purchasing power of wages in terms of traditional export products. Real wages in Argentina rose by 50 per cent between 1944 and 1947, while domestic prices of traditional export items (though not other farm products) were prevented from following the upward trends in overseas prices. Argentina therefore never fully recovered its pre-war markets for agricultural commodities, especially grains. Imports, on the other hand, rose to a high level, and there was a swift decline in foreign reserves (from $1,700 million at the end of 1946 to $700 million at the end of 1949). This rise in imports relieved the wartime shortages mentioned above; nevertheless, as wage increases were greater than the increases in productivity, production costs rose. Moreover, other forces were at work promoting inflation. A good deal of equipment was worn out and much economic and social capital was below the levels appropriate to postwar incomes. Public investment was heavy but, being badly planned, it widened the budget deficit without curing these shortages. Despite the import surplus and the use of controls from 1947 onward, price rises averaged over 20 per cent a year in the period 1945–1950.

Chile was a different case again. Foreign reserves had not been built up so much during the war; exports shrank slightly in volume after it ended; and the terms of trade improved only moderately. Consequently, the volume of imports could hardly be expanded at all and supply problems continued to restrict the government's room to maneuver. Investment was only moderate and the increase in the national product was slow. Although imported foods were subsidized, prices continued to rise at much the same rate as in war years. In Bolivia and Paraguay, too, near-stagnation was associated with inflation. Apart from supply problems, cumulative forces had now emerged in these three countries because of the duration and pace of inflation, and these forces in turn propelled inflation farther forward. The saving propensity was low, budgets were difficult to balance, and investment tended to be directed to projects yielding high and quick returns, rather than to developing the basic industries and services which were needed.

Some other countries in this group did much better. Their exports expanded more quickly, and they made use of the opportunity thus provided. Investment was high and better balanced in Brazil, Mexico, and Uruguay, and the national product grew at about 5 or 6 per cent a year. In these cases, now that imports could be obtained in sufficient quantities and internal supply problems were eased, price rises became more moderate (5 to 11 per cent a year).

Still, in retrospect, it seems that the region failed to profit fully by the opportunity presented by the export boom of 1945–1950. A large proportion of reserves was spent on consumer durables, such as motor vehicles, instead of being used to strengthen economies against the lean period that obviously lay ahead, in the not-so-distant future, after the reconstruction period, when the industrial countries would have built up their inventories to normal peacetime levels.

The Position at the Start of the Nineteen-fifties

Despite the developments of the nineteen-thirties and nineteen-forties the structure of the Latin American economies still showed many of the shortcomings of the pre-Depression period. Capital was lacking in basic sectors of the economy. The inadequacies of the educational system were shown by the low ratio of teachers to children of school age, and the consequences in a specific sector can be inferred from the very low figures, particularly in certain countries, for professionally trained personnel in agriculture. The level of training of the labor force is indicated by the low level of literacy, especially in the rural areas.

The distribution of income continued to be highly unequal because of the concentration of property in a few hands, monopolistic profit margins, and the lack of educational opportunities. A large proportion of personal income still accrued to those accustomed to heavy personal spending on foreign travel or imported luxuries. The internal market for domestic industries was correspondingly limited and it was broken up, because different qualities were demanded by the various social groups. The mass-production techniques needed, especially in the metal-using industries, could therefore hardly be established.

The same contrast can be looked at on another plane as the difference between urban and rural incomes. In the cities, incomes were very much higher and consumption patterns were distinctly different. City-dwellers ate different foods, were accustomed to wearing shoes (for example), and used far more electricity.

But despite the inflexibility of an economy fissured in this way, the pattern of demand changed rapidly as the migration to the cities accelerated.

Despite the degree of industrialization already achieved, economic structures were still unable to cope with rising demand. Even in the more developed countries, conspicuous gaps could be found—for instance in industries for making heavy equipment and heavy chemicals.

The market mechanisms were highly imperfect, as was shown by a wide range of different prices in various parts of the same country. Mining sectors, usually dominated by foreign capital, formed what amounted to separate enclaves within the economies concerned.

There was a considerable degree of fragmentation in the region's economies. If perfect mobility existed in the labor and capital markets, it might be expected that there would be a marginal productivity and, therefore, a more or less equal average productivity in the various sectors, as in the industrialized countries. For Latin America as a whole, however, output per capita still varied widely, and data for individual countries would show striking contrasts.

Socioeconomic structures of this type were obviously not well suited to cope with the strains—sometimes severe—of the new stages upon which the process of import substitution was entering.

The Stagnation of Exports in the Nineteen-fifties: The Acute Economic Policy Dilemma

These strains, however, were late in making themselves felt. The postwar commodity boom continued into the early nineteen-fifties. The United States economy rebounded from the recession of 1949, and the recovery in the Federal Republic of Germany was gathering speed. Then the Korean hostilities led to the adoption of armament programs in the industrial countries and had a more immediate impact on commodity prices. But in 1951, as fears of a general war diminished, prices of primary commodities fell back. In some cases they recovered later. There was a boom in nonferrous metals in 1955 and 1956; and free-market petroleum and sugar prices rose during the Suez crisis. Coffee prices rose to a peak in 1954 and remained relatively high until 1957. But broadly speaking, there was no sustained rise in commodity prices after the first few months of 1951. The volume of exports continued to expand but in most cases the rise was only moderate. On the other hand, although the upward trend in import prices slowed down, reflecting an increased emphasis on price stabilization overseas and the slowing down in the rate of growth of the world economy, it was not actually halted. So Latin America's terms of trade started to deteriorate.

In the countries of Group O (the countries of the Caribbean area and Central America, which followed conservative financial practices), price rises leveled off almost completely, in the sense that any further rises were within the margin of statistical error, owing to the unreliability of price indices. Price changes closely followed those in the United States, the main customer and supplier of these countries.

Appreciation of the success enjoyed by these economies in holding inflation in check and then eliminating it must be tempered by the consideration that the closer the adherence to the dollar standard, the more not only price movements but also economic growth will depend on external developments. An upward trend in the value of exports raises incomes and reserves, increases the demand for locally produced goods and also leads to rising imports. The whole set of variables can keep moving upward. But, because of the preponderance of manufactures in imports, the income-elasticity of demand for imports tends to be greater than unity, despite attempts to protect local industries. So the rate of expansion of the value of exports tends to limit the rate of growth of the gross product. Account must also be taken of import prices, since, if they rise, this will tend to depress the rate of growth even more by absorbing foreign exchange. Thus, "the purchasing power of exports"—the value of exports deflated by an index of import prices—is likely to be the main determinant of changes in the domestic product of a dollar-standard country.

The inflow of capital would also, of course, stimulate growth, just as the outflow would depress it. But data on capital movements are particularly scanty, so this is difficult to allow for statistically. In any case, the effect of capital inflow trends is not comparable with that of export trends, especially if allowance is made for the rising expenditure of foreign exchange in the form of profits and interest, associated with growing foreign investment. Moreover, the progress of exports very much determines the extent of foreign investment even in industries producing for the home market. So the purchasing power of exports can still be considered the main determinant.

For Venezuela, a big rise in domestic income was associated with a more or less equivalent rise in exports, although, with the heavy investment in the Venezuelan petroleum industry in 1956 and 1957, a bigger rise in the former variable might have been expected. Equally large increases in both income and exports occurred in El Salvador, Guatemala, Nicaragua, and Panama. In other cases, the extent of import substitution appears to have caused a faster (or slower) growth in income than in exports. In Costa Rica and the Dominican Republic, the growth of income appears to have substantially exceeded that of exports, while the reverse was true in Ecuador. In Cuba, Haiti, and Honduras, the purchasing power of exports hardly changed and may have declined; total real income nevertheless rose somewhat in these cases, but the substantial reduction in the backing for their currencies indicates again that the temptation to relax monetary practices is strong when exports stagnate. Despite these signs of some monetary expansion, the increase in the total product was so small in the three countries concerned that there was little change, perhaps even a fall, in per capita terms. Since there was quite a close relation between change in income and the purchasing power of exports for the largest economy (Venezuela) and for most countries of the group, this was also true for the group as a whole.

After the middle of 1957, the exports of several of these countries fared badly. Prices of free-market petroleum and sugar fell back from the peaks attained in the Suez crisis; coffee prices weakened as the world market became saturated, and exports were restricted in volume by international agreement; cotton prices declined; and among tropical commodities only the banana market remained moderately strong. The penalty for failing to diversify the economy now became apparent in terms of economic stagnation and social unrest. It appears from preliminary figures that, in most countries of this group, the rate of growth of income slowed down considerably.

Its biggest members, Cuba and Venezuela, have in fact taken independent action to stimulate an expansion of internal activity. In these two cases, political and economic developments have been intermixed, and it cannot be said that it is purely for economic reasons that the dollar standard has been relaxed. Moreover, in the case of Venezuela, the measures taken have not so far been incompatible with the principles of this standard. The government has failed to balance the budget, but the deficit was partly attributable to repayment of the external debt. Import controls have been tightened, tariffs raised, and exchange controls introduced, but the import surplus, like the budget deficit, has been covered by depleting reserves and borrowing. Although prices started to rise in 1958, the rise has been moderate. However, banking legislation has been reformed, to allow a lower ratio of reserves to central bank liabilities (33 per cent instead of 50 per cent) and to permit lending by the Central Bank to the government.

The experience of Group U was very different. Prices continued to rise and, in several cases, the pace of inflation accelerated. There was quite a different relationship between the growth of income and exports. Industrialization was a more deliberate policy, even in the face of difficulties in marketing exports. Governments refrained from taking steps to reduce internal activity when exports declined, so that a policy of compensation was in fact practiced. Budgets slipped into deficit, or deficit grew, particularly in Chile, where taxes on profits of export companies form a big source of revenue. Moreover, the base of the monetary structure was further reduced by allowing credit to increase when reserves were falling.

The main problem was not, however, that exports slipped back from time to time, but rather that the trend was no longer definitely upward. Taking this group as a whole, the change in the purchasing power of exports over this period was virtually zero. Yet population increases were accelerating, except in Argentina and Uruguay, as death rates were driven down by improvements in health services. The growth of cities, once under way, gains a certain momentum and a check to industrialization soon leads to serious social problems. Consequently, governments had little option but to promote development and further diversification, and import substitution became an increasingly deliberate aim. Brazil, in particular, established a program of priority targets for the basic sectors of the economy (steel, petroleum, and transport).

Indeed, the purchasing power of exports did not rise greatly for any member of this group, except Mexico, and in this case it is partly explained by the fact that the tourist industry has been included in exports. In Chile and Peru, moderate rises in exports were paralleled by similar increases in income. The exports of other countries showed only small rises, or actually fell, but experience with income was much better. Brazil and Colombia, especially the former, achieved the most significant increases in their domestic incomes, considering the poor performance of their exports. Argentina achieved some increase in income, and Bolivia averted a decline, although exports fell somewhat in both cases.

The total product of this group rose about 28 per cent (or over 4 per cent a year), even though the purchasing power of exports was unchanged.

A Summary of External and Internal Trends in the Main Economic Indicators, 1929–1959

It was not until after the Second World War that the purchasing power of Latin American exports recovered the levels reached at the end of the nineteen-thirties, as a result solely of the improvement in the terms of trade. After these swung back against Latin America in the nineteen-fifties, there was no further significant increase in the purchasing power of the region's exports. In fact, if Venezuela is excluded, there was little change over the whole thirty years. Some countries were particularly severely affected. In Argentina, the purchasing power of exports in 1958 was only half what it had been thirty years earlier; and in Chile, too, exports—in this sense—never recovered their pre-Depression level.

Much the same long-term trends are shown by the volume of imports, since this depends very largely on exports and the terms of trade. Total imports for the region in 1958 were not much greater in quantity than in 1928, if Venezuela is excluded. In Argentina and Chile, the volume of imports actually fell over the three decades, and in Brazil the rise was limited.

The evolution of imports must be contrasted with the expansion of the region's gross product, which more than trebeled in the same period. This was accompanied by the rapid growth of cities, which resulted not merely in a rapid increase in total demand but in an accelerated expansion of demand for manufactures (especially equipment), processed foodstuffs, and professional services.

In the "open economies" of Group O, rising demand was accommodated by imports increasing more quickly than the output of goods for internal consumption. So imports formed a growing proportion of total supply. No doubt a similar trend would have been observable in Group U, if foreign exchange supplies had permitted, but in all members of this group, except Peru, which was really an "open economy" for much of the nineteen-fifties, the opposite happened. The import coefficient, defined in this way, fell almost throughout the period, being approximately halved from 1928–1929 to 1957–1958. Only in Mexico did the coefficient cease falling after 1938–1939.

Producers in this group of countries were therefore confronted with a major task, both during and after the Depression: they had to provide substitutes for imports which were unobtainable. In some cases the task was harder by price controls and subsidies that stimulated consumption of enegry, for example. Within the stationary or contracting total of imports, petroleum imports grew rapidly, especially in Argentina and Brazil. Import substitution in steel also lagged in Argentina and Chile, although in the latter case it increased greatly in the nineteen-fifties. Output of capital equipment rose everywhere after 1939, but demand also expanded very quickly, so that imports continued to climb, except in Argentina. Nevertheless, because of the shortage of equipment, there was growing pressure on capacity in several key industries, especially electric-power production, and the railways.

One consequence of this series of developments was that the heavy industries had to be expanded rapidly. Thus, in Mexico, the number of workers employed in the metallurgical, machinery, and vehicle industries rose from below 10,000 in 1930 to 173,000 in 1955. The impact was, however, wider than this: industrial expansion on this scale means changes in many other industries, in fact a transformation of the whole economy. Another consequence was that the composition of imports changed greatly. While consumer goods accounted for almost half of all imports in 1928, by 1957–1958 this proportion had fallen to 7 per cent in Brazil, 10 per cent in Argentina, and only slightly more in Colombia, Chile, and Mexico. On the other hand, the share of capital equipment rose from about 20 per cent of total imports in 1928 in the countries of Group U to more than one-third in 1957–1958 (over 40 per cent in Chile and Mexico). The only exception was Argentina, where the shortage of foreign exchange was especially acute. The share of petroleum in total imports also grew considerably in Argentina, Brazil, and Chile, though not in the traditional producers such as Colombia, Mexico, and Peru. Finally, there were rapid increases in imports of raw materials—of metals in Argentina because of the need for ore, pig iron, and steel products, and of nonmetal materials elsewhere.

This forced shift in the structure of imports indicates the strain produced in many countries by their attempts to achieve rapid growth during a period of foreign exchange shortage, especially in those—notably Argentina—where the necessary rate of production growth had not been achieved in key sectors. Although the deterioration in export markets was not so spectacular in the second half of the nineteen-fifties as in the first half of the nineteen-thirties, the impact was nevertheless comparable in some countries, because it came at a time when it was difficult to reduce imports, whereas the import structure in 1929 had afforded room for substantial reductions.

There has been a close relationship between the import coefficients in various periods and the rate of price increases. One obvious exception is Argentina. Before 1945, plentiful supplies of food and a fairly well-equipped economy meant that structural problems were only of limited importance in Argentina, and in the early nineteen-fifties price and wage controls were being used to suppress inflation. But in general it appears that, in the countries of Group U, an import coefficient of less than 10 per cent has been associated with inflation. At levels below this, there is little possibility of using foreign exchange for imports that would relieve internal structural problems.

CHAPTER VII

SOCIAL CONDITIONS AND EFFECTS OF ECONOMIC DEVELOPMENT

Social Realities in Economic Development[1]

The Need to Include Social Questions in Developing Problems

The progress made by the Latin American countries in their movement to promote economic growth has now reached a stage when it is perhaps necessary to consider certain aspects of this process which have so far received scant attention. Since any exploratory work must start from known ground, in this case the point of departure may be the established fact that public opinion in the Latin American countries has generally adopted certain economic concepts, which some of the ECLA publications endorse. First, there is the tenet that income redistribution is insufficient in itself to raise the average level of living of the masses and that the only lasting solution to this problem is to increase the average per capita product, or, what amounts to the same thing, to accelerate the growth of the whole economic system. Second, it is believed that economic growth posits an energetic development policy, directed with the greatest possible foresight and maintained

[1] "Progress Report on the Study on Social Conditions of Economic Development," (E/CN.12/374), pp. 1–8 and 12–14.

with flexibility and continuity. The third idea is that policy of this kind must be founded upon a firm basis of programming, the nature and technique of which have been defined with increasing precision over the last few years.

From the foregoing suppositions, which are undoubtedly fairly realistic, little effort of the imagination is required to pass to others. Let it be assumed, for instance, that a given country has for some time been following a consistent development policy, guided in all its aspects by a well-planned program, and that, even so, the growth rate is falling short of the proposed target. What has gone wrong? A searching examination may fail to reveal errors in the projections or calculations, or inaccuracies in the working data, and there may be no unforeseen internal or external factors that explain the phenomenon. Would it not in this case be legitimate to look beyond the mere working data for factors which were disregarded or simply taken for granted? May not the answer lie in the economic behavior of the various social groups which were expected to react rationally to the new conditions proposed? What were their actual conduct and motivations? An investment target does not set in motion an automatic process requiring help from individuals with the will to invest and entrepreneurs with initiative, ready to seize favorable opportunities; a savings program cannot be carried out without people who are willing to modify their consumer habits and income levels to a reasonable extent; finally, the required increase in productivity cannot be achieved by mechanical procedures alone, but entails a responsible attitude to work, and people who are drawn by their own aspirations to submit themselves voluntarily to the requisite discipline.

All these factors—will, habits, aspirations, and sense of responsibility—fall outside the economist's usual sphere of interest and working concepts. But to acknowledge that this boundary has been overstepped can serve neither as an excuse nor as a facile condonation for having expected too much, for the field is not an impossible one to explore, survey, and in one way or another take into account. The problem is not, of course, new to the economist, but it presents itself in an acute and possibly different form in underdeveloped countries. It can by no means be dismissed with the usual reference to the gap between an economic model and reality: precise mathematical computation and statistical projections are at all times in opposition to the unforeseeable contingencies of life, its forces of inertia, its conflicts and anomalies. In the underdeveloped countries—whose backwardness is not altogether a historical accident—not only is this acknowledged and the unavoidable gap between theoretical model and reality far greater, but the assumptions and conditions required for any economic model to function may be wholly or partially lacking. Faced with this situation, students of underdeveloped economies have virtually despaired of overcoming the difficulties involved. Nevertheless, there appears to be no justification for such discouragement. Although certain values and particular attitudes, habits, and traditions can be singled out as powerful obstacles to economic development, they are neither incomprehensible nor immutable. The first essential is to understand them, to know how they operate, and to determine their effects; they can then be modified as expedient, slow though the process may be.

When the pursuit of this hypothetical line of thought revealed the need to investigate the actual behavior of the different social groups that are essential to the economic life of a given country, the existence of negative motivation was mentioned. What motives did these people have for not doing what was expected of them? A study of their motives, and of the charges wrought in them through the elimination of the forces of inertia and the introduction of incentives, should not be regarded as a task for the psychologist, and hence traditionally alien to the economist. The motives, activities, and beliefs by which men are influenced do not exist in a vacuum, but represent the demands of specific customs and institutions. The analysis of such motives necessarily entails an analysis of the social structure, a question which is obviously close to the economist's habitual concerns and field of training. Hardly anyone will deny that the broad principles of contemporary social science are based on two fundamental tenets: first, that social structure and character—as it is termed today—are closely related, each being a correlative of the other; second, that the social structure is formed by a nexus of institutions which cannot be changed unless more or less radical modifications are made simultaneously in each of its parts. Hence, when the economist encounters behavior which is not in accordance with his assumptions and requirements, the implication is that he is faced with a character—a system of attitude and motives—which was shaped by a different social structure from the one he is looking for and needs. And when, for purposes of development, the economist attempts to introduce into a country the instruments that it requires for its economic growth, he is actually introducing factors of institutional change which can only operate with complete success if the other components of the social structure are modified in the same direction.

Thus it is not surprising that research workers and institutions are becoming increasingly aware of the integral nature of the problem of the underdeveloped countries. The expression "integrated development" has already become current usage, and many efforts are being made—sometimes of a rather confused kind—to define the concept it represents. But before elucidating further, a short disgression may usefully be made.

It not infrequently happens that the first reaction to the difficulties posed for current economic development by more or less obsolete social structures is to refer to the past to find a model for guidance in the social evolution of the advanced countries. According to this approach, if the social and cultural conditions which governed the appearance and development of modern capitalism were such-and-such, and followed this or that course in their internal evolution, it will be necessary to wait for them to recur spontaneously, or, at best, to induce them to reappear by shortened stages. The evolutionary theories of the nineteenth century and the phasic interpretation of economic growth by a number of prominent economic historians consciously or unconsciously still exert a strong influence on present-day thought. For example, the order recommended for the process of industrialization is usually no other than the order of historical development itself. Some may hold this belief in its most extreme form, namely, that for a country to obtain the entrepreneurial cadres it requires, it will have to await a new religious reform or the creation of certain heterodox and marginal groups.

The foregoing remarks do not, of course, deny in any way the value of historical research and knowledge for Latin America and its problems, but are intended to draw attention forthwith to the fact that in most cases these problems are completely new, and cannot be solved by reference to the past or imitation of the supposedly real models offered by the more advanced countries. The trend of events is the same in the field of social institutions and human relations as in that of economics and technology. The countries of the periphery represent a new situation in relation to the dynamic centers of the world economy. Consequently, although they can benefit from loans of capital and technique, they are not absolved as a result from the obligation of continually exercising their own ingenuity. In the sphere of economic theory itself, they have had to seek and find new variants based on their own actual situation, while, as regards technology, the urgent need for them to find solutions better adapted to their own technical problems has repeatedly been emphasized. In the field of social customs and human relationships, entirely new situations have also emerged, which preclude the recurrence of others arising from different circumstances, and for which there is no precedent that can be followed. In this respect, it sometimes happens that models are held up which merely represent imaginary conditions, or have been crystallized in academic theory, when they have already crumbled away in actual fact. For instance, the exact entrepreneurial model it is hoped to imitate may have ceased to exist in the milieu where it is being sought, while the image of the industrial worker or the rural community, as presented, may be distorted by failure to take later changes duly into account. The warnings of a Riesman on the dangers of using the United States as an example for the underdeveloped countries may, despite their perspicacity, be somewhat exaggerated or paradoxical, but they underline a vital fact. There is no reason to suppose that the power of creating new social and cultural patterns in the drive to propagate the industrial society has been exhausted. The new social problems bred in the peripheral countries by their eagerness to share actively in the industrialization process can be dealt with not by looking backward, but by an effort of the imagination focused on the future. But as imagination and invention must be kept in contact with reality to be effective, it is necessary to make a searching and detailed examination of the facts. This digression thus ends as it began, with the realization on many sides that it is essential not to overlook the fundamental social and human factors of economic development in the task of promoting growth.

The interest aroused by the social and cultural aspects of economic development has not yet begun to follow a definite line, nor is it always clear and undivided. Moreover, it may seem to have arisen belatedly. For this reason, a brief outline of the way in which concern for such factors has developed will be given below.

A Synopsis of Past History

It is not surprising, first, that the study of the social aspects of economic development has been relegated well to the background in the special world of the economist; and second, that its initial stages reproduce to some extent the evolution of economic theory itself. In the last analysis, it is invariably the most topical issues that form the point of departure, and contemporary interest has therefore been aroused by the urgent practical problems rather than by the advance of theory. This is acknowledged by numerous economists, who point out the extent to which the current analysis of economic development theory has been spurred on by the burning questions of the day. The interest and concern displayed in relation to the so-called underdeveloped countries is the outcome of a particular set of circumstances, which stemmed from the consequences of the Second World War, and has therefore become a *fait accompli.* Economic development theory was thus conceived—or revised—in response to immediate requirements, and for that very reason was inevitably colored by ideological dogma in certain cases. Accordingly, it would be worth while to examine carefully a trend that will merely be summarized in a few words here: namely, the twofold effort made by current economic thinkers to forge as comprehensive and precise a body of ideas as possible, and at the same time to free it from all traces of extraneous influence.

In the sociological analysis of development—to use a single term for the sake of convenience—exactly the same stages are reproduced, with a certain time lag. A cursory review of the official and private publications that have touched upon the subject in one way or another in the last few years shows clearly that current interest in the social aspects of economic development emanates from three sources.

One point of departure—possibly the first in order of time and of empirical importance—is practical action itself. The interest thus aroused has taken different forms. It is useful, however, to emphasize those manifestations deriving from the reactions produced by the technical assistance which international organizations and the governments of advanced countries have been giving to underdeveloped countries of late. Many of those involved agree on a point which only a few have put in writing: namely, that the success of technical assistance depends upon a broader and more comprehensive social vision of the countries that receive it. Some have expressly recognized that to this end closer cooperation should be established between the various specialists in the social sciences. It is certainly very significant that the unified and integrated concept of the social sciences which was once a lodestar—now rechristened "interdisciplinary research"—is repeatedly urged as a requisite today by those engaged in the more practical type of action.

A second point of departure is to be found in economic theory itself, that is, among certain economists who are working on the construction of a satisfactory and integrated theory of development. Detailed consideration of this question would be impractical here; it would entail closer study, because of the wide variations in the terminology used and in the breadth of the approach adopted. Recognition of the importance of social aspects is sometimes even carried so far as to be tantamount to a repudiation of economic methods, with the resultant loss of value from the standpoint of development theory. One school of thought actually aims at dovetailing social aspects with the theory of development itself, in the hope of finding measurable values for its component factors. Another recognizes the importance of these factors, but cannot see how to use them as parameters in constructing its model. The majority, however, are content to indicate the need for complementary approaches, and, as before, hope for an integration of the piecemeal findings of the social sciences. The antecedents of these different positions are to be found in the history of economics itself, and this is drawn upon more or less explicitly.

For the purposes of the present summary, however, no more need be said. The salient point to note is that history, sociology, and psychology are once again being used as fields of reference by some of the economists who are currently engaged in formulating development theory.

The third point of departure is to be found, as might be expected, among the specialists in the various social sciences—apart from economists—who adopt different lines of approach in studying one of the major and universal issues of our time, or who are awake to what C. Brinkmann has recently termed "the sociological dimensions of human disciplines." However, the suggestions put forward by the social scientists are still inclined to be vague and confused, a fact which is readily understandable simply because, generally speaking, the social scientists have no unified position. Furthermore, as a result of special circumstances, the rationale and working methods of the anthropologist and, to a certain extent, of the social psychologist have taken pride of place over the traditional approach of the sociologist. The bibliographies and some of the attempted syntheses recently published clearly show the disconnected and heterogeneous nature of this whole school of thought. Finally, there are the contributions made by certain writers who look at economic development from the angle of a particular codes of values, and from there tackle the far from insignificant question of the type of economic growth that should be encouraged: for example, they may advocate only the kind that would simultaneously foster and make possible the materialization of those personal values which form the moral basis of any given culture. To state this in objective terms, what is the price in human values which must be paid for each type of development and for the rate of growth it demands?

These brief considerations show that although the study of the social aspects of development has advanced comparatively quickly to a new stage, much still remains to be done, from the theoretical standpoint, in the way of elaborating and systematizing the fragmentary observations that have been made. For without a minimum theoretical background, it is obviously impossible to guide specific research, to marshal the findings of studies carried out in an uncoordinated and random fashion, and to distinguish between what is really essential and what is of little or no importance. Moreover, this insistence on scientific precision is a *sine qua non* for practical action, since the social and political aspects of economic development are more apt than those of a strictly economic or technical character to acquire ideological overtones or to evoke interested or emotional responses that are overhasty and ill-defined. The only way to ensure that the action taken is characterized by vision and continuity is through the shifting process that can be carried out by sound research.

The Two Major Issues

The method followed up to now has been retrospective and exploratory, and the impression it has left may have been predominantly one of vagueness and doubt. This was inevitable, however, and therefore the least compromising terminology was deliberately and voluntarily chosen. The time has now come, however, to make some points clear, and to escape from the imprecision of such platitudes as "the interest in the social aspects of economic development." The best way of shedding the necessary light at the outset is doubtless to give a definite answer to the following question: what are the basic issues involved? Plainly, there are two: the social conditions of economic development, and the social effects of that development. Both, while quite different, strictly demarcate the field of research. The ground thus cleared, a firm starting point can be established.

Both questions have already been raised on various occasions, but particular emphasis has been laid on the first. The variety of views that have been expressed on the relationship of economic activity with human character and motivations, and with the customs, traditions, and usages of a society, amount in the end to an inverse recapitulation —at times purely descriptive—of the theme that made Weber's study of capitalism a classic: what are the social conditions that enable this system to function? To pose the same question from the standpoint of modern economic development implies the continuity of an extremely precise theoretical tradition.

In this sense, the preference of some writers for the term "obstacles" to denote the development difficulties of the less advanced countries is debatable. These obstacles certainly exist, but theoretically they are only special features of those conditions which must be examined as a whole. They are, so to speak, negative conditions, whose effects differ considerably according to whether they constitute lacunae or opposing forces. Moreover, apart from the fact that the construction of a theory demands an extremely broad and general basis, the stress laid on "obstacles" leads to the adoption of a dogmatic or militant position, sometimes tinged with a pessimism that is prejudicial to the maintenance of a scientific attitude.

The second question, that of the social effects of development, simply relates to a specific example of the results inherent in any process of change, whatever its nature. Economic development is a process of induced change and entails an examination, not only of its primary and willed effects, but also of its secondary and unforeseen consequences. In fact, as was pointed out before, economic change inevitably has repercussions—sought or unsought—on the institutions that make up the social structure. Can these be predicted? Apart from such abstract considerations, which will be reverted to later, the outstanding practical problem of the underdeveloped countries, which has been viewed from many different angles, can perhaps be stated most flexibly and directly in the following terms: countries in course of development must progress by using Western methods of industrialization, but should not have to pay the same price as did the West for its industrial revolution. In the words of E. Heimann, industrialization must not destroy the moral and social structure of the newcomers, as it did in the older industrial countries. This is the idea which in one form or another dominates the consideration of the social effects of economic development.

The Situation in Latin America

If an attempt is made to establish a list of the studies undertaken from this viewpoint on the present social situation in Latin America, it will be seen that they are few in number and, on the whole, inadequate. The region's situation in this respect cannot be compared with those of Africa and Asia, which, as international abstracts and bibliographies testify, have formed the subject of most of the research work carried out in recent years. Although this is largely due to the pattern of world events and to a new policy on the part of certain countries that still retain territories overseas, a contributory cause lies in the peculiar features of Latin America's own situation, which can mislead those who have no intimate knowledge of it. Its compound of unity and diversity in social and cultural respects, the contrasts between its huge rural population and its thriving industrial centers, and, above all, the fact that the culture to which this region belongs is, up to a point, a peripheral version of Western culture, make up a picture that is not always easy to understand, and to which the standards formed elsewhere in the world do not apply. The social and cultural questions raised by Latin America's economic development can only be dealt with in this context, because they are neither the same as those of the more developed countries nor wholly identifiable with those proper to some of the industrial centers' more primitive accretions.

The reasons for the lack of sociological studies on Latin America cannot be explored any further here. Whatever they are, however, the fact remains that the gap exists and must be filled as soon as possible.

With this in mind, it was thought timely to embark on a closer, if still preliminary, examination of the questions that have been raised. The following pages are devoted to the pursuit of this end.

Economic Development and the Structure of Employment[2]

This study is merely tentative and introductory in scope. It attempts to consider from the sociological standpoint the data gathered in the course of a statistical study on manpower problems, in the hope that, from this fresh point of view, it may be possible to discern the shape and depth of several of the more important sociocultural questions associated with economic development. Manpower surveys undertaken from an economic standpoint are justified by their intrinsic value; this point need not therefore be stressed. What is of interest is to open a new line of approach, since if such studies are viewed from a

2 "Three Sociological Aspects of Economic Development," *Economic Review of Latin America*, special issue (August 1955), pp. 56–65.

more properly sociological angle, not only can they emphasize in their own terms some of the main social elements of any development policy, but they also call for a strict definition of the concepts indispensable to their classification and understanding.

A study of the structure of employment and occupations from the sociological point of view shows that there are three broad social aspects of economic development (disregarding other minor questions for the moment) which require different types of economic and psychosocial analyses. Economic development may be considered as: (1) the adjustment of a society to new functions; (2) the creation of new patterns of living within the society; and (3) the formation of a new social structure. These are the questions which this study attempts to outline.

The first two aspects require a microanalysis, since they refer to individual action or finite social relationships; while the third necessitates macroanalysis, since it deals with the social structure as a whole. A more detailed analysis would make it necessary to resort to different psychosocial approaches. The problems of adjustment can be studied through the psychology of automatic selection, though this is not the only way. On the other hand, all questions involving new patterns of living require the help of social psychology and fall within the field of the sociology of relationships and of sociometric research. Finally, the third aspect will inevitably lead to the classic subjects of structural or historical sociology. This line of thought will not be followed here, since only an initial, general exploration will be attempted, and stress will be laid on the fact that these phenomena are to a certain extent social obstacles to the economic process.

Social Adjustment to New Functions

Data on the structure of employment and occupations within a country, if extended over a certain period, give the best indication of the meaning of economic development as a phenomenon of social change. It is primarily a question of changing an institution, in this case the economic institution; and the change may be large or small, according to whether there are complete structural transformations or merely minor amendments not affecting the over-all pattern. But in every case it is soon evident that these changes will inevitably transform the other institutions of the same society. Therefore the effort of adjustment to be made by the individuals making up this institution is not limited to the initial sphere of change but is extended and branches out to very different and apparently distant sectors.

It is not necessary to linger over this point or to rebut the objection that a unilateral criterion is being used, since the course of the process outlined above is set at the point of departure, and there is nothing to prevent other starting points from being chosen and a different course set.

For present purposes, on the contrary, it is advisable to bear in mind the significance of any institutional change. In effect, an institution is a complex or orderly pattern of functions required for its continued existence and growth, which from the individual point of view appear as different roles to be played. Any change in an institution therefore consists in a modification of the functions which support it or of the reciprocal links between them. For the individual, each social role involves certain material aspects and a complex of human relationships, varying in scope, which are not limited merely to the necessary distribution of rights and obligations; consequently, every institutional change will imply greater or lesser changes for the individual at the different levels already indicated.

From the sociological standpoint and at the most abstract level, society is only a systematic pattern of roles and functions which must be fulfilled in order that it may subsist. It is also a commonplace that such roles take precedence over the individual, on whom they are imposed, very often with complete disregard for the individual nature of his personal fate. In order to make these statements completely intelligible and acceptable, numerous comments and reservations would have to be made, but they will have to suffice as they stand, in view of what follows, since it is only a question of defining the scope of the phenomenon of "induced" change, implied in the acceleration of economic progress in the underdeveloped countries. This phenomenon in reality involves two factors. First, the process implies the continual emergence of social roles and functions far in advance of the individuals needed to take them on. Expressed in another way, the creation of new social roles very often precedes the training of individuals capable of performing them. This time lag between the creation of new roles and functions and the training of individuals to carry them out is the origin of the first social bottleneck, which varies in intensity according to the inherent complexity of each function.

But, in the second place, given the conditions of modern life, it is no longer possible to await the slow, spontaneous disappearance of such maladjustment, as it was in other periods. This is mainly because of the almost total lack of any ascribed status of functional importance outside the family today, and the irreparable seriousness of the mistakes made in the technical activity of our society. In previous communities of another type, when a similar emergency arose which was a matter of life and death to society, the common expedient was to resort to the principle of heredity and to fill any gaps by ascription. In present society, which is ruled by the principle of functional adequacy, of the knowledge and skills peculiar to each task (performance or merit, from the standpoint of the role), the old procedure can no longer be used without risk, and the only possible solution is to find the best means of selection and training as the occasion arises. The induction of an economic change should be accompanied by a parallel induction of the necessary social change. In other words, economic development planning should contain the minimum sociological programming required to foresee and forestall as far as possible any social obstacles to development.

In order of complexity, the adjustments required of society for the creation of new functions, purely from the socioeconomic point of view, are as described below.

SIMPLE MODERNIZATION OF EXISTING ACTIVITIES

This is not a matter of creating new roles or completely new activities, but of modifying the methods of carrying them out, which requires an adjustment from the individual in the shape of new habits and automatic responses. An examination of the data available on the structure of employment and occupations reveals some of the main features. The best-known case is that of agricultural mechanization, in which the traditional tasks remain the same although different methods are used. It is advisable to consider this example in some detail, if only for purposes of illustration. The recent introduction of modern methods into agricultural operations may be perfectly evaluated by the mechanization process, which in turn is measured by the expansion of the tractor park. In Latin America there were 35,000 tractors in 1938–1939, 64,000 immediately after the war, and about 190,000 in 1953. These changes are still greater if consideration is given only to the block of countries where mechanization has made the most rapid strides (Argentina, Brazil, Mexico, and Uruguay). For the region as a whole, 20 per cent of the arable land is already being cultivated with tractors, but in Uruguay, relatively the most advanced country in this respect, the proportion rises to 80 per cent. These few data are enough to indicate the effort of adjustment already made and that which will be required in future if this trend is to be maintained. The mechanization process creates a large mass of drivers and mechanics in the farm environment, and requires from all some degree of familiarity with agricultural machines. Except in Mexico, this process until now has been confined mainly to large holdings, and has thus transformed the work-habits of the employees. But the establishment of pools of agricultural machinery in some countries (Brazil, Chile, Cuba, and Peru) not only brings the benefits of progress to small holders, but also introduces a new professional category into the rural milieu, since the drivers and mechanics of those pools fulfill a public function.

The same is true when internal improvements—by means of machines and electricity—are introduced into nonmechanized industries, as this not only increases productivity but also, with the introduction of new automatic responses, gives rise to a different mental attitude toward the same task. The interest shown in some countries in these small forms of development is based to a large extent on the educational effect obtained.

A similar adjustment, although on a smaller scale, is required when obsolete equipment is replaced in existing industries. The workers must then adapt their skills to more modern machinery, without thereby abandoning their previous activities.

The other two most important cases in this connection occur in the modernization of business methods and public and private administrative procedures. Not even by citing specific cases would it be possible to indicate the full significance of the changes entailed by economic development in both cases. It is enough to bear in mind that it is not so much a question of the creation of new functions as of the alteration, whether gradual or abrupt, of traditional ones. No better illustration could be furnished than the development of office techniques in both sectors in industrialized countries, through the constant introduction of new and faster typewriters, filing and classification equipment, calculating machines, and tabulators, not to mention the new electronic equipment. It has been observed that even the physical characteristics of offices are changing and becoming similar to those of factories: it is possible that the typical desk will be replaced by a kind of assembly line which will make the office worker's task similar to that of the factory hand.

The serious problem in underdeveloped countries largely calls for reforms of this type—of functional adjustment rather than simple expansion—for its solution.

CHANGE OF ACTIVITY WITHIN THE SAME FIELD

This aspect is particularly interesting from the standpoint of development, although in practice it is sometimes imprecise or confused with the preceding one. A typical example is the conversion of a homeworker into an industrial worker within the same activity: textiles, or ceramics, for example. In this case it is not only a question of an adjustment to new working techniques, but—which is sociologically still more important—of a change in social status, which requires wider adjustments in other spheres of behavior. All statistics on the disappearance of nonmechanized industries should be interpreted from the sociological angle as an expression of this effort of adjustment.

A similar case is the change in the position of casual workers when they become permanently employed. This change plays a part in reducing the marginal population. In Latin America, a typical example is that of the building industry, where stability of employment varies greatly from country to country, resulting in a different degree of productivity. A final example, also in Latin America, is the change from small- to large-scale mining operations.

CHANGE OF OCCUPATION

Social adjustment is much greater in this case than in the previous ones, since it implies not only a move to a new environment, but a total transformation of material activities and human relationships. The classic example is the shift from rural labor to nonagricultural types of employment. This shift has reached tremendous proportions in Latin America.

Another type of move to a new environment, also related to employment, is that associated with interregional migrations of the population. These generally are made by marginal populations which, in their region of origin, are unable to rise above a mere subsistence level, and therefore try to settle on virgin land or seek new and better-paid employment. Suffice it to recall that in Brazil this kind of movement has assumed such significance that it more than counterbalances the decline in international immigration in the receiving areas.

CREATION OF NEW ROLES AND FUNCTIONS

As the title indicates, these are entirely new activities, which therefore require a maximum effort of social adjustment. This is where the greatest temporary disequilibrium may arise, although it is also the easiest to handle, between the creation of new roles and functions and the necessary training of the individuals for their fulfillment.

Of the wide range of functions necessary for the subsistence of a modern economy, only a few examples will be given, in the order of their importance to developing countries.

(*a*) There is first the question of training a modern entrepreneurial class in the main branches of economic activity. To speak of such training is in no way unreasonable since the problem is posed in the same terms, though for different reasons, in more advanced countries. As Sargant Florence has said, one hundred years ago it would have seemed grotesque to discuss the problem of entrepreneurial training, although today it is of vital importance.

(*b*) Next comes the training of a professional class, according to current needs, in the various fields of the economy—the executives whose work at present ranks second only to that of managers and directors. A similar significance attaches to the training of administrators able to deal with present-day economic problems and rapid social changes.

(*c*) The third aspect relates to the very complex category of intermediate technicians and specialists, indispensable in every kind of enterprise, and who must be available in large numbers in order to attain the successive targets of economic development. They include all supervisory and coordinating personnel: overseers, mechanics, and assemblers, as well as bookkeepers, and other administrative and laboratory staff with training at the intermediate level.

(*d*) Finally, skilled and manual labor, for the operation of special machinery, and highly skilled artisans.

The most vital task which the Latin American must face in order not to retard his economic development is that of foreseeing the obstacles which may beset the accomplishment of all these functions and of promptly solving any temporary disequilibria which may appear.

The Creation of New Patterns of Living

If at first sight economic development appears to be the continuous formation of roles and functions, it also consists, at a more complex level, in the creation of new patterns of living. In this rapid review of the principal functional changes only a rough idea has been given of the technical and professional aspects of the effort for adjustment required of society and its individual members. In this respect, it should not be forgotten that an occupation is not only a method of work but also a way of life. A brief reference to this point is the best possible introduction to the present theme. In the analysis of an occupation, such as that made by industrial sociologists, not only the working routine, but also the distinctive social milieu in which this takes place, and the influence which it exerts on the nonprofessional activities of the individual should be borne in mind. The result of all these factors is what is called the pattern of professional life. But it is also evident that the adjustment of the individual to this behavioral pattern is in itself a much slower process than mere professional training.

As a first approximation it may be contended that these patterns of living are only the uniform repetition, collectively or as a whole, of similar professional modes of life. This, however, involves two consequences: first, when new roles and functions are developed within a society, patterns of living are necessarily created; second, their complete assimilation tends to be relatively slow. Patterns of living—social customs or mores—do not produce their full effects—personal, social, or economic—until they are firmly established.

The full significance and scope of the creation of new patterns of living can now be appreciated from the standpoint of economic development, since the greater delay in their stabilization and the greater effort of adjustment required may constitute a more serious social obstacle to economic development than those already described. The problem is one of the pace of adjustment—of delays, undue haste, and synchronization—but it is much more difficult to control, although not totally impossible, in some aspects.

It might be considered that a way of facilitating this task would be to compare the two major patterns of living, the rural and the urban, whose various elements are thought to be generally known. But this illusion must be dispelled before the problems presenting themselves can be fully grasped. At first sight, for instance, the urbanization process in Latin America may seem to be relatively rapid and encouraging, insofar as it is analyzed in relation to economic development. By 1950, the urban population represented about 41 per cent of the total population, and about 45 per cent of the urban population lived in large cities of more than 100,000 inhabitants. These figures, however, tell only a small part of the story. It would first be necessary to make an analysis of the occupational structure of certain urban units, to see whether or not they resemble the traditional patterns of typical modern cities. Two urban centers with the same population may in fact represent two very different patterns of living. Other indices, such as those on consumption, would shed further light on the question. And once this has been done, it would still be necessary to determine the influence of the traits revealed in the analysis on the formation of social character within a specified urban form. It should be remembered that what is of interest is the moment of complete assimilation of a pattern of living by a sufficiently large mass of individuals, since only then are the full effects felt. This is not meant to discourage an optimistic interpretation of certain phenomena, but to indicate the fertile field for research which has been opened up, and which must be explored if the progress of economic development is to be correctly construed.

PATTERNS OF LIVING AND CONSUMPTION

What has already been said about the contrast between rural and urban patterns of living would have to be repeated in any attempt to describe other modes or ways of life which are of equal importance to the socioeconomic interpretation of development, ranging from complete patterns of living peculiar to a specific type of civilization to those relating to certain key occupations—the entrepreneur or the foreman—through others which are proper to certain social strata of decisive significance from the economic standpoint. However, this subject lies outside the scope of this study and could be undertaken only by compiling a relatively complete list of the necessary studies. However interesting this might be, it would not serve the purposes of this article, which is mainly concerned with showing the link between the purely sociological considerations of patterns of living and the questions which economists must study for purposes of development.

Fortunately this link is not difficult to find and is not entirely *terra incognita*. Consumption is an essential component of any pattern of living and, together with the structure of demand which it determines, provides the link from the economic standpoint between some of the consequences indicated above concerning the nature of patterns of living. It is therefore advisable to consider this point in some detail.

All these patterns of living, however widespread, are composed of three different elements, which may be termed the cultural, social, and material, in order to avoid using esoteric, though more exact, terminology. The individual, subject to a pattern of life and to its conventions, accepts certain beliefs—ways of seeing or apprehending the world, or that part of it which comes within his ken—enters into personal contacts, known as human relationships, and makes use of these and material objects: goods produced and material means of production. It should be recalled, in addition, that the essential characteristic of these patterns of living, as of every collective phenomenon, is their compulsive or obligatory nature. When they are fully established, they impose themselves even in the tiniest details on the individual who desires to conform to society, and they therefore mold or shape him, even if he is not fully conscious of the process. Thus, consumption is merely the economic counterpart of the prevailing patterns of living and corresponds exactly with each constituent element. It depends on ideas and convictions, is stimulated and provoked by social relationships, and manifests itself through the use of material goods. In turn, consumption patterns are also compulsive and exert constant pressure on personal tastes and inclinations. This, however, is only fully true when the patterns of living have become stable. This, incidentally, is why the Duesenberry theory of the influence exerted on the propensity to consume by certain forms of emulation can be valid only to the extent allowed by the socioeconomic structure and is not true of the prevailing structure in underdeveloped countries, since in these countries, according to the terms of this article, the corresponding patterns of living have not yet been stabilized.

If, instead of going this roundabout way, the procedure were adopted of starting from consumption and accepting the most common description of its determinants, identical results would be achieved; and at least these—at the usual determinants-level of income-acquired habits, consciousness of status, and level of aspirations—would be fully intelligible, and make it necessary to revert, in varying degrees of detail, to the subject of the patterns of living as a whole.

What is the general significance of the connection between the social adjustment required and the rapidity of the economic process? Here it is advisable to repeat some facts which are perhaps already well known.

Of the different ways of establishing this connection, the following should be mentioned: the volume and structure of consumer demand; the volume and structure of savings; the nature and extent of stimuli or incentives encouraging human effort; and the values, both material and spiritual, determining the quality of the work.

There is no need to insist on the aspects of consumption already mentioned; but it is worth emphasizing that the patently multiple character of the links between patterns of living and economic development makes the problem extremely complex and not always susceptible of statistical analysis.

Thus a single change in the patterns of living may be favorable or unfavorable to economic development, depending upon the other prevailing circumstances. First of all, naturally, consideration should be given to the general economic conditions of the country in question, but still more important are the conditions produced by a coordinated planning process which gives rigid priorities to specific sectors of production. In such a case, one of two situations may arise: first, the too-rapid growth of certain consumer trends may take place at the expense of other goods and services which are considered of crucial importance for economic development. Second, and conversely, there may be insufficient demand for certain goods and services, of which greater consumption would have a generally stimulating effect on the economy. It is always a question of imbalance between consumer demand and the needs and possibilities of the economy, with negative and disturbing effects on development.

This is one particular aspect of the problem of social adjustment already defined. The adjustment of a community to a new consumption pattern may sometimes be extremely quick, but since at other times it may be slow, and hampered by social bottlenecks, a question arises as to the rolè of consumer education, which is undoubtedly most urgently needed in underdeveloped countries.

STAGES IN THE DEVELOPMENT OF DEMAND

The consideration of patterns of living through their concrete expression in the structure of demand makes it possible to outline the temporal phases of their development, which, although they may be indistinguishable in practice, are of interest for analytical purposes. Such an attempt will also make it possible to consider some of the questions already dealt with separately as a logical whole. Thus social adjustment to change of occupation reappears in a new guise, the typical case being the transfer of agricultural labor to industrial occupations, which is considered crucial for development problems. This approach also classifies what has already been explained about the relative slowness of the stabilization of the patterns of living when viewed from the economic standpoint. It not only gives a clearer indication of the points at which social and economic bottlenecks are most likely to appear, but also stimulates the formulation of such strategies as consumer education or training. Finally, it may show the economist, who habitually tends to consider the direct relationship between per capita income and the demand for various products, that he should remember that, in fact, the composition of demand by groups of products generally evolves in accordance with socially conditioned stages of development.

These stages are the following:

1. *Concentration.* Perhaps the most important factor in the creation of new patterns of living and their far-reaching repercussions on the structure of demand is the concentration of the population in large centers. This is the beginning of the "urbanization process," and the reason why large cities grow more rapidly than medium-sized and small towns.

It is well known that this process is a result of the fact that demand for labor in industry and services is much more intense than in agriculture. To this must be added the attraction of the large cities for the rural population, particularly its marginal sectors. It is the exodus of this population which has caused the spontaneous growth of the cities.

2. *Stabilization.* At the outset, a large proportion of the rural population which arrives in the cities in search of nonagricultural occupations is semi-skilled and is usually employed as casual labor in a variety of tasks. In other words, they lack specialization and adequate stability in the various branches of economic activity. Since the income of even the marginal population in towns is relatively higher than in rural areas, they are better able to satisfy their most urgent dietary needs, in contrast with their former very low nutritional standards. It cannot be expected, however, that when the surplus rural population moves to the cities the chronic malnutrition of the marginal population

will quickly disappear. This will be possible only after employment has become stabilized, when new forms of demand begin to be created.

Stabilization depends to a large extent on the general level of economic activity and, consequently, on the current phase of the business cycle and on the economic policy in force. Thus, stabilization will be relatively quickly achieved in times of prosperity and will be delayed during periods of depression.

This stabilization of employment arises concurrently with specialization and with the development of branches of activity which can provide more permanent employment; the new situation coincides with the period when unskilled labor is capable of adjusting to new types of employment requiring semiskilled labor or minimum training.

In certain cases the process of stabilization may coincide with concentration, but more often the disparity between both processes gives rise to a large floating reserve of underemployed which, over and above the actual unemployed, constitutes the main source of the labor needed for the development of industries and services.

Stabilization results in better wages and prompts new and greater requirements. Once nutritional needs have been more or less adequately covered, city life channels consumption toward an improvement in clothing. In addition, demand for cultural goods and services first appears, although only at a relatively low level.

3. *Resettlement.* The rapid growth of cities inevitably causes an acute housing shortage, reflected in an abnormal density of inhabitants per housing unit or in the proliferation of slum districts, which are called by different names in the various Latin American countries. This tragic phenomenon has been described repeatedly since the first analyses of the human consequences of the industrial revolution and is still of primary importance in any social policy, owing to its complex repercussions.

In general, once the urban population achieves stabilization of employment and higher incomes, it is possible to apply private and public capital to the improvement of housing, either directly, by the construction of low-cost housing for the working classes, or indirectly by the creation of new residential districts for the middle classes so that their former dwellings may become available to those in the lower-income brackets.

This whole process of resettling city dwellers has great social significance, since it enables many of them to have an adequate home, perhaps for the first time, and channels demand toward new types of goods and services, which, while improving the level of living, are at the same time an important stabilizing factor.

4. *Increase in comforts.* In most cases, the satisfaction of minimum housing requirements must precede higher levels of demand for durable goods. The two phenomena are not always exactly parallel, but a detailed analysis will not affect the general thesis from the sociological point of view. Incidentally, in industrial countries there has been a significant link between the economic and social consequences of the production of some of these goods, resulting in the gradual emancipation of women.

It is probably at this stage that consciousness of status or of levels of living begins to be formed. This converts the mass of consumers into one homogeneous body which can respond in a uniform and foreseeable manner to successive changes in the market. In other words, a truly integrated market is then established, which is equally accessible to all social classes.

5. *Private transport.* The last phase in the development of demand and in the transformation of patterns of living begins with the appearance of interest in private means of transport. The acquisition of private transport has vast implications for all aspects of life—work, recreation, culture,—and it is necessarily reflected in the structure of demand.

Time and space forbid detailed consideration of the expansion in the demand for public services which accompanies the final stages of this process. But mention must be made of the fact that it is during these stages that the concept of the future first becomes important. Just as individuals can plan their lives only when there is a minimum of security for the future so in the major forms of collective life it is the emergence of thought for the morrow which perhaps represents the moment of true stabilization. In the economic sphere, the arrival of this stage is of vital importance for the whole process of development, since the propensity to save, interest in social security schemes, and, equally important, increased demand for education, all depend on it. Individual and collective investment in the future undoubtedly represents one of the most powerful tools for the adjustment of a society to new patterns of living.

The foregoing should not be interpreted as a denial of the possibility of similar progress in the rural environment. But conditions in Latin America and the rapid growth of the cities have made it advisable to stress the significance of this process.

The New Social Stratification

The central idea of this section has already been touched upon in the two previous sections, since, if economic development involves the continual formation of new roles and functions and the concomitant creation of new patterns of living, the result of these processes for society as a whole is a different arrangement of social strata. All economic development, therefore, inevitably gives rise to a new social stratification.

This approach is, however, much more abstract and complex, since it means that social structure must always be viewed as a whole. The risks incurred in this type of macroanalysis are in direct relation to the simplifications required, but if they are kept in mind, it is worthwhile venturing an over-all approach—because of the light it sheds on the general picture and on the broad relationships between the phenomena already studied. This is what happens when the arrangement of social strata is viewed from the standpoint of economic development. The difficulties which might arise and which must be identified and the social obstacles reflecting unfavorable arrangements of social strata now loom so large that they would lead to complete discouragement, unless it is remembered that the concepts employed simplify the picture for specific purposes.

Apart from its controversial aspects, which are to some extent inevitable, the subject of stratification is in itself extremely complex. Various factors need to be considered, such as status, income, occupation, and power, which, depending upon the purpose of the research, lend themselves to different combinations and to different methods of study. However, a brief outline is sufficient for the purposes of this study, and excessively complicated theoretical refinement and all unnecessary details will be avoided.

The thesis should therefore be stated concisely. A comparative study of the structure of employment in countries at different stages of economic development shows that in those less developed there is a fundamental phenomenon which has a dual aspect: first, that social stratification tends not to be economically integrated at the national level; and second, that a social class which at present wields a decisive influence in industrialized countries—namely, the so-called new middle class—is totally lacking or at least only incipient. This class is characterized by its functional diversity, by its dependence on income from employment, and by the nature of its work, which deals with symbols or with the coordination of other people's activities.

SOCIAL STRATIFICATION IN UNDERDEVELOPED COUNTRIES

In primitive and traditional societies stratification presents a homogeneous aspect, whatever the predominating formative factor. This factor may be blood or family ties, or the land, with its fundamental relationships of ownership and neighborhood, or the status ascribed to the main occupations. What is important—though it is impossible to go into the subtle distinctions drawn by specialists—is the uniform nature of the stratification criteria during fairly lengthy periods of social stability. In contrast with this homogeneity, which is also characteristic of more advanced countries, social stratification in developing countries is essentially heterogeneous and complex. That is to say, numerous isolated and completely unrelated vestiges of traditional and primitive stratifications tend to remain embedded in the new fabric created by the exigencies of modern life. It goes without saying that the complications resulting from this situation vary according to the stage of development reached by these countries. Generally speaking, it may be said that three parallel systems of social stratification exist in underdeveloped countries: (a) the old residual forms, which in the Latin American countries may be either primitive or a product of the colonial period; (b) intermediate patterns of recent origin, doomed to disappear under the conditions of modern life, and (c) new emergent forms, adjusted to these conditions.

The existence of such a mixture creates a typical social bottleneck in underdeveloped countries which hampers economic development in various ways and can only be overcome gradually through technical and cultural progress. The trend is always toward greater simplicity, since stratification in more advanced countries always presents a simpler structure, so simple, in fact, that it can be assessed by one criterion only: income distribution. It should be recalled that modern society is integrated as follows: first, by the formation of a nationwide market for goods and services, which stimulates the formation of a common pattern of tastes and preferences; second, by the formation of a labor market, also nationwide, owing to the intense mobility of the labor force; and third, by the creation of a stratification in accordance with income and the level of living of the different occupations.

When the modern social structure achieves full functional integration, it continues to maintain a close relationship with the structure of economic development. But until this stage has been reached, and while anachronistic vestiges remain, the social structure will continue to present serious obstacles to rapid development. A false structure produces a vicious circle of negative conditions for economic progress, which often persist despite the existence of favorable natural conditions.

THE SITUATION IN LATIN AMERICA AND THE PROBLEM OF THE MIDDLE CLASS

An examination of the data provided by existing studies on the structure of employment and occupations in Latin America reveals, of course, that at the present time stratification generally displays the characteristics peculiar to underdeveloped countries which have been described above. Only a brief outline will be made of the results of such an examination.

For the moment, it will be sufficient to bear in mind the percentage distribution of total manpower (59 per cent of the active male population was employed in agriculture or related activities in 1950) in order to obtain a preliminary view of the still considerable importance of relatively primitive economic patterns and of their corresponding social structures.

Data on the structure of agriculture show to what extent the agricultural population of many Latin American countries is forced to live in extremely primitive conditions. A large proportion of this population farms extremely small holdings, which, in addition, are in most cases distributed over vast areas, with insufficient means of communication, and where the nearest markets do not yet possess the modern characteristics of those in the towns and the more densely populated areas; not to mention the still numerous remnants of primitive and semi-primitive jungle communities.

On the other hand, the agricultural sector is still much influenced by the inertia of its colonial past. Its structure is characterized by the coexistence of large holdings, worked by numerous hired laborers, and small holdings, whose farmers—whether owners, tenants, or sharecroppers—cannot, because of the size of the holdings, attain more than a subsistence level of living.

With certain well-known exceptions, medium-sized family farms producing for the market, which are the basis of the agricultural economy in the United States and a large part of Western Europe, are very rarely found in Latin America. Thus, from the sociological standpoint, there is practically no middle class in the agricultural sector, and this is a typical feature of most Latin American rural communities. This class is already in existence or is beginning to emerge only in some of the more advanced regions, where it is composed mostly of European immigrants or their descendants, who brought with them not only their techniques and a willingness to work, but also the traditions of their class. Similar reasons explain the little contribution made by fishing and forestry activities to the development of a middle class in the rural environment.

The rapid expansion of industry in Latin American countries would seem to imply the existence of a strong middle class, made up of small entrepreneurs, professionals, and well-paid specialists, as was the case in more advanced industrial nations. But this does not seem to be the case at present. It is true that industrialization has created an entrepreneurial class, and that some small- and medium-scale industrialists already constitute a middle class with all the traditional characteristics, but their number is very limited. In addition, a large proportion of these persons, who in the European tradition, for example, would permanently adopt the living patterns of the middle class, take advantage of the business opportunities provided by deficiencies in the market, shortage of technical skill, and privileged political situations to participate in the upper-class way of life, thanks to their rapid and abundant earnings. Although this aspect is very interesting from the socioeconomic point of view, it will not be developed further, since all that matters is that this phenomenon restricts even more the possibility of creating a middle class with stable traditions.

Moreover, the artisan group, which in Europe and the United States made a substantial contribution to the formation of the middle classes, is virtually nonexistent in Latin America, since it still occupies a very low level with the characteristic features of the lower urban groups from which it springs.

Professionals and intermediate specialists—technicians of all kinds, who in industrial countries represent the core of the middle class—are found only in small numbers in the industries so far developed in Latin America. It is to be hoped that such technical cadres will be formed with greater speed with the present development of the metallurgical industry, basic chemical industries, and production of mechanical and electrical equipment.

All this is equally applicable to the formation of the upper strata of the working class, who are indispensable in modern industry because of their qualities of leadership and their roles as teachers and technical instructors. Socially, they also constitute an intermediate link, ambitious to push the new generation up into the middle class. The present stage of Latin America's industry has not yet created a sufficiently large demand for the kind of occupation typified by foremen and various highly skilled workers. Apparently, in the more advanced areas (as Venezuela), mining and building activities have stimulated the formation of a large number of well-paid technicians, who have reinforced the volume and stability of the middle classes and upper working classes.

This brief outline of the over-all situation in Latin America confirms the extreme weakness of the middle classes—both old and new—in the sectors concerned with the production of goods. Most of the existing middle class is connected with the services sector: commerce, public administration, and other personal and public services. Thus, the services sector is not only more developed than the industrial, but also ties up a large proportion of the social strata urgently needed in industry. There is thus an imbalance within the Latin American middle class itself, which, accentuated by the force of family tradition, prevents it from making the adjustments required for economic development.

This means that in addition to quantitative deficiencies in stratification there are others of a qualitative order, which are more difficult to analyze, but which are reflected in the difficulties of effecting a rapid adjustment to new economic conditions. As is well known, the essential characteristic of the middle classes in modern industrial countries is their great flexibility, which makes them capable of adjusting easily to the continual changes brought about by technical progress. Considered as a whole, it is improbable that the Latin American middle class with its current structure will be able to respond fully to the demands of present-day economic development policy. In this respect, therefore, intelligent intervention is vital for strengthening the middle classes and for providing the necessary training.

CHAPTER VIII

PROBLEMS AND POLICIES RELATING TO WORLD TRADE[1]

The second session of the United Nations Conference on Trade and Development marked a crucial stage in the international community's attempts to speed up economic and social progress and improve living conditions in the developing regions of the world. The end of the 1960's was near, and all too clearly the radical changes in international economic policy required to facilitate the development of the economically less advanced countries were still a long way off, with new obstacles looming ahead. From Latin America's standpoint, the Conference met at a time when circumstances were once again such as to perpetuate and strengthen the influence of certain external

[1] This chapter has been taken almost verbatim from the address delivered by Mr. Carlos Quintana, Executive Secretary of ECLA, at the second session of UNCTAD (New Delhi, India, February 1 to March 25, 1968). World trade problems, particularly those connected with trade relationships between the developing and the industrialized countries, have been the focal point of ECLA's activities over the last few years. The studies entitled "Latin America and the United Nations Conference on Trade and Development" (E/CN.12/-693, February 1964) and "Latin America and the Second Session of UNCTAD" (E/CN.12/803, December 1967) are among the tangible evidences of this concern. The statement made by the Executive Secretary at the second session of UNCTAD summarizes the most important of the questions raised and the proposals put forward by ECLA in this connection.

factors which had been distorting and retarding the region's development for centuries.

The Weakness of Latin America's Economic Growth

If Latin America is viewed as a whole, it will be seen that its economic growth has been slow and uncertain since the mid-nineteen-fifties. Recently, the annual growth rate of the domestic product has barely reached 4.5 per cent, which means that the development of Latin America has been less dynamic than in the postwar period, up to 1955. This growth pattern is particularly unsatisfactory, inasmuch as the population is increasing at the high annual rate of 3 per cent, so that any improvement in living conditions is only very slight, and the increment in the active population resulting from the population explosion cannot be absorbed in productive occupations.

It is true that the growth rates of some countries (including Mexico, and several others of less geographical and economic importance) have been above average; but it must be borne in mind that the rate of population increase is relatively higher and that income levels are lower in the smaller countries, that the diversification of their economies is only beginning, and that the underdevelopment of their economies in the past was more marked.

Exports, External Financing, and Growth Rate During the Nineteen-Sixties

The main causes of Latin America's erratic and sluggish economic development are the inadequate expansion and diversification of its exports, the fluctuations in its export earnings, the deterioration of its terms of trade, and the lack of a genuine technical and financial co-operation policy. It should be noted, in this context, that during the first six years of the current decade Latin America's export earnings rose relatively fast. In terms of dollars, the annual rate of increase exceeded 5 per cent, as against barely 1.5 per cent in the second half of the nineteen-fifties. In addition, these more favorable trends were recorded in almost all the countries of the region, whereas in 1955–1959 the improvement was largely confined to petroleum exports.

This was one of the factors that helped to increase the rate of economic development in several countries. Other determinants included certain external financing facilities promoted through regional cooperation programs, a greater readiness to come to grips with development problems of institutional and structural origin, progress in integration, and the introduction of planning procedures. Thus the Latin American economies have given proof of their capacity to increase investment and production when the external-sector bottleneck is relieved.

Some aspects of Latin America's experience had a very important bearing on the topics discussed at the Conference. Paradoxically, despite the expansion of export earnings and the inflow of external financing, the economic growth rate of the region as a whole has been even lower than in previous years. The explanation lies in four basic circumstances: the deterioration of the terms of trade; the increase in service payments on external debts; the need to replenish monetary reserves; and the brief duration of the boom in export earnings. The depressive effects of anti-inflationary policies must also be taken into account. The influence of these factors has made itself felt, in greater or less degree, in a number of countries (including some of those that carry considerable weight in the aggregate figures for the region), and has caused contractions in their economic activity or, in many cases, has kept their growth rates below the over-all average.

Latin America's external terms of trade have steadily deteriorated since the mid nineteen-fifties, falling lowest in 1962, when the over-all index showed a decline of 22 per cent in relation to the average level for the period 1950–1954. The subsequent improvement did not extend to all products, and for petroleum and certain agricultural commodities the downward trend continued. Thus the adverse terms of trade affected some countries more severely than others, and the purchasing power of their exports was reduced—very considerably in the case of Venezuela.

The aggregate inflow of external funds in the shape of loans and investment has increased considerably during the present decade. Between 1960 and 1966, annual gross inflows averaged $2,950 million (excluding Venezuela, where there was a substantial outflow of capital from the petroleum industry). This is a much higher figure than the average of about $2,000 million recorded during the second half of the nineteen-fifties; but if amortization payments are deducted, the net inflow of funds works out to $1,560 million, which is about the same as in the previous decade. A comparison of these net inflows with the amounts represented by interest and profits on loans and investment will show that the net balance of all these movements represented an average annual contribution to the over-all balance of payments of only $610 million, while in the second half of the last decade these additional resources averaged $730 million.

If Venezuela is taken into account, it will be seen that Latin America has been transferring abroad, under the head of amortization, interest payments, and profits, sums exceeding the gross inflows of funds it has received.

This is the result of the calculation for the region as a whole. But in certain countries, the movement of external funds has been still more unfavorable; net inflows of capital have dwindled in recent years until, in some cases, they have been replaced by outflows, and the balance-of-payments position has been further aggravated by transfers of profits and the growing burden of interest payments on the accumulated debt. Moreover, this situation has often arisen at times when monetary reserves were at a critically low ebb, and it has been combined with the depressive impact of fiscal and anti-inflationary policies. All this explains why it has been so difficult for these countries to increase their growth rate, notwithstanding any increase in their export earnings.

On the other hand, another group of countries—comprised of Mexico and many smaller States—has made more intensive use of external financing in recent years, and the resulting supply of external funds may have helped to increase external purchasing power and push up the rate of growth.

In short, the point that must be stressed is the shakiness of the balance-of-payments position of the Latin American countries. Notwithstanding a few discrepancies, the following aggregate figures give an enlightening picture of this state of affairs. Between 1960 and 1966, while export earnings increased by 35 per cent, profits and interest on foreign investment and loans rose by almost 70 per cent, and amortization payments on noncompensatory loans by over 40 per cent. Thus, in 1966 total payments under the heads of amortization, interest, and profits amounted to one-third of the income accruing from exports.

It is becoming clear, therefore, that unless financial cooperation programs are launched in which the amount, costs, repayment procedures, and other features of external financing are tailored to the needs of development policy and of development itself, and unless external action is effectively coordinated with internal measures, it will be impossible to establish conditions in which foreign capital can help to augment investment and promote domestic saving.

Limitations on Economic Growth and the Potential Balance-of-Payments Deficit

Consideration must therefore be given to the prospects which the external sector may hold out for a lasting and more satisfactory process of growth in Latin America. In this respect, the increase in export earnings over the past few years might be regarded as a promising sign of a more favorable trend. But after study of the factors underlying the export situation and the principles and procedures governing international trade and financial policy, it must be concluded that those prospects are not satisfactory.

Although the greater demand stemming from the economic growth of the industrialized countries had a certain impact on Latin American exports, it is nevertheless true that transitory or fortuitous factors, likely to disappear quickly, exerted a significant influence on export earnings. Thus, for example, shortages in the Soviet Union and mainland China were responsible for a temporary increase in exports of cereals; a contraction in the supply of meat in Europe and Argentina raised meat prices; trade union and other disputes and demand for military purposes were reflected in the world prices of metals, particularly copper; and coffee prices rose temporarily as a result of a fall in production due to adverse weather conditions.

However, the disappearance of these factors caused the prices of many agricultural and mining products—which had already begun to slide in 1966—to drop even lower in 1967. This trend, in combination with the weakness of demand in the industrialized countries because of the recent decline in their growth rate, explains, in large measure, why the growth of Latin America's export earnings came to a standstill in that year. They remained at the 1966 level; and the fall in prices also affected foreign exchange reserves in 1967.

The terms of trade, which were recovering somewhat from their previous low levels, became once again unfavorable for Latin America. And, as in the past, this deterioration affected investment and earnings, with a consequent reduction of the real contribution from external financing.

Other factors restricting the expansion and diversification of Latin America's exports have aggravated these unfavorable effects. Among these are the protection and development policies of the industrialized countries, which are trying, regardless of higher costs, to become more self-sufficient in those important commodities which are the traditional exports of the developing countries and to promote subsidized exports; also the restrictions, quotas, taxes, and other measures which limit consumption of products exported only by the developing countries; the progressive replacement of natural products by synthetics; the special preference which some of the developed countries accord to other developing countries and which are being extended to more and more countries and products; the shipping practices and policies which injure Latin America's trade; and the increasing difficulties and unfair treatment hampering Latin American attempts to diversify export trade by introducing new exports of manufactures. And further, there are the policies which lead the developed countries to restrict financial cooperation and aid, raise interest rates, and impose conditions on the use of external funds.

These features of the world economy are preventing the developing countries from expanding their trade and securing the financial and technical cooperation which, in conjunction with internal institutional reforms and the mobilization of their domestic resources, would enable them to attract more investment, assimilate new techniques, and increase production and employment on the required scale.

It is clear from the technical studies that have been carried out since the first session of the Conference and new studies presented at the second session that a considerable potential trade or balance-of-payments deficit would preclude a satisfactory rate of growth over the next decade.

This creates a very delicate situation for Latin America. Import substitution has forged ahead in the large and medium-sized countries and is continuing in the others along traditional lines. In the former group, no further impetus of any significance can be expected from that source, and in the remainder, for obvious reasons, the prospects are extremely dim. It is true that regional integration is opening up new possibilities; but here, too, difficulties are bound to arise, unless trade with the rest of the world is expanded and adequate financial and technical cooperation is forthcoming.

The Need for a Reorganization of World Trade and for Substantial Changes in the Economic Policy of the Developed Countries

At its first session, four years ago, UNCTAD adopted principles and recommendations which, had they been put into effect, would have led to a reorganization of world trade and would have promoted the economic growth of the developing countries. Unfortunately, those undertakings were not translated into policy decisions, and other measures and restrictions increased the obstacles to the expansion of Latin America's exports. The appropriate instruments have yet to be drawn up to give effect to recommendations that were adopted without opposition, such as those on the reduction and elimination of obstacles to trade in products of export interest to developing countries, and on the negotiation of international commodity agreements or arrangements. The delay is disheartening, for if it can happen in a field in which there is general agreement regarding the action that should be taken by the international community, still graver doubts may be felt as to the implementation of other recommendations which contain escape clauses that may be invoked unilaterally by the developed countries.

These clauses, and other provisos, have been used to some extent as an excuse for taking no action with regard to the formidable problems that remain to be solved. It is necessary, therefore, to establish objective criteria and determine the circumstances under which such clauses may be invoked. They should not be applied on the unilateral decision of one country but only after prior consultations or negotiations between the parties concerned.

The results of the Kennedy Round of tariff negotiations were a source of deep satisfaction to the developed countries inasmuch as great strides were made toward the liberalization of world trade. Unfortunately, the developing countries could not fully share this feeling, because only marginal consideration was given to their interests.

The most important tariff reductions were granted on highly processed products whose manufacture is capital-intensive and fairly complex in technique, and which are exported exclusively by the developed countries. In respect to primary commodities and manufactures and semimanufactures of special interest to the developing countries, the concessions are minimal, and in some cases merely represented the consolidation of tariff reductions already in force on a temporary basis. Moreover, as a result of the application of the most-favored-nation clause, many of the concessions are likely to encourage trade between developed countries more than the developing countries' trade. The hoped-for tariff reductions in favor of the developing countries have not been achieved, and no progress has been made in relaxing the protectionist policies of the developed countries, or in reducing or eliminating duties and other restrictions on agricultural commodities of vital interest to the developing countries.

Although the developing countries did obtain fairly sizable tariff reductions for some of their products, no solution has yet been found for the serious problems connected with the access of their traditional exports to the markets of the industrialized countries, and with the stabilization of prices at remunerative levels, or for those which impede the establishment of new export flows of manufactures and semimanufactures.

If this goes on, the relative position of the Latin American countries in world trade and development will continue to deteriorate. The world community cannot remain indifferent to this paradoxical state of affairs: while the industrialized countries have agreed upon decisions of enormous importance for the liberalization of their trade, which will certainly promote a new surge of rapid technical progress and economic growth in the developed areas of the world, no such agreement has been reached for adopting the measures or establishing the institutions which would make for equal progress in the developing countries.

If the developed nations have decided to liberalize their trade, despite the industrial competition and adjustments which such a process entails, why should not similar action be undertaken in favor of the less advanced countries, and why should they not be given equitable treatment, as their development is only just beginning, so that they also may share in the benefits of technical progress and infuse the necessary dynamism into the development of their economies?

In this regard two particularly significant facts emerge from Latin America's past experience: first, that the growth rate of investment and income can be stepped up immediately if a cure is found for the lack of dynamism in the external sector; and second, that the rate of growth must be increased so as to facilitate the institutional reforms and the mobilization of domestic resources which are an urgent necessity if there is to be any easing of the social tensions that dominate the Latin American scene.

ECLA and the Second Session of UNCTAD

The second session of UNCTAD afforded an opportunity for adopting decisions to lay new bases for world trade and finacial cooperation with the developing countries. Definite programs of action, and practical procedures were agreed upon, so that recommendations of the first session and any formulated at the second, could be put into effect through specific government measures. It was emphasized that the developing countries could no longer confine their aspirations to a modest improvement of their current rate of growth; that the promotion of conditions that would enable lasting progress to be achieved in the coming decade would entail a coordination and redoubling of effort in the next few years, with more ambitious objectives. It was pointed out that, in Latin America's case, employment problems and the need to improve living conditions—both at the material and at the cultural level—made it urgently necessary that the annual per capita growth rate should average more than 3 per cent.

Since the date of its establishment, ECLA has explored these practical problems and studied world trade in relation to development. In the year or two before the second session of UNCTAD, at ECLA's express request, its secretariat concentrated even more attention on the preparatory work for that session. The document entitled "Latin America and the second session of UNCTAD" (E/CN.12/803) is the outcome of a process of research, exchange of views, and consultation which began in mid-1966 at the third meeting of experts of the *Ad Hoc* Committee on Latin American Co-ordination (CECLA), and was continued at the twelfth session of ECLA, in May 1967—where it was the keynote of the proceedings—and at the fourth meeting of CECLA at the expert level. It culminated in the meeting of government experts from the developing countries' members of ECLA, held in December 1967.

At all these gatherings, the ECLA secretariat put forward ideas and proposals relating to items on the agenda for the Conference, and a provisional text of the document was examined at the twelfth session of ECLA. In the first part of the study, recent trends in Latin America's foreign trade were reviewed, together with the economic and financial policy of the industrialized countries. Special attention was devoted to problems connected with the fulfillment of commitments assumed at the first session of UNCTAD and under GATT, and to procedures for applying escape clauses. The results of the Kennedy Round were also analyzed from the standpoint of the developing countries in general and the Latin American countries in particular. The second part of the document dealt with the various items on the agenda for the second session of UNCTAD, and specific ideas and suggestions were included as to the decisions that the ECLA secretariat felt should be adopted.

Owing to the course followed in preparing the ECLA document, the proposals it puts forward with respect to trade policy and financing differ little, in the main, from those formulated by the Latin American countries in the Charter of Tequendama, or from the essential content of the Charter of Algiers. However, some points were emphasized as being of special importance for the success of the UNCTAD session.

It was again emphasized that an indispensable step toward solving the problems of the developing countries would be the adoption of effective measures to ensure an immediate and progressive increase in export earnings and to provide instruments for the implementation of a financial and technical cooperation program on lines adapted to development needs. It was suggested that the international community should establish practical procedures and some kind of institutional machinery for the coordination of essential aspects of external action in the light of national development programs or targets, so that developing countries might be able to rely on obtaining coordinated (and not conflicting) support to enable them to carry out their national programs.

At the second session of the Conference, specific decisions could not be taken concerning all the agenda items, either on account of pressure of time, or because headway had first to be made in certain basic technical studies; but at all events, it would have been extremely discouraging if the session had ended with the adoption of general declarations or recommendations more or less echoing the agreements reached nearly four years before, at the first session. Disappointment of this kind would generate a profound and dangerous sense of frustration in the developing world, because the fiasco that it caused would occur just after the developed countries had concluded negotiations of vital importance for their own interests.

Consequently, certain lines of action were mapped out beforehand. The Board decided that discussion would be concentrated on those basic issues where the problems had been sufficiently elucidated and enough information collected for there to be a likelihood that definite decisions could be reached. It was agreed that, as regarded other important items, basic directives should be adopted with a view to expediting research and discussion, and that they should include precise guidelines and time schedules for the convening of any meetings of experts considered necessary and for the various phases of the work, right up to the actual application of decisions by governments.

Mr. Carlos Quintana, Executive Secretary of ECLA, explained fully his ideas about the nature and scope of the decisions to be adopted at the second session of UNCTAD in alluding briefly to some of the following items on the agenda.

COMMODITIES

There seems to be a consensus of opinion that in dealing with commodity problems the product-by-product approach should be adopted. The developing countries should be guaranteed a minimum share in the consumer markets of the industrialized countries for commodities which are produced by both. Moreover, a specific plan of action should be agreed upon, on a product-by-product or market-by-market basis, with a view to reaching government-supported decisions which will remove the mass of obstructions impeding trade in such commodities. With regard to those other primary products which are exported mainly by the developing countries, the aim should be to secure the reduction or elimination of the customs duties, internal taxes, and other restrictions which limit their access to the markets of the developed countries. An imperative necessity here is to devise appropriate procedures for the elimination of the existing special preferences. In addition, steps should be taken to prepare a specific program of action to improve the competitive position of natural products vis-à-vis substitutes and synthetics. Another point that must be mentioned is the pressing need for effective decisions to ensure closer cooperation in concluding commodity agreements or agreeing upon other market organization arrangements to secure the expansion of exports and the stabilization of prices at remunerative levels.

MANUFACTURES AND SEMIMANUFACTURES

I am fully confident that at the present session, agreement will be reached concerning the essential principles of a system of general preferences in favor of manufactures and semimanufactures from the developing countries. The suggestions formulated in the ECLA document largely coincide with the proposals put forward in the Charters of Tequendama and Algiers. They relate to the following points: the preferences should be general and nondiscriminatory, without reciprocity; free access to the markets of the industrialized countries should be granted, although quotas may be established for certain products; and preferential treatment should be unconditionally extended to all manufactures and semimanufactures produced by the developing countries. Provision may be made for exceptions to this last rule, provided that they are subject to consultation and negotiation with the developing countries.

At the present session, tedious discussions of detail which might hold up the entry into operation of the system should be avoided. The best plan would be to agree on the basic principles of the system and establish directives for the program of negotiations that should be undertaken, so that the preferences may be applied as from the beginning of next year.

TRADE WITH THE CENTRALLY PLANNED ECONOMIES

Latin America is aware of the importance that may be assumed by trade with the centrally planned economies. Some procedures conducive to the expansion of such trade have recently been introduced. However, the familiar difficulties still keep it down to very low figures. Consideration should therefore be given to new modes of action, and more specific commitments and decisions should be arrived at, so that the centrally planned economies may, *inter alia*, include in their purchasing programs increasing volumes of products from the developing countries, reduce the unduly wide margins between import and domestic market prices, and introduce more flexible procedures in payments agreements to facilitate multilateralism both inside and outside the socialist area.

FINANCING OF DEVELOPMENT

The only other question I should like to touch upon is that of financing, a subject on which information and technical studies are not lacking of the kind required to pave the way for decisions to establish the necessary institutional framework and provide a permanent solution for problems threatening to become more acute. Among the various proposals, I would highlight those relating to the conversion of the International Bank of Reconstruction and Development (IBRD) into a bank for the developing countries, and to the expansion of the net flow of external funds to these countries until established targets have been attained. Above all, I think enough progress has been made for the Conference to take at this session a final decision to establish a system of supplementary financing. Moreover, we all feel that it is urgently necessary to adopt measures to modify the terms and procedures of external financing and, in particular, to establish a fund by means of which interest payments on loans to developing countries can be substantially reduced.

The mention of these specific points does not mean that I assign less importance to other items on the agenda for this session; I would merely stress that what I feel to be indispensable is the adoption of decisions on subjects of particular importance, and the establishment of bases for reaching agreement on others through programs of action which also must be very precisely defined.

Out of indifference, or for want of effective action, no international economic and financial machinery has yet been set up to ensure the observance of principles of economic rationality and a fair deal for peoples that constitute the vast majority of mankind.

Today the time is ripe for us to find effective solutions for the vital problems of the developing countries, and I am confident that coordinated action on the part of these countries themselves, together with the constructive cooperation of the developed countries, in accordance with the claims of equity and the responsibility they bear within the international community, will help to ensure that the achievements of this session of UNCTAD will mark it as an epoch-making event. And thanks to these achievements, the developing regions of the world will at last emerge from their economic stagnation and share in the technical and economic progress which is now enjoyed by only a privileged few.

CHAPTER IX

TOWARD A DYNAMIC DEVELOPMENT POLICY FOR LATIN AMERICA[1]

Structural Reforms to Clear the Way for Development

The ills besetting the Latin American economy are not determined by circumstantial or transient factors. They are an expression of the critical state of affairs in our time and of the incapacity of the economic system—owing to structural defects that it has been beyond our ability or our power to remedy—to achieve and maintain a rate of development consonant with the growth of the population and with its demands for a speedy improvement in its levels of living.

The increase in the population has been phenomenal. At the beginning of the century, there were 63 million inhabitants in Latin America, and the annual rate of demographic growth was 1.8 per cent. Now we number 220 million, and we are multiplying at an annual rate of 2.9 per cent, which shows signs of rising even higher.[2]

On the basis of conjectural data, it may be estimated that about half the existing population has a tiny average personal income of $120

[1] Raúl Prebisch, *Towards a Dynamic Development Policy for Latin America* (United Nations publication, Sales No.: 64.II.G.4), pp. 3–20.

[2] In 1900 the population increased by 1.1 million inhabitants, and in 1960 by 6.4 million.

a year.[3] And this vast social aggregate accounts for only about one-fifth of total personal consumption in Latin America, showing the highest coefficients of undernourishment, poor clothing and worse housing, and disease and illiteracy; and, at the same time, the highest rate of reproduction.

It is here that development effort must primarily be concentrated. The notion, which dies hard, that development takes place spontaneously, without a rational and deliberate effort to achieve it, has proved to be an illusion, both in Latin America and in the other peripheral regions of the world. For a century now our economies have been linked to the international economy, and 50 per cent of the population is still stagnating in precapitalist conditions which are incompatible with its growing economic and social aspirations.

Even so, average per capita income in Latin America is appreciably higher than in other peripheral regions, and thus affords an advantageous starting point for the realization of what is no longer a utopian dream: the eradication of poverty and its inherent evils, by virtue of the tremendous potential of contemporary technology—and the possibility of assimilating it more quickly than was the case with the capitalist evolution of the more advanced countries.

However, this rapid penetration of technique demands and carries with it radical changes: changes both in the pattern of production and in the structure of the economy, which could not be effectively brought about without a basic reform of the social structure.

The prevailing social structure in Latin America constitutes a serious obstacle to technical progress and, consequently, to economic and social development. This shows itself in three main ways:

(*a*) The structure of society considerably hampers social mobility, that is, the emergence and rise of the dynamic elements in society, men of drive and initiative, capable of taking risks and responsibilities both in technical and economic matters and in the other aspects of community life;

(*b*) the social structure is largely characterized by a situation of

[3] See the chapter entitled "Income Distribution in Latin America" in *The Economic Development of Latin America in the Post-War Period* (United Nations publication, Sales No.: 64.II.G.6), pp. 62–74.

privilege in the distribution of wealth and therefore of income. Privilege weakens or destroys the incentive to economic activity, to the detriment of the efficient utilization of human resources, land, and machinery;

(*c*) This state of privilege in regard to distribution is reflected not in a rapid rate of net capital formation, but in extravagant patterns of consumption in the upper strata of society, contrasting with the unsatisfactory living conditions of the broad masses of the population.

In these days of zeal for planning there is a great deal of talk about the prime importance of the role of private enterprise in Latin America and the need to keep it intact. But what is meant by this, in the last analysis? Does it mean that the present system, under which individual initiative is cramped by social stratification and privilege, should be kept intact? Or is the way to be cleared for this initiative by the above-mentioned structural reforms, so that the system may acquire the full dynamic force it lacks at present?

Capital Formation and Income Distribution

The test of a system's dynamic strength lies in its ability to accelerate the rate of development and improve progressively the distribution of income. If the annual rate of growth of average per capita income could be raised from the very low figure of 1 per cent, recently recorded, to a minimum of 3 per cent in Latin America as a whole, by means of a rational redistribution policy, the personal income of the underprivileged half of the population could be doubled in seventeen years, and the lot of the middle-income groups could be improved likewise, although at a less rapid rate.

This is where the first step toward reform of the social structure becomes essential, since such a rate of growth is not feasible without substantial restriction of the consumption of the higher-income groups.

The social contrast is striking indeed. While 50 per cent of the population accounts for approximately two-tenths of total personal consumption, at the other end of the scale 5 per cent of the inhabitants of the region enjoy nearly three-tenths of that total, according to the estimates referred to above. A policy of austerity mainly affecting this latter social group, and supplemented by the contribution of international resources, would permit an increase in net capital formation and the attainment of the above-mentioned growth target for per capita income, while at the same time redistribution policy would ensure that the income increment thus obtained was passed on to the lower strata of the community.

Herein lies the essence of redistribution policy. It is not a matter of taking income away from the upper minority and simply distributing it among the broad masses of the population, for with per capita personal income in Latin America as a whole barely amounting to $370 a year, the benefits of such a redistribution would not stretch very far. But if, on the other hand, restrictions on the consumption of the privileged groups were reflected in a steady increase in net capital formation, the standard of living of the bulk of the population would rise progressively faster.

Technology has made this dynamic concept of redistribution viable for the first time in history, for without the immense potential it places at the disposal of developing countries, the effects of the redistribution operation would be very limited in their scope. Thus, the problems of capital formation and income distribution assume very different forms from those they took during the capitalist evolution of the more advanced countries.

At that time it was capital formation that came first, and the gradual redistribution of income followed. Now, on the other hand, both these requirements present themselves—as they are bound to do—simultaneously, under the increasing political and trade-union pressure exerted by the lower-income groups.

The only available means of meeting them is by directly combating one of the anomalies that most affect the development of Latin America, namely, the marked failure of capital formation to reach the levels demanded by contemporary technology, as against the extravagant pattern of consumption of the high-income groups.

Among these upper strata (5 per cent of the population) which account for about three-tenths of Latin America's total consumption, average consumption per household is fifteen times greater than that of the lower strata (50 per cent of the population). If this ratio were reduced to 11 to 1, by the restriction of consumption in favor of increased investment, the annual rate of growth of per capita income could rise from 1 per cent to 3 per cent. And if restriction of consumption brought the ratio down to 9 to 1, the rate of growth might reach 4 per cent, or even more, according to the political feasibility of this operation and the capacity of each country to put it into effect.

International Cooperation and the Structure of Trade

This capacity might be seriously handicapped by the external bottleneck in development, which, in conjunction with the limitations of domestic production of capital goods, would make it impossible for all the additional savings obtained to be invested in such goods. Hence the vital need for international resources, until the structural reforms advocated here permit full advantage to be taken of the increase in savings.

The contribution to be made by international resources is thus of a temporary nature. It would cease to be necessary, once the reforms had borne the full crop of results to be expected of them. They are not a matter for Latin America alone, since it is also essential to work for the elimination of the external bottleneck by changing the existing structure of international trade.

The countries in which industrialization advances most rapidly tend to be affected more and more by this bottleneck. Their difficulties do not originate solely in the social structure, but also in the type of trade structure which characterized the epoch of externally geared development that preceded the world depression of the thirties. Here again, as in other aspects of Latin America's development problems, a whole constellation of out-of-date ideas survives. It is true that the industrialization of the peripheral regions has at last been accepted as an indispensable requisite for economic development. But what is still perpetuated is the anachronistic trade pattern inherent in the peculiar concept of the international division of labor which was prevalent up to a short time ago—the trading of primary commodities against manufactured goods. This is the framework within which the industrialization of the Latin American countries has been taking place. And the obstacle to economic development that it represents is now beginning to loom larger at every turn, for whereas the upward trend of demand for the manufactures we import is very sharp, primary exports are expanding relatively slowly, largely for reasons over which the Latin American countries have no control. Thus there is a latent tendency toward disequilibrium which is aggravated as economic development gains speed.

This is a new phenomenon not experienced by the more advanced countries in the past. Hence it is only now that its significance is beginning to be understood, and recognition accorded to the vital need to encourage the industrial exports of the peripheral countries, especially those which have completed the first stage of the industrialization process.

This encouragement of industrial exports, in addition to exports of primary commodities, cannot be achieved within the narrow bounds of the existing markets. It is essential to alter the geographical structure of trade, as well as its composition by products.

Latin America's exports are of course affected by the universal slowness of the growth of demand for primary commodities, in contrast with the buoyancy of demand for manufactures as per capita income rises. But this circumstance combines with other factors of considerable importance. In the first place, the moderate rate of economic development of the United States and the import restrictions it has imposed have exerted an adverse influence on Latin America's export trade. And, in the second place, the protectionism and discrimination practiced by the European Common Market prevent Latin America from taking full advantage of the steady expansion of demand for primary commodities in the vast economic area it represents.

Without prejudice to measures aimed at eliminating or reducing these barriers to trade, it is a matter of urgent necessity to explore, with the utmost diligence, the possibilities for trade with other regions of the world, especially those—the socialist economies, for example—which show a high rate of development.

While it is true that basically the solution of such problems depends upon the great industrial countries and the degree to which their trade policy favors liberalization, it is no less certain that the Latin American countries too must put forth a tremendous effort in the same direction. In this sense, the formation of a common market is an undertaking that brooks no delay. Its importance has been realized by the Central American countries, whose determination to establish such a market has been bold and resolute. The problem of the Latin American Free-Trade Association is more difficult, for the very reason that the development of industrialization in watertight compartments has created vested interests and prejudices which oppose reciprocal trade without taking account of the serious effects of such an attitude on economic development. This is not merely a technical matter; it is a question of important policy decisions which must follow up the Montevideo Treaty. The technical groundwork for these decisions is basically complete; all that remains to be done is to study and select the best ways of putting them into practice.

The Closed Type of Development in Latin America

The external bottleneck in development is not due solely to the slow upward trend of exports of primary commodities as against the rapid expansion of industrial imports from the great centers, or to the low level of inter-Latin American trade; it has also largely been determined, in recent years, by the deterioration of the terms of trade and its serious effects on the purchasing power of exports. The action of all these factors in combination reduced the per capita value of Latin America's exports from $58 in 1930 to $39 in 1960 (at 1950 prices).

The recent decline in the terms of trade is yet another indication of the peripheral countries' inherent incapacity to retain the whole of the benefits accruing from their technical progress. There is not much consolation to be had from the reflection that in the future, when the Latin American countries reach more advanced stages of development and their industrialization process is complete, this state of affairs will some day be brought to an end; it will take a long time, and meanwhile the deterioration of the terms of trade is aggravating the external bottleneck and exerting a marked depressive influence on domestic capacity for capital formation, to the detriment of development itself.

From a different angle, the other notion that still survives in some circles, to the effect that the external bottleneck and the disequilibria in international accounts in which it is reflected are mere matters of monetary operation, has had deplorable consequences, since its practical application—besides adversely affecting economic development—has diverted attention from the basic solutions which this structural phenomenon demands.

This is a point of considerable importance for Latin America, for unless the solutions in question are resolutely sought, Latin American countries will be swept by the force of circumstances toward an increasingly closed type of development, and a steady contraction of their share in trade with the rest of the world, which will add further difficulties to those inherent in such a process. In default of sufficient international cooperation to overcome these difficulties, in the fields of trade and of financing, all kinds of authoritarian measures might supervene, with grave consequences for the progressive development of democracy in Latin America.

Internal Bottlenecks

The intensification of development is not simply a question of increasing net capital formation. While this is necessary, it is by no means sufficient, since development may be cramped by a variety of factors. Those of an external kind have already been mentioned, but there are also internal bottlenecks that circumscribe or hamper the expansive force of net capital formation.

Furthermore, there is usually a wide margin for the immediate growth of production in the Latin American countries, because of idle capacity in a number of branches. But the factors that have been mentioned either rule out this production or bring inflationary pressures of a nonmonetary kind in their train if a policy directed toward the full utilization of idle capacity is put into force.

There is no doubt that the most persistent bottleneck in the whole of Latin America's development process is generally to be found in agricultural production.[4] A combination of several factors is responsi-

[4] This internal bottleneck—in common with others frequently encountered in the Latin American development process—has frustrated a number of attempts to redistribute income; these have been limited to improving the monetary level of wages and salaries, irrespective of the investment required to raise production, especially in the agricultural sector, and to satisfying the increase produced in popular demand by the redistribution of income, without inflationary pressure.

ble for this: the system of land tenure, which makes it difficult for modern techniques to be assimilated; inadequate State aid in the work of adapting and diffusing these techniques; and the unsatisfactory investment situation. However thoroughly these three problems may be dealt with, unless farmers are given proper incentives, efforts to accelerate development are likely to find their most formidable stumbling block in the agricultural sector, as in a number of countries with differing economic systems.

The incentives may be of various kinds, but the most important is that agriculture should reap the benefits of the technical progress it makes, both externally and in the interplay of internal economic forces. This is the only way the wide gap between average-income figures in rural and in urban areas can be gradually narrowed. The fact is that the impoverished half of the population is largely to be found in rural areas.

With a little thought, it will be clear that the externally geared growth of earlier periods, based on the characteristic types of foreign enclave which do not allow technical progress to spread to the internal economy, broke up the original precapitalist integration of the countryside with the town. And industrialization tends to widen rather than reduce the breach by aggravating the social and economic dichotomy. Steps must now be taken to remedy this.

The widening of the gap is due not only to the structural features of the rural sector, but also to the fact that internal development has not been dynamic enough to raise the farmer's income. Furthermore, it is usually the farmer who is called upon to bear a considerable part of the cost of import substitution, excessive protection, and unfair marketing practices, and also of social security and other State services —from which the rural worker reaps virtually no benefit, because he can exert no trade-union pressure and has no political contacts. In fact, he continues to be the Cinderella of urban politics.

No exhaustive examination has yet been made of all the repercussions of these factors on the drift from the countryside to the bigger Latin American towns, which is a striking and disquieting sign of economic and social disequilibrium. There is no doubt that such migration is bound to take place; nor is there any doubt that the increased technical progress of the rural areas will tend to give it greater momentum. But is it necessary for the displaced population to congregate in the big towns? Why should they not stay in the rural milieu, living in small or medium-sized communities, and employed in industries and services that would satisfy some of the requirements of that milieu itself? Why have the bigger towns in Latin America grown, at the expense of the medium-sized and small towns, to an extraordinary extent that is quite disproportionate to the trend in more advanced countries?

These questions cannot be answered satisfactorily without careful research. Perhaps the weakness of rural demand, or, to put it another way, the concentration of demand in the big towns as a result of the structural[5] and adventitious factors mentioned above, may have played an important part in this phenomenon. And, as in the case of other social phenomena, there have been no countervailing reactions, but a self-perpetuating spiral, since the agglomeration of people in big towns concentrates its own increasing demand, and this in turn leads to further population congestion. It may therefore be concluded that the geological redistribution of income is also of great social importance.

Why Should Development Forces Be Deliberately Controlled?

One dominant idea runs through the whole of this book: Latin America must quicken its rate of economic development and redistribute income in favor of the broad masses of the population. The attainment of these objectives cannot be indefinitely postponed, nor are there grounds for expecting that economic development will take place first and be followed in the natural course of events by social development. Both must be achieved gradually and side by side. This will entail rational and deliberate action to influence the forces of development; the spontaneous interplay of these forces will not suf-

[5] With respect to these structural factors, it should be borne in mind that, because of the existing system of land tenure, much of the income from the land—particularly that of the big landowners—is spent in the towns and not in the countryside.

fice here, as it did in the capitalist evolution of the advanced countries.

The notion that this type of evolution could be repeated in Latin America has been very misleading. In the advanced countries economic development has been essentially a spontaneous phenomenon, but the same is not true of social development, which has largely been shaped by deliberate policy measures. And it is clear that in those countries the need for action of this sort, the need for planning, is also gaining recognition.

There is one overriding argument: today, when man is acquiring a hitherto undreamed-of power over the forces of nature, he cannot resign himself to remaining at the mercy of the unfettered play of economic forces, with their manifest incapacity, to maintain or achieve a satisfactory rate of growth, reduce cyclical fluctuations, or bring about equitable income distribution.

As history cannot repeat itself in this respect, there are very cogent reasons for finding new paths. The assimilation of an already highly developed technique in a fairly short space of time is a very different matter from the gradual development of such a technique, since serious incongruities or disparities appear which have to be dealt with by State action.

First, during the evolution of the capitalist economies, technology was gradually incorporated into the production process as the necessary capital formation took place. The countries now developing, on the other hand, have to assimilate a technology that is ready-made. And if they are to climb progressively toward the higher stage already reached by the more advanced countries, the rate of increase of per capita income will have to be more rapid than it was in the industrial countries in the past.

Then, too, this technology and the continual innovations it entails call for substantial capital investment per head, which the advanced countries can easily build up on the strength of their high per capita income. The developing countries, on the other hand, in face of the same extremely capital-intensive technology, have an average per capita income barely comparable to that of the advanced countries about a century ago. Hence there is no way out now but for the State deliberately to reduce the consumption of the higher-income groups in the community, whereas there was no necessity for this when the capitalist economies were developing, since saving on the part of those same groups was spontaneous and almost automatic.

These incongruities bring in their train another, to which reference has already been made. Whereas in the advanced countries net capital formation came first and the redistribution of income later, in Latin American countries the two problems have now to be solved simultaneously, particularly with the model of the Soviet method of economic development forever before our eyes.

To add to this, there is the rapidity with which techniques for the prevention and cure of disease are spread, and the ensuing sharp drop in the mortality rate, a phenomenon that took place very slowly during the evolutionary stage of the more advanced countries, accompanied by an equally gradual fall in the birthrate. There the increase in income fostered changes in the psychological attitude to family formation not yet in evidence among the masses of the Latin American population with their meager resources. This explains the disparity between the exceptionally high rate of population growth in Latin America and the relatively moderate rate prevailing during the evolution of the capitalist economies.

The high rate of demographic growth entails a more intensive capital-formation effort and enhances the incongruity between the inexhaustible supply of manpower in Latin American countries and the technology to be assimilated, as evolved in the big industrial centers under the spur of an everincreasing labor shortage.

Lastly, mention must be made of the incongruity or disparity between import and export demand, which was likewise no problem in the past. Thus the big centers, as they grew, did not show that trend toward the formation of external bottlenecks which is characteristic of the Latin American countries.

The task of coping with these incongruities and promoting development entails three forms of State action. First and foremost, action to reform the social structure and thereby remove the obstacles to development; this consists essentially in making full use of the savings potential, encouraging the intensive utilization of land and capital and freeing the huge potential of individual initiative which now goes to waste, so as to give the system its full dynamic force.

These changes in the social structure pave the way for others, affecting the production pattern and structure of the economy, which are inherent in the spread and absorption of contemporary technology.

Lastly, State action is indispensable if the marked disparities in income distribution are to be progressively remedied by virtue of the increase in income accompanying the changes introduced.

Opposition to Reforms and Responsibility for Carrying Them Out

This book is designed as much for those who resist such changes within their own countries as for those who propose to carry them out. It is also directed toward those outside the region who fail to grasp the nature and gravity of events in Latin America.

To the first of these groups, we should like to demonstrate the ineluctable necessity of introducing these changes into the social structure so that the pattern of production and the structure of the economy can respond to development requirements. If they are anxious to keep their position in the distribution scale inviolate, we would emphasize for their benefit that a point in history has been reached when it is no longer feasible to maintain consumption patterns that imply the dissipation of a substantial capital formation potential in a fashion totally incompatible with the region's vast capital formation requirements. And if they are concerned for the future of democracy, it will not be amiss to suggest that nothing will do more to strengthen it in Latin America than social mobility, the emergence and rise of the dynamic elements of society, by virtue of the reforms in question; and that stubborn opposition to such measures might compel other men, whose ultimate motive was the same, to ride roughshod over democratic procedure in order to achieve this aim, perhaps in the illusory belief that the opportunities for sound democratic development which would be lost in social strife could in the course of time be recovered.

Those who are resolved to carry out the reforms are faced with a tremendous responsibility. Considerable emotional force is building up in Latin America, the emotional force of great mass movements. It must be channeled toward clear and constructive ends. Nothing can be accomplished without thought and rational planning. But neither can bold decisions be taken—such decisions as our countries need—without the driving-power of this force. The acid test of ultimate effectiveness will lie in the ability of the leaders to fuse these elements into a development policy.

There is, of course, always the risk that such reforms and the necessary follow-up action may be bungled if the primary objectives are lost sight of. There will be no genuine reforms in the structure of society if all that happens is that the existing privileges change hands or that new privileges and sinecures are added to the old.

Furthermore, it must be understood both in Latin American countries and outside them that in all this we are confronted with new requirements. In the evolution of the capitalist economies a development policy was not essential, because of the spontaneity of the process itself. This type of evolution cannot be repeated in the Latin American countries.

Outside Latin America, naturally enough, it may seem not only posssible but desirable for the region to follow the path which led the developed countries to achieve such impressive results. There are also some who look to international cooperation to produce results which have some virtue, viewed from the political angle, but which, however effective as stopgaps, would be self-defeating over the long run. The only admissible political meaning of such cooperation, from the Latin American standpoint, is that it should contribute to the political viability of an intensive internal development effort.

A System of Ideas and a Changed Outlook

All this presents Latin America with a new set of problems, very different from that with which previous generations were faced. In the midst of the world Depression we did not know the true nature of Latin America's development difficulties: the dominant idea was simply to restore normal conditions, to return to the past. Fifteen years ago we were able to attempt a definition of the set of problems in question and to point with deep conviction to certain basic solutions. And today sufficient progress has been made to work out a system of ideas, a dynamic view of economic and social development leading to practical action. Now the task is to promote public discussion and, above all, to gain the ear of political and trade-union leaders. What has to be done is to overcome the ideological poverty that prevails in our countries in this field, the traditional propensity to introduce from abroad nostrums that are largely alien to the real requirements of Latin America's situation.

If the ideas that we Latin American economists have worked out are to serve as a guide to the State in acting on the forces of development, they must be presented in a clear and easily understood form. There is no idea in the development field that cannot be explained in simple terms, even though its working-out may have required complicated reasoning and mathematical procedures to improve the level of thinking—not to reduce the need for it. We economists must acquire this ability to make ourselves understood; if we do not succeed, the failure should be attributed to our own confused ideas rather than to the limitations of others. In fact, if our arguments are not concise and lucid, this is generally because they have not been properly sifted, or because we have not altogether freed ourselves from the frame of mind that looks to the esoteric for the material of intellectual prestige. Or perhaps confusion results from the play of economic or political interests, or from a certain tendency to wrap one's thoughts in vague terms in order to shun the responsibility for definite views.

This, too, involves a new problem. There was no need for public discussion of development when it took place of its own accord as the capitalist economies evolved; there was no reason then to expound the problem of capital formation, since the solution came about spontaneously.

This is undoubtedly the crucial problem of Latin American development. Admitting that very firm measures must be adopted to increase the flow of savings, we see that steps must also be taken to ensure that the funds thus obtained are in fact used to augment capital, and that this capital is devoted to achieving the aims of the development plan.

Here we must watch for an ever-present risk. The social tensions of today may make for the use of an excessively high proportion of such funds to improve present consumption, or to effect social investment for immediate welfare purposes, at the expense of economic investment which would promote welfare at a later date. To yield to this pressure would spell utter failure in attaining the social objective of a steady, vigorous improvement in the living conditions of the masses of the population.

In addition, military expenditure often absorbs an appreciable proportion of total income, to the detriment of economic development. Certain very significant questions arise in this context. Does the evolution of military technology call for a searching review of its prevailing ideas? Would this involve increasing expenditure, or might it not be possible, by virtue of this technology and a limitation of armaments, to reduce the armed forces, at the same time increasing their effectiveness and curtailing military expenditure in favor of economic development?

All these questions disclose, for the first time in our countries, a very broad field in which public awareness of development can be shaped. This does not apply solely to the lofty ideas and grand designs that capture the popular imagination. The practical process of development also provides varied opportunities for channeling the energies of the community into the many tasks that are part of a development plan. There are visible signs in Latin America of a vast, latent wealth of enthusiasm and initiative, springing less from personal interest than from a community spirit. The women of Latin America too are showing this spirit by their increasing participation in political and social life.

Furthermore, community action, like a cooperative movement, will permit simplification of State action by confining it to the efficient manipulation of the machinery of the system, leaving to individuals the tasks that can better be performed by them on their own initiative and responsibility, as the State is already taking on some very thorny problems as part of development planning. Generally speaking, the State is not equipped for this, in the Latin American countries, and in this respect, too, sweeping changes will have to be made if it is to assume new and exacting responsibilities.

In fact neither structural reforms nor planning can be approached on the basis of simple formulas. But, once crystallized in the form of legislation and decrees, they will operate automatically, by virtue of the mere fact that a plan has been approved and international funds have been promised. In periods of externally geared development, this typical expectation that all problems will somehow solve themselves is strongly entrenched. This is a danger inherent in planning itself.

We must clear our minds of such illusions. There is no easy way out for Latin America. Planning means a strictly methodical—although not a straitjacketed—approach to development problems, and an unremitting discipline in State action. It consists in a series of acts of foresight, of anticipation of future needs, of rationally relating the method of meeting those needs with the scanty resources available.

All this shows that the development is a vast undertaking in terms of both time and scope. It requires not only changed structure but also changes in outlook, approach, and modes of action. Are such changes feasible in our countries? This question often evokes a feeling of discouraged skepticism. But the attempt must be made, for there is no other way. Reliance on the mere play of market forces, on foreign private investment, and on a "hands-off" State policy is no solution.

Latin America Must Find Its Own Paths to Development

Development policy must be based on a correct interpretation of the real state of affairs in Latin America. The theories that we have absorbed and are still absorbing from the big centers, often claim, quite wrongly, to be generally applicable. The fundamental task of those of us who are on the periphery is to play our part in pondering these theories and in introducing the dynamic elements needed to bring them into line with our own situation.

The same is true of the practical side of development. The uncompromising opposition to the industrialization of our countries has already been overcome, and we are now successfully combating the reluctance to recognize the significance of the deterioration in terms of trade. But we have a long way to go—and perhaps very little time to lose—in the field of monetary policy, where it is still the practice to impute inflationary leanings to those who refuse to admit that inflation is a phenomenon unconnected with the social structure.

In the actual planning for development it is obvious that we must find our own way. In the most advanced Western countries, planning experience is expanding, but under conditions different from those existing in Latin America. This experience must be closely followed, and so must that of the socialist countries, where planning is of longer standing and is based on direct economic action by the State and the political system that would appear to be inherent in this.

In Latin America the propensity to import ideologies is still very strong—as strong as the propensity of the centers to export them. This is an obvious legacy from the times of externally geared development. Let us be quite clear: this is not a question of closing our minds to what is being thought and done in other countries. But in the great centers there is a growing interest in development theory and problems, and it would be a serious mistake not to take advantage of the valuable assistance thus made available to us. Nothing can absolve us from the intellectual obligation to analyze our own phenomena and forge our own image of what we seek, in our endeavor to change the existing order. Let us make intelligent use of the thought and experience of others, but only as a means of crystallizing our own ideas.

This does not apply to the economic field alone. The vital problem is a much broader one, and we must not lose sight of the real object of development or fail to project, in addition, the image of what we want the Latin American citizen to become within the next few generations.

The rapid assimilation of technology entails new patterns of living and new attitudes of mind. Nevertheless, there is nothing in this vast process of change that requires human values to take second place. On the contrary, present-day technology opens up infinite possibilities for a variety of ways of life and a freedom of individual choice that, until recently, in terms of history, were confined to a small fraction of mankind.

But the production technique of today also makes possible an enormous concentration of economic power in a few hands, and this is perhaps even more true of information techniques and mass communication of ideas. Everything depends on the use we make of such techniques for the purpose of exercising conscious and deliberate control over the forces of economic and social development—on whether we use them to place some men under the dominion of others, or to enhance the dignity of man as an individual.

The Concentration of Economic Power and Its Political Effects

However, circumstances might well lead Latin America to take decisions that are not based on an objective view of such arguments. Resistance to the structural reforms postulated in the Charter of Punta del Este is all too well known in our countries. It may safely be assumed that some of the avowed opposition to State intervention is due at times to the simple fact that the prime purpose of such intervention is to effect these reforms. Ideological beliefs are invoked to dress up a basic opposition rather than because they are deeply held. Possibly the authoritarian State, and the disintegration of democracy, would not be regarded as nearly so distasteful by some critics if they thought that by such means it would be possible to achieve their goal—fantastic and illusory as this is—of keeping the present structure intact.

This dissentient note often meets with a response in certain circles outside Latin America, where it is only to be expected, since the economic and social complex that hampers development also includes certain exogenous elements. Thus the old argument emerges once more, both at home and abroad: first, we must complete the stage of economic development, and social reforms will follow; to speak of them now is to discourage private initiative.

This is a profoundly mistaken belief. There can be no acceleration in economic development without a change in the social structure. And it is also a cause of deep concern for those who envisaged the Charter of Punta del Este as heralding a new policy of international cooperation with those countries that were resolute in undertaking such structural reforms. It is easy to understand that certain private investments may be delayed while there is uncertainty as to the issue of these reforms. Without attempting to establish a strict parallel, it may be pointed out that equal uncertainty prevailed in the countries of Western Europe after the war; but the immediate threat that existed then was banished, not by private investment or appeals to repatriate fugitive European capital, but by the superb daring of the Marshall Plan. It was after this development that private investment began to flourish and fugitive capital return.

We are living in an epoch that is, and will continue to be, decisive, and that calls for a long-term approach. The postponement or emasculation of reforms for fear of temporarily discouraging private investment would not create an atmosphere favorable to foreign private investment. On the contrary, it would jeopardize the very existence of private enterprise, not to mention the endeavor to give it full dynamic impetus.

Let us not deceive ourselves. This is not a question that can be resolved on a doctrinaire level; it is essentially political. The political banner under which Latin American development is carried out is not a mere matter of intellectual preference, but will depend largely on the actual course of events in the next few years. There is a certain element of determinism in these events, and the only way to circumvent it is to act with forethought so as to influence their course.

I have already stressed this point in these early pages, and there is no need to labor it further. Suffice it to recall the many serious difficulties that are attending the trend toward closed development. A supreme effort is called for to reverse this trend in national, Latin American, and international plans, since if this is not done, and done in time, the outcome may be the authoritarian State, and incentives to economic activity may be superseded by compulsion.

We have spoken of determinism in relation to events; and perhaps there is an inexorable logic in their consequences. For if development were to become progressively more closed, we should also have to withdraw to some extent from the outside world, to avoid the contamination of new tastes, new needs, or new aspirations, and this withdrawal would be woven into the fabric of an ideology that, on the basis of the same repressive machinery, would have to be similarly safeguarded from the harsh breath of criticism.

There are many paths leading to the authoritarian State; this is not the only one. Another is resistance to the structural changes that fling wide the gate for the forces of development. But in this case the starting point is political, not economic, although both paths lead to the same destination. If there were unyielding opposition, either to the reforms as such, or to their execution, extremely critical situations might arise.

And the men who acquire political power to carry out these reforms as the result of a possibly irresistible tide of popular feeling may be forced to concentrate economic power in their own hands in order to strengthen and consolidate their political power, and perhaps also in order to use the whole of the savings potential of the community, in face of the magnitude of the problem confronting them and the contraction of private investment—an economic power far exceeding any the State possessed during the evolution of the capitalist economies.

The concentration of economic power in any form is always a threat to the true spirit of democracy. The State is not an abstract and disembodied entity, and those who operate its machinery are inevitably swayed by interests and passions as well as by community aims. It is hardly conceivable that when they hold the economic power in their hands, when they have seized it under the spur of these interests and pressures, they will refrain from imposing their will on others, or that these others can be independent in their outlook and decisions if their every activity and their very means of existence depend on those in power, and any alternative is denied them.

The basic question lies here, not in planning, since even those who hold deep and firm democratic convictions, who believe in political freedom and human rights, might find themselves compelled to compromise, first of all by force of circumstance, and second by the actual logic of events.

This is certainly not the state of affairs we would wish to substitute for the *status quo*. It would be a tragedy if, in order to free man from want, we had to sacrifice other values and subject him to the demands of arbitrary power. The very idea is fundamentally incompatible with the genius of the Latin American peoples, with their latent urge to shake off the trammels of poverty in order to liberate the human personality and give full rein, by means of economic development, to democracy and human rights, especially as regards the underprivileged of the population; in order to ensure that both there and in all strata of society, social mobility will allow the best elements to move upward, for the good of economic development and of democracy. The goal must be a social order free from privilege, and not only economic privilege, but also that baneful sort whereby some men usurp dominion over the ideas of the rest, over the creative forces of the spirit, and over the deepest feelings of the heart.

ANNEX

ECLA PUBLICATIONS 1948–1967

Annual Surveys

ECONOMIC SURVEY OF LATIN AMERICA, 1948

1949 — 279 pages
E/CN.12/82 — Sales N°: 1949.II.G.1
(Divided into two parts:
Part one: Trends in production
Part two: Other economic aspects)

ECONOMIC SURVEY OF LATIN AMERICA, 1949

11 January 1951 — 536 pages
E/CN.12/164/Rev.1 — Sales N°: 1951.II.G.1
(Divided into three parts:
Part one: Growth, disequilibrium and disparities: interpretation of the process of economic development
Part two: Economic development of selected Latin American countries
Part three: Recent changes in the economic condition of Latin America)

ECONOMIC SURVEY OF LATIN AMERICA, 1951-1952

December 1953 — 217 pages
E/CN.12/291/Rev.2 — Sales N°: 1953.II.G.3
(Divided into three parts:
Part I: The gross product, investments and consumption in Latin America
Part II: The impact of recent world economic events on Latin America
Part III: Trends in the principal sectors of production)

ECONOMIC SURVEY OF LATIN AMERICA, 1953

April 1954 — 246 pages
E/CN.12/358 — Sales N°: 1954.II.G.1
(Divided into two parts:
Part I: The gross product, foreign trade and the monetary situation
Part II: The main branches of production)

ECONOMIC SURVEY OF LATIN AMERICA, 1954
July 1955 203 pages
E/CN.12/362/Rev.1 Sales Nº: 1955.II.G.1
(Divided into two parts:
Part I: Latin America as a whole
Part II: Analysis by countries)

ECONOMIC SURVEY OF LATIN AMERICA, 1955
May 1956 176 pages
E/CN.12/421/Rev.1 Sales Nº: 1956.II.G.1
(Divided into two parts:
Part I: Economic trends in Latin America during 1955
Part II: Government income and expenditure 1947–1954)

ECONOMIC SURVEY OF LATIN AMERICA, 1956
September 1957 183 pages
E/CN.12/427/Rev.1 Sales Nº: 1957.II.G.1
(Divided into three parts:
Part one: Economic trends in Latin America during 1956
Part two: Trends of the main production sectors
Part three: Two special studies
A. Preliminary study of the effects of post-war industrialization on import structures and external vulnerability in Latin America
B. Productivity of labour and land in Latin American agriculture)

ECONOMIC SURVEY OF LATIN AMERICA, 1957
1959 292 pages
E/CN.12/489/Rev.1 Sales Nº: 59.II.G.1
(Divided into three parts:
Part I: Latin America and the world economy
Part II: Survey of the international economic situation in Latin America as a whole and in selected countries
Part III: Pressures on the balance of payments
Special study on trade in agricultural commodities in Latin America)

ECONOMIC SURVEY OF LATIN AMERICA, 1958
September 1959 160 pages
E/CN.12/498/Rev.1 Sales Nº: 59.II.G.1
(Divided into two parts:
Part I: The foreign exchange problem in Latin America
Part II: The internal situation in Latin America)

ECONOMIC SURVEY OF LATIN AMERICA, 1961[a]

Prepared jointly by the secretariats of the Organization of American States (OAS) and of the Economic Commission for Latin America (ECLA) under the editorship of OAS, OAS Official Documents. OAS/Ser.H/X.3.

ECONOMIC SURVEY OF LATIN AMERICA, 1963

1965 — 289 pages

E/CN.12/696/Rev.1 — Sales N°: 65.II.G.1

(Divided into four parts:

Part one: The economic development of Latin America in recent years

Part two: Sectoral evolution

Part three: Commodity trade and the balance of payments

Part four: The Cuban economy)

ECONOMIC SURVEY OF LATIN AMERICA, 1964

1966 — 381 pages

E/CN.12/711/Rev.1 — Sales N°:66.II.G.1

(Divided into three parts:

Part one: The Latin American economy 1963–64

Part two: Foreign trade, world markets and balance-of-payments trends in 1963–64

Part three: Economic policy and planning in Latin America)

ECONOMIC SURVEY OF LATIN AMERICA, 1965

1967 — 404 pages

E/CN.12/752/Rev.1 — Sales N°: 67.II.G.1

(Divided into three parts:

Part one: Latin America as a whole

Part two: The recent economic situation in selected countries

Part three: Evolution of the main economic sectors)

THE LATIN AMERICAN ECONOMY IN 1965

(Excerpt from ECLA Survey)

May 1966 — 49 pages

E/CN.12/754 — Sales N°: 66.II.G.8

[a] The 1959 and 1960 *Surveys* were not printed. The mimeographed versions are out of stock.

ECONOMIC SURVEY OF LATIN AMERICA, 1966
(In the press)
E/CN.12/767
(Divided into four parts:
Part one: The major trends of recent economic growth
Part two: Recent changes in the economy of selected countries
Part three: The major sectors of economic activity
Part four: Agriculture in Latin America)

THE LATIN AMERICAN ECONOMY IN 1966
(Excerpt from ECLA Survey)
March 1967 — 55 pages
E/CN.12/768 — Sales N°: 67.II.G.5

THE LATIN AMERICAN ECONOMY IN 1967
(Excerpt from ECLA Survey)
March 1968 — 62 pages
E/CN.12/806–E/CN.12/AC.61/2 — Sales N°: 68.II.G.12

Economic Development

THE ECONOMIC DEVELOPMENT OF LATIN AMERICA AND ITS PRINCIPAL PROBLEMS
April 1950 — 59 pages
E/CN.12/89/Rev.1 — Sales N°: 50.II.G.2

THEORETICAL AND PRACTICAL PROBLEMS OF ECONOMIC GROWTH
18 May 1951 — 113 pages (mimeographed)
E/CN.12/221

INTERNATIONAL CO-OPERATION IN A LATIN AMERICAN DEVELOPMENT POLICY
September 1954 — 147 pages
E/CN.12/359 — Sales N°: 1954.II.G.2
(Divided into two parts:
I: Preliminary report of the secretariat of the United Nations Economic Commission for Latin America;
II: Explanatory statement and recommendations of the Preparatory Group appointed by the Commission's secretariat.
Prepared for the Meeting of Ministers of Finance or Economy, at

the IVth Extraordinary Meeting of the Inter-American Economic and Social Council of the Organization of American States, held at Rio de Janeiro, November 1954.)

MANUAL ON ECONOMIC DEVELOPMENT PROJECTS
1958 — 242 pages
E/CN.12/426/Add.1/Rev.1 — Sales N°: 58.II.G.5

EL DESEQUILIBRIO EXTERNO EN EL DESARROLLO ECONOMICO LATINOAMERICANO. EL CASO DE MEXICO
May 1957 — 386 pages
E/CN.12/428 and Add.1 — Sales N°: 61.II.G/Mim.1

ECONOMIC DEVELOPMENT, PLANNING AND INTERNATIONAL CO-OPERATION
1961 — 65 pages
E/CN.12/582/Rev.1 — Sales N°: 61.II.G.6

THE ECONOMIC DEVELOPMENT OF LATIN AMERICA IN THE POST-WAR PERIOD
1964 — 147 pages
E/CN.12/659/Rev.1 — Sales N°: 64.II.G.6

TOWARDS A DYNAMIC DEVELOPMENT POLICY FOR LATIN AMERICA
1963 — 103 pages
E/CN.12/680/Rev.1 — Sales N°: 64.II.G.4

EXTERNAL FINANCING IN LATIN AMERICA
1965 — 247 pages
E/CN.12/649/Rev.1 — Sales N°: 65.II.G.4

Social Development

EL DESARROLLO SOCIAL DE AMERICA LATINA EN LA POSTGUERRA
Document E/CN.12/660 published by Ediciones Solar and Libreria Hachette, Buenos Aires, 1963

ECONOMIC DEVELOPMENT IN LATIN AMERICA: SOCIOLOGICAL CONSIDERATIONS
This document was presented at the Commission at its tenth session, May 1963
E/CN.12/646

EDUCATION, HUMAN RESOURCES AND DEVELOPMENT IN LATIN AMERICA
(In the press)
1968
E/CN.12/800

Analyses and Projections of Economic Development

I. AN INTRODUCTION TO THE TECHNIQUE OF PROGRAMMING
June 1955 — 52 pages
E/CN.12/363 — Sales N°: 1955.II.G.2

II. EL DESARROLLO ECONOMICO DEL BRASIL
April 1956 — 176 pages
E/CN.12/364/Rev.1 — Sales N°: 56.II.G.2

III. THE ECONOMIC DEVELOPMENT OF COLOMBIA
November 1956 — 454 pages
E/CN.12/365/Rev.1 — Sales N°: 57.II.G.3

IV. EL DESARROLLO ECONOMICO DE BOLIVIA
February 1958 — 301 pages
E/CN.12/430 and Add.1/Rev.1 — Sales N°:58.II.G.2

V. EL DESARROLLO ECONOMICO DE LA ARGENTINA

Volume I.	129 pages	Sales N°: 59.II.G3/Vol.I
Volume II.	259 pages	Sales N°: 59.II.G.3/Vol.II
Volume III.	181 pages	Sales N°: 59.II.G.3/Vol. III

VI. THE INDUSTRIAL DEVELOPMENT OF PERU
1959 — 323 pages
E/CN.12/493 — Sales N°: 59.II.G.2

VII. EL DESARROLLO ECONOMICO DE PANAMA
December 1959 — 203 pages
E/CN.12/494/Rev.1 — Sales N°: 60.II.G.3

VIII. EL DESARROLLO ECONOMICO DE EL SALVADOR
December 1959 — 175 pages
E/CN.12/495/Rev.1 — Sales N°: 60.II.G.2.

IX. EL DESARROLLO ECONOMICO DE NICARAGUA
November 1966 — 220 pages
E/CN.12/742/Rev.1 — Sales N°: 67.II.G.2

X. EL DESARROLLO ECONOMICO DE HONDURAS
December 1960 222 pages
E/CN.12/549 Sales N°: 61.II.G.8

Agriculture

AGRICULTURAL REQUISITES IN LATIN AMERICA
Report of the Joint ECLA/FAO Working Party
February 1960 156 pages
E/CN.12/83/Rev.1 Sales N°: 50.II.G.1

THE SELECTIVE EXPANSION OF AGRICULTURAL PRODUCTION IN LATIN AMERICA
Joint report of the Economic Commission for Latin America and the Food and Agriculture Organization of the United Nations
February 1957 69 pages
E/CN.12/378/Rev.2 Sales N°: 1957.II.G.4

COFFEE IN LATIN AMERICA: PRODUCTIVITY PROBLEMS AND FUTURE PROSPECTS
Reports prepared under the Joint Program of the Economic Commission for Latin America and the Food and Agriculture Organization of the United Nations.

I. COLOMBIA AND EL SALVADOR
1958 144 pages
E/CN.12/490 Sales N°: 58.II.G.4

II. BRAZIL, STATE OF SAO PAULO
Part I. The state and prospects of production
December 1960 111 pages
E/CN.12/545 Sales N°: 60.II.G.6/Vol.I
Part II. A. Case study of thirty-three coffee farms
B. Analysis of the functions of production
December 1960 109 pages
E/CN.12/545/Add.1 Sales N°: 60.II.G.6

LIVESTOCK IN LATIN AMERICA: STATUS, PROBLEMS AND PROSPECTS
Reports prepared in accordance with the Joint Program of the Economic Commission for Latin America and the Food and Agriculture Organization of the United Nations

I. COLOMBIA, MEXICO, URUGUAY AND VENEZUELA
1962 — 94 pages
E/CN.12/620 — Sales N°: 61.II.G.7

II. BRAZIL
1964 — 76 pages
E/CN.12/636 — Sales N°: 64.II.G.3

AGRICULTURE IN LATIN AMERICA: PROBLEMS AND PROSPECTS
This document was presented at the Commission at its tenth session, May 1963
E/CN.12/686 — (Mimeographed)

EL USO DE FERTILIZANTES EN AMERICA LATINA
Document prepared by the Joint ECLA/FAO Agriculture Division in collaboration with the Inter-American Development Bank
December 1966 — 96 pages
E/CN.12/760 — Sales N°: 67.II.G.3

Reports of Seminars and Workshops

WORKSHOP ON BUDGETARY CLASSIFICATION AND MANAGEMENT IN SOUTH AMERICA
Santiago, Chile, 27 May to 5 June 1959
E/CN.12/538 — 38 pages

REPORT OF THE WORKSHOP ON BUDGETARY CLASSIFICATION AND MANAGEMENT IN SOUTH AMERICA
Santiago, Chile, 3–14 September 1962
E/CN.12/634/Rev.1 — 62 pages

REPORT OF THE WORKSHOP ON BUDGETARY CLASSIFICATION AND MANAGEMENT IN CENTRAL AMERICA AND PANAMA
San José, Costa Rica, 18 to 30 September 1963
E/CN.12/692 — 83 pages

REPORT OF THE LATIN AMERICAN SEMINAR ON HOUSING STATISTICS and PROGRAMMES
Copenhagen, Denmark, 2–25 September 1962
February 1963 — 87 pages
E/CN.12/647/Rev.1 — Sales N°: 63.II.G.14

Transport

EL TRANSPORTE EN AMERICA LATINA
May 1965 — 348 pages
E/CN.12/703/Rev.1 — Sales N°: 65.II.G.7

Trade

A STUDY OF TRADE BETWEEN LATIN AMERICA AND EUROPE
January 1953 — 117 pages
E/CN.12/225 — Sales N°: 1952.II.G.2

STUDY OF THE PROSPECTS OF INTER-LATIN AMERICAN TRADE: SOUTHERN ZONE OF THE REGION
April 1954 — 134 pages
E/CN.12/304/Rev.2 — Sales N°: 1953.II.G.4

FOREIGN CAPITAL IN LATIN AMERICA
November 1954 — 164 pages
E/CN.12/360 — Sales N°: 1954.II.G.4

STUDY OF INTER-LATIN AMERICAN TRADE
April 1956 — 313 pages
E/CN.12/369/Rev.1 — Sales N°: 1956.II.G.3

INTER-LATIN AMERICAN TRADE: CURRENT PROBLEMS
January 1957 — 105 pages
E/CN.12/423 — Sales N°: 1957.II.G.5

THE LATIN AMERICAN COMMON MARKET
1959 — 146 pages
E/CN.12/531 — Sales N°: 59.II.G.4

FOREIGN PRIVATE INVESTMENT IN THE LATIN AMERICAN FREE-TRADE AREA
1961 — 30 pages
E/CN.12/550 — Sales N°: 60.II.G.5

MULTILATERAL ECONOMIC CO-OPERATION IN LATIN AMERICA
Volume I. TEXTS AND DOCUMENTS
1962 — 165 pages
E/CN.12/621 — Sales N°: 62.II.G.3

HACIA LA INTEGRACION ACELERADA DE AMERICA LATINA
(Published by Fondo de Cultura Económica, Mexico City, 1965
Proposals submitted to the Presidents of the Latin American republics by José Antonio Mayobre, Felipe Herrera, Carlos Sanz de Santamaría and Raúl Prebisch, together with a technical study by ECLA)

EL COMERCIO INTERNACIONAL Y EL DESARROLLO DE AMERICA LATINA
(Published by Fondo de Cultura Económica, Mexico City, 1964)
Contains the Spanish text of the following documents prepared by ECLA: "Latin America and the United Nations Conference on Trade and Development"[b] (E/CN.12/693) and "Report by the secretariat on the Meeting of Latin American Government Experts on Trade Policy"[b] (Brasilia, 20 to 25 January 1964) (E/CN.12/694)

Industry

LABOUR PRODUCTIVITY OF THE COTTON TEXTILE INDUSTRY IN FIVE LATIN AMERICAN COUNTRIES
April 1951 — 294
E/CN.12/219 — Sales N°: 1951.II.G.2

THE TEXTILE INDUSTRY IN LATIN AMERICA

I. CHILE — (Spanish only)
November 1962 — 97 pages
E/CN.12/622 — Sales N°: 63.II.G.5

II. BRAZIL
October 1963 — 137 pages
E/CN.12/623 — Sales N°: 64.II.G.2

III. COLOMBIA — (Spanish only)
August 1964 — 120 pages
E/CN.12/698 — Sales N°: 64.II.G/Mim. 2

IV. URUGUAY — (Spanish only)
December 1964 — 125 pages
E/CN.12/691 — Sales N°: 64.II.G/Mim.5

V. PERU — (Spanish only)
October 1964 — 118 pages
E/CN.12/700 — Sales N°: 64.II.G/Mim.3

[b] English text in mimeograph only.

VI. BOLIVIA (Spanish only)
October 1964 51 pages
E/CN.12/699 Sales N°:64.II.G/Mim.4

VII. PARAGUAY (Spanish only)
July 1965 42 pages
E/CN.12/736 Sales N°: 65.II.G/Mim.6

VIII. ARGENTINA (Spanish only)
August 1965 228 pages
E/CN.12/735 Sales N°: 65.II.G/Mim.7

IX. ECUADOR (Spanish only)
August 1965 80 pages
E/CN.12/738 Sales N°: 65.II.G/Mim.8

X. VENEZUELA
December 1965 136 pages
E/CN.12/729 Sales N°: 65.II.G/Mim.9

XI. MEXICO
February 1966 58 pages
E/CN.12/745 Sales N°: 66.II.G/Mim.1

POSSIBILITIES FOR THE DEVELOPMENT OF THE PULP AND PAPER INDUSTRY IN LATIN AMERICA
November 1953 151 pages
E/CN.12/294/Rev.2 Sales N°: 1953.II.G.2
(A joint study by the Economic Commission for Latin America and the Food and Agriculture Organization of the United Nations)

PULP AND PAPER PROSPECTS IN LATIN AMERICA
October 1955 465 pages
E/CN.12/361/Rev.1 Sales N°: 1955.II.G.4
(Divided into two parts:
First part. Report of the Latin American Meeting of Experts on the Pulp and Paper Industry sponsored by the secretariats of the Economic Commission for Latin America, the Food and Agriculture Organization of the United Nations and the Technical Assistance Administration
Second part. Working papers submitted to the Meeting)

PULP AND PAPER PROSPECTS IN LATIN AMERICA
December 1962 81 pages
E/CN.12/570/Rev.1 Sales N°: 63.II.G.7
(A joint study by the Economic Commission for Latin America and the Food and Agriculture Organization of the United Nations)

LATIN AMERICAN TIMBER TRENDS AND PROSPECTS
1962 117 pages
E/CN.12/624 Sales N°: 63.II.G.1
(A joint study by the Economic Commission for Latin America and the Food and Agriculture Organization of the United Nations)

A STUDY OF THE IRON AND STEEL INDUSTRY IN LATIN AMERICA
Volume I. Report of the Expert Working Group held at Bogotá, 1952
December 1954 123 pages
E/CN.12/293/Rev.1 Sales N°: 1954.II.G.3, Vol. I

Volume II. Proceedings of the Expert Working Group held at Bogotá
November 1954 449 pages
E/CN.12/293/Rev.1/Add.1 Sales N°: 1954.II.G.3, Vol. II
(Sponsored by the secretariat of the Economic Commission for Latin America and the Technical Assistance Administration)

PROBLEMS OF THE STEEL-MAKING AND TRANSFORMING INDUSTRIES IN LATIN AMERICA
Volume I. Report of the Latin American Meeting of Experts on Steel Making and Transforming Industries, Sao Paulo, 1956
March 1957 62 pages
E/CN.12/425 Sales N°: 1957.II.G.6/Vol.1

Volume 2 Siderurgia 258 pages (Spanish only)
Sales N°: 1957.II.G.6/Vol.2
(Sponsored by the secretariats of the Economic Commission for Latin America and of the Technical Assistance Administration in collaboration with the Associação Brasileira de Metais)

ENERGY DEVELOPMENT IN LATIN AMERICA
1956 268 pages
E/CN.12/384/Rev.1 Sales N°: 1957.II.G.2

ESTUDIOS SOBRE LA ELECTRICIDAD EN AMERICA LATINA

Volumen I. Informe y documentos del seminario latinoamericano de energía eléctrica
October 1962 — 576 pages
E/CN.12/630 — Sales N°: 63.II.G.3

Volumen II. Documentos del seminario latinoamericano de energía eléctrica
October 1964 — 520 pages
E/CN.12/630/Add.1 — Sales N°: 64.II.G.10

(This Seminar was held under the joint auspices of the Economic Commission for Latin America, the Bureau of Technical Assistance Operations, the Resources and Transport Branch of the United Nations and the Government of the United States of Mexico)

LOS RECURSOS HIDRAULICOS EN AMERICA LATINA

I. CHILE
October 1960 — 190 pages
E/CN.12/501 — Sales N°: 60.II.G.4

II. VENEZUELA
November 1962 — 127 pages
E/CN.12/593/Rev.1 — Sales N°: 63.II.G.6

III. BOLIVIA Y COLOMBIA
September 1964 — 177 pages
E/CN.12/695 — Sales N°: 64.II.G.11

THE MANUFACTURE OF INDUSTRIAL MACHINERY AND EQUIPMENT IN LATIN AMERICA

I. BASIC EQUIPMENT IN BRAZIL
November 1962 — 71 pages
E/CN.12/619/Rev.1 — Sales N°: 63.II.G.2

II. LAS MAQUINAS-HERRAMIENTAS EN EL BRASIL
November 1962 — 49 pages
E/CN.12/633 — Sales N°: 63.II.G.4

III. LOS EQUIPOS BASICOS EN LA ARGENTINA
December 1963 — 85 pages
E/CN.12/629/Rev.1 — Sales N°: 64.II.G.5

IV. LAS MAQUINAS-HERRAMIENTAS EN LA ARGENTINA
October 1967 — 62 pages
E/CN.12/747 — Sales N°: 68.II.G.4

LA INDUSTRIA QUIMICA EN AMERICA LATINA
August 1963 — 307 pages
E/CN.12/628/Rev.1 — Sales N°: 64.II.G.7

THE PROCESS OF INDUSTRIAL DEVELOPMENT IN LATIN AMERICA
1966 — 272 pages
E/CN.12/716/Rev.1 — Sales N°: 66.II.G.4

PROBLEMAS Y PERSPECTIVAS DEL DESARROLLO INDUSTRIAL LATINOAMERICANO
(Published by Ediciones Solar y Libreria Hachette S.A., Buenos Aires, 1964. Document E/CN.12/664 submitted to the Commission at its tenth session, May 1963)

Studies on Central America

MEMORIA DEL SEMINARIO CENTROAMERICANO DE CREDITO AGRICOLA
Volume I. General conclusions
January 1954 — 94 pages
E/CN.12/305 — Sales N°: 1953.II.G.1/Vol.I

Volume II. Survey of agricultural credit in countries in the area
January 1954 — 159 pages
E/CN.12/305 — Sales N°: 1953.II.G.1/Vol.II

Volume III. Legislation pertaining to agricultural credit in countries in the area
January 1954 — 194 pages
E/CN.12/305 — Sales N°: 1953.II.G.1/Vol.III
(The Central American Seminar on Agricultural Credit was held under the aegis of the Government of Guatemala, the Food and Agriculture Organization of the United Nations and the Economic Commission for Latin America)

EL TRANSPORTE EN EL ISTMO CENTROAMERICANO
September 1953 — 244 pages
E/CN.12/356 — Sales N°: 1953.VIII.2
(Report of the Technical Mission nominated by the Economic Commis-

sion for Latin America and the Technical Assistance Administration, in collaboration with the International Civil Aviation Organization, and report of the Seminar on Transport held in San José, Costa Rica, from 9 to 20 June 1953)

NOMENCLATURA ARANCELARIA UNIFORME CENTROAMERICANA (NAUCA) Y SU MANUAL DE CODIFICACION
November 1955 — 416 pages
E/CN.12/420 — Sales N°: 1955.II.G.3

LA INTEGRACION ECONOMICA DE CENTROAMERICA: SU EVOLUCION Y PERSPECTIVAS
November 1956 — 98 pages
E/CN.12/422 — Sales N°: 56.II.G.4

LA POLITICA TRIBUTARIA Y EL DESARROLLO ECONOMICO EN CENTROAMERICA
September 1956 — 141 pages
E/CN.12/486 — Sales N°: 1957.II.G.9

COMPENDIO ESTADISTICO CENTROAMERICANO
August 1957 — 125 pages
E/CN.12/487 — Sales N°: 1957.II.G.8

SEGUNDO COMPENDIO ESTADISTICO CENTROAMERICANO
January 1963 — 62 pages
E/CN.12/597 — Sales N°: 63.II.G.11

HUMAN RESOURCES OF CENTRAL AMERICA, PANAMA AND MEXICO 1950–1980, IN RELATION TO SOME ASPECTS OF ECONOMIC DEVELOPMENT
1960 — 155 pages
E/CN.12/548 — Sales N°: 60.XIII.1

POSSIBILITIES OF INTEGRATED INDUSTRIAL DEVELOPMENT IN CENTRAL AMERICA
November 1963 — 54 pages
E/CN.12/683/Add.1 — Sales N°: 63.II.G.10

EVALUACION DE LA INTEGRACION ECONOMICA EN CENTROAMERICA
January 1966 — 295 pages
E/CN.12/762 — Sales N°: 66.II.G.9

Reports of the Central American Economic Co-operation Committee

REPORT OF THE CENTRAL AMERICAN ECONOMIC CO-OPERATION COMMITEE
30 January 1956 to 24 February 1957[c]
E/CN.12/431, Annex Sales N°: 1957.II.G.7
Contains draft texts of:

I. Central American Multilateral Free Trade and Economic Integration Treaty

II. Agreement on Central American Integration Industries

III. Regional Central American Agreement on Road Signs and Signals

REPORT OF THE CENTRAL AMERICAN ECONOMIC CO-OPERATION COMMITTEE
25 February 1957 to 10 June 1958
E/CN.12/492 Sales N°: 1958.II.G.3
Contains:

I. Multilateral Treaty on Free Trade and Central American Economic Integration

II. Agreement on the régime for Central American Integration Industries

III. Central American agreement on road traffic

IV. Central American agreement on uniform road signs and signals

REPORT OF THE CENTRAL AMERICAN ECONOMIC CO-OPERATION COMMITTEE
11 June 1958 to 2 September 1959
E/CN.12/533 Sales N°: 59.II.G.5
Contains:

I. Central American agreement on the Equalization of Import Duties and Charges Schedule A and Schedule B

II. Protocol to the Central American Agreement on the Equalization of Import Duties and Charges

[c] The English text, in mimeograph form only, does not contain the texts of the agreements mentioned here.

III. Addresses delivered at the inaugural and the closing meetings of the sixth session of the Central American Co-operation Committee

REPORT OF THE CENTRAL AMERICAN ECONOMIC CO-OPERATION COMMITTEE

3 September 1959 to 13 December 1960

E/CN.12/552 Sales N°: 60.II.G.7

Contains:

I. General Treaty on Central American Economic Integration

II. Protocol to the Central American Agreement on the Equalization of Import Duties and Charges

III. Agreement establishing the Central American Bank for Economic Integration

REPORT OF THE CENTRAL AMERICAN ECONOMIC CO-OPERATION COMMITTEE

13 December 1960 to 29 January 1963

E/CN.12/672 Sales N°: 63.II.G.12

Contains:

I. Protocol to the Agreement on the Régime for Central American Integration Industries

II. Protocol to the Central American Agreement on the Equalization of Import Duties and Charges (San Salvador Protocol)

III. General situation and future outlook of the Central American Integration Programme (note by the ECLA secretariat)

IV. Instruments of Accession of Costa Rica to the General Treaty on Central American Economic Integration and to the Agreement establishing the Central American Bank for Economic Integration

V. Protocol of Accession of Costa Rica to the Protocol on the Equalization of Import Duties and Charges, signed at Managua on 13 December 1960

VI. Protocol to the Central American Agreement on the Equalization of Import Duties and Charges, signed at San José, Costa Rica, on 31 July 1962

VII. Central American Agreement on Fiscal Incentives to Industrial Development

VIII. Protocol to the General Treaty on Central American Economic Integration: Schedules of goods subject to special interim régimes of exemption from free trade as between Costa Rica and each of the other Signatory States

EVALUACION DE LA INTEGRACION ECONOMICA EN CENTROAMERICA

E/CN.12/762 Sales N°: 66.II.G.9

Contains:

Report of the Central American Economic Co-operation Committee 29 January 1963 to 31 January 1966

Economic Bulletins for Latin America

ECONOMIC REVIEW OF LATIN AMERICA

Special Issue

1. Review of the economic situation in Latin America during the early months of 1955
2. Recent trends in the exports and prices of some products
3. Impact of coffee exports on the economies of Brazil and Colombia
4. Some aspects of the recent evolution of Cuba's economy
5. Three sociological aspects of economic development

August 1955

Vol. I, N° 1

1. The economic situation in Latin America during 1955
2. The situation in Argentina and the new economic policy
3. Some aspects of the inflationary process in Chile
4. Colombia in a year of balance-of-payments disequilibrium
5. The meat problem in Latin America
6. Recent trends in the exports and prices of some products

January 1956

Vol. I, N° 2

1. The economic situation in Latin America during 1956
2. The input-output model
3. Concepts and methods used by ECLA
4. Energy consumption in Latin America

5. United States imports of Latin American products
6. Exports and prices of some products

September 1956

Vol. II, Nº 1

1. The economic situation in Latin America during 1956
2. Changes in employment structure in Latin America, 1945–1955
3. Possibilities for the expansion of wheat production in Brazil
4. Recent developments and prospects in trade between Latin America and Japan

February 1957

Vol. II, Nº 2

1. Latin America's foreign trade in the early months of 1957
2. The economic development of Bolivia
3. Index clause on deferred payments

October 1957

Vol. III, Nº 1

1. The Latin American regional market
2. Latin America's trade with the Common Market countries of Europe
3. Development policies and programs, by Hollis B. Chenery

March 1958

Vol. III, Nº 2

1. Latin America's foreign trade in the first half of 1958
2. The international banana market—its evolution and prospects
3. Statistical supplement

October 1958

Vol. IV, Nº 1

1. Progress towards the Latin American common market
2. The problem of the economic development of Argentina
3. Some observations on the industrial development of Peru
4. Coffee in Latin America: the producers' problem
5. Statistical supplement

March 1959

Vol. IV, Nº 2

1. Rolled iron and steel products in Latin America
2. The Central American Economic Integration Programme

3. The economic development of Panama
4. Statistical supplement

October 1959

Vol. V, Nº 1

1. Heavy industry in the Latin American Common Market, by Jan Tinbergen
2. The Free-Trade Area
3. Economic developments in Venezuela in the 1950's
4. Some applications of the input-output model to the Argentine economy
5. Statistical supplement

March 1960

Vol. V, Nº 2

1. Economic trends in Latin America in 1959
2. Central America's post-war exports to the United States
3. The coffee industry in São Paulo

October 1960

Vol. V—Statistical supplement

November 1960

Vol. VI, Nº 1

1. Economic development or monetary stability: the false dilemma, by Raúl Prebisch
2. Relationship between social and economic institutions. A theoretical model applicable to Latin America, by José Medina Echavarría
3. Economic policy and the price system, by Thomas Balogh
4. Report of the Expert Working Group on Social Aspects of Economic Development in Latin America

March 1961

Vol. VI, Nº 2

1. An agricultural policy to expedite the economic development of Latin America
2. The demographic situation in Latin America
3. Development of commodity trade between Latin America and the United States, by David H. Pollock
4. Productivity of the agricultural sector in Ecuador

October 1961

Sales Nº 61.II.G.5

Vol. VI—Statistical supplement
November 1961
Sales Nº: 61.II.G.4

Vol. VII, Nº 1

1. The economic development of Latin America and its principal problems, by Raúl Prebisch
2. Inflation and growth: a summary of experience in Latin America
3. Latin America's position in relation to world changes in trade policy, by Esteban Ivovich
4. Hydroelectric resources in Latin America: their measurement and utilization

February 1962
Sales Nº: 62.II.G.1

Vol. VII, Nº 1—Statistical supplement
October 1962
Sales Nº: 63.II.G.9

Vol. VII, Nº 2

1. Latin American Institute for Economic and Social Planning
2. The creation of a United Nations Economic Projections and Programming Center and the technique of projections
3. The achievement of co-ordination in Latin American trade policy: Relations with the European Economic Community
4. Short-term economic fluctuations in Latin America during 1948 to 1959
5. Report of the Latin American Seminar on Planning
6. Conference on Education and Economic and Social Development in Latin America
7. Economic development and education in Latin America

October 1962
Sales Nº: 62.II.G.4

Vol. VII, Nº 2—Statistical supplement
December 1962
Sales Nº: 63.II.G.9

Vol. VIII, Nº 1

1. Stabilizing the terms of trade of under-developed countries, by Nicholas Kaldor

2. General situation and future outlook of the Central American Economic integration programme
3. Planning in France, by Francois Le Guay
4. Geographic distribution of the population of Latin America and regional development priorities
5. Technological research in Latin America
6. ECLA's recent activities:
   I. Workshop on Budgetary Classification and Management
   II. Conference on Fiscal Policy
   III. Latin American Seminar on Housing Statistics and Programmes
   IV. Relation between community development and national development programmes
   V. Problems of the electricity industry
7. Methodological notes. The concept of terms of trade and methods of computation

March 1963
Sales N°: 63.II.G.8

Vol. VIII, N° 2

1. The new Executive Secretary of ECLA
2. Some aspects of the Latin American economic situation in 1962
3. Progress in planning in Latin America
4. Agriculture in Latin America: problems and prospects
5. A measurement of price levels and the purchasing power of currencies in Latin America, 1960–62
6. Informative note: The United Nations Conference on Trade and Development
7. Recent activities of ECLA:
   I. Tenth session of the Economic Commission for Latin America (Mar del Plata, Argentina, 6–17 May 1963)
   II. Seminar on Industrial Programming (São Paulo, Brazil, 4–15 March 1963)
8. Methodological notes: The adoption of machine tabulation for national foreign trade statistics, by Mario Movarec

October 1963
Sales N°: 64.II.G.1

Vol. IX, N° 1

1. The growth and decline of import substitution in Brazil

2. Protectionism and industrialization in Latin America, by Santiago Macario
3. Tax incentives in Latin America, by Pedro Mendive
4. Central America: industrial policy problems
5. Recent ECLA activities:
   I. Workshop on Budgetary Classification and Management in Central America and Panama (San José, Costa Rica, 18–30 September 1963)
   II. Working Group on Classification of Manufactured Products (Santiago, Chile, 4–15 November 1963)
   III. Meeting of Latin American Government Experts on Trade Policy (Brasilia, Brazil, 20–25 January 1964)
6. Activities of the Latin American Institute for Economic and Social Planning

March 1964
Sales N°: 64.II.G.8

Vol. IX, N° 2

1. Fifteen years of economic policy in Brazil
2. Dual exchange rates and economic development, by Nicholas Kaldor
3. Popular participation and principles of community development in relation to the acceleration of economic and social development
4. Latin America's coffee exports to countries members of the European Economic Community
5. The United Nations Conference on Trade and Development
6. Recent ECLA activities

November 1964
Sales N°: 65.II.G.3

Vol. X, N° 1

1. Rural settlement patterns and social change in Latin America: notes for a strategy or rural development
2. The Central American Common Market for agricultural commodities
3. Foreign trade of Argentina and Australia, 1930 to 1960, by Ruth Kelly
4. The programming of short-term financing, by Angel Monti
5. Rural electrification in Latin America
6. Recent activities of ECLA:

I. Second Inter-American Seminar on Civil Registration (Lima, 30 November to 11 December 1964)

II. Seminar on the Development of the Chemical Industries in Latin America (Caracas, 7 to 12 December 1964)

III. Study Tour and Workshop on Organization and Functions of National Housing Agencies for the Implementation of Housing Programmes (Copenhagen, Oslo and Stockholm, 30 August to 10 September 1964)

March 1965
Sales N°: 65.II.G.6

Vol. X, N° 2

1. Aspects of development and trade in the Commonwealth Caribbean, by Alister McIntyre
2. Structural changes in employment within the context of Latin America's economic development
3. Foreign trade of Argentina and Australia, 1930 to 1960 (II), by Ruth Kelly
4. Recent ECLA activities
5. Activities of the Latin American Institute for Economic and Social Planning

October 1965
Sales N°: 66.II.G.3

Vol. XI, N° 1

1. The recent evolution of the Latin American economy
2. International monetary reform, by Robert Triffin
3. Social development and social planning: A survey of conceptual and practical problems in Latin America
4. Social service in Latin America: Functions and relationships to development, by Virginia A. Paraiso
5. Income distribution in Argentina

April 1966
Sales N°: 66.II.G.7

Vol. XI, N° 2

1. The training of human resources in the economic and social development of Latin America
2. Economic planning in Brazil at the level of the states
3. The housing problem in Latin America in relation to structural development factors, by Rubén D. Utria

4. Methodology of the national economic budget, by Frederico J. Herschel and Juan J. Santieri

October 1966

Sales N°: 67.II.G.4

Vol. XII, N° 1

1. The new Executive Secretary of ECLA
2. Concepts and methods of area programming for community development
3. Fiscal incentives for export
4. Latin America's hydroelectric potential
5. Small-scale industry in the development of Latin America
6. Recent activities of ECLA:
   - I. Latin American Seminar on Small-Scale Industry (Quito, Ecuador, 28 November to 3 December 1966)
   - II. Latin American Seminar on Industrial Statistics (Quito, 7 to 16 December 1966)
   - III. Seminar on the Latin American Petroleum Industry (Santiago, Chile, 15 to 23 February 1967)
   - IV. Meeting of the Group on the Application of Science and Technology to Development
7. Activities of the Latin American Institute for Economic and Social Planning

May 1967

Sales N°: 67.II.G.7

Vol. XII, N° 2

1. Planning in Latin America
2. Planning and plan implementation in Latin America
3. Discussion and resolution on development planning at the twelfth session of the Commission
4. Income distribution in Latin America
5. The economic policy of Bolivia in 1952–64
6. The economic policy of Colombia in 1950–66
7. The measurement of Latin American real income in U.S. dollars
8. Recent activities of ECLA:

(In the press) Twelfth session of the Economic Commission for Latin America

SESSIONS OF THE COMMISSION AND OF THE COMMITTEE OF THE WHOLE

Sessions Commission Committee of the Whole	Date and place	Report
First	7–25 June 1948, Santiago, Chile	A report on the first session. E/840/Rev.1
Second	29 May to 14 June 1949, Havana, Cuba	Annual report (26 June 1948–14 June 1949). E/1330–E/CN.12/158/Rev.1[d]
Third	5–21 June 1950, Montevideo, Uruguay	Annual report (15 June 1949–21 June 1950). E/1717–E/CN.12/190
Fourth	28 May to 16 June 1951, Mexico City, Mexico	Annual report (22 June 1950–16 June 1951). E/2021–E/CN.12/266
First	11–14 February 1952, Santiago, Chile	Annual report (17 June 1951–14 February 1952). E/2185–E/CN.12/AC.16/15
Fifth	9–25 April 1953, Quitandinha, Brazil	Annual report (15 February 1952–25 April 1953. E/2405 and Corr.1–E/CN.12/324 and Corr.1
Second	8–10 February 1954, Santiago, Chile	Annual report (26 April 1953–10 February 1954). E/2536–E/CN.12/AC.24/9 /Rev.1
Third	30 July 1954, Santiago, Chile	Special *interim* report. E/CN.12/AC.25/5

[d] On 10 January 1949 the Commission submitted a provisional annual report to the Economic and Social Council at its eighth session (E/1099–E/CN.12/80).

Sessions Commission Committee of the Whole	Date and place	Report
Fourth	9–10 May 1955, Santiago, Chile	Annual report (10 February 1954–10 May 1955). E/2756–E/CN.12/AC.26/8/Rev.1
Sixth	29 August to 16 September 1955, Bogotá, Colombia	Report of the sixth session (29 August–16 September 1955). E/2796/Rev.1–E/CN.12/387/Rev.1
Fifth	14–15 May 1956, Santiago, Chile	Annual report (10 May 1955–15 May 1956). E/2883/Rev.1–E/CN.12/AC.34/9/Rev.2
Seventh	15–29 May 1957, La Paz, Bolivia	Annual report (15 May 1956–29 May 1957). E/2998–E/CN.12/451
Sixth	7–8 April 1958, Santiago, Chile	Annual report (30 May 1957 to 8 April 1958). E/309/–E/CN.12/AC.40/13/Rev.1
Extraordinary	1–3 October 1958, New York (United Nations Building, Santiago, Chile)	Annual report of the Commission (9 April 1958–23 May 1959). E/3246–E/CN.12/530/Rev.2 Annex VIII (E/CN.12/AC.41/3)
Eighth	14–23 May 1959, Panama City, Panama	Annual report (9 April 1958–23 May 1959) E/3091–E/3246/Rev.2–E/CN.12/530/Rev.2
Seventh	28–29 March 1960, Santiago, Chile	Annual report (24 May 1959–29 March 1960) E/333–E/CN.12/AC.45/13/Rev.1
Extraordinary	28–30 June 1960, New York (Earthquakes in Chile, 21–23 May 1960)	Report on the third extraordinary session E/3402–E/CN.12/AC.46/4

Sessions Commission Committee of the Whole	Date and place	Report
Ninth	4–15 May 1961, Santiago, Chile	Annual report (30 March 1960–15 May 1961) E/3486–E/CN.12/573/Rev.1
Eighth	14–16 February 1962, Santiago, Chile	Annual report (16 May 1961–16 February 1962) E/3581/Rev.1–E/CN.12/AC.50/11/Rev.1
Extraordinary	21–22 March 1962, Santiago, Chile (Election of the Governing Council of the Latin American Institute for Economic and Social Planning)	Report on the fourth extraordinary session. E/3582/Add.1–E/CN.12/AC.51/2/Rev.2
Ninth	6–7 June 1962, New York (Latin American Institute for Economic and Social Planning)	Report on ninth session. E/3649–E/CN.12/AC.52/3
Tenth	6–18 May 1963, Mar del Plata, Argentina	Annual report (17 February 1962–17 May 1963) E/3766/Rev.3–E/CN.12/690/Rev.3
Tenth	12–14 February 1964, Santiago, Chile	Annual report (18 May 1963–14 February 1964) E/3857/Rev.2–E/CN.12/AC.57/15/Rev.2
Eleventh	6–18 May 1965, Mexico City, Mexico	Annual report (15 February 1964–17 May 1965) E/4032/Rev.1–E/CN.12/731/Rev.2 and E/4032/Rev.1/Add.1–E/CN.12/731/Rev.2/Add.1

Sessions Commission Committee of the Whole	Date and place	Report
Eleventh	10–12 May 1966, Santiago, Chile	Annual report (18 May 1965–12 May 1966) E/4181–E/CN-.12/AC.58/9/Rev.1
Twelfth	2–13 May 1967, Caracas, Venezuela	Annual report (13 May 1966–13 May 1967) E/CN.12/784/Rev.1 and E/4359/Add.1–E/CN.12/784/Add.1

INDEX